Commercial Property Valuation

Founded in 1807, John Wiley & Sons is the oldest independent publishing company in the United States. With offices in North America, Europe, Australia and Asia, Wiley is globally committed to developing and marketing print and electronic products and services for our customers' professional and personal knowledge and understanding.

The Wiley Finance series contains books written specifically for finance and investment professionals as well as sophisticated individual investors and their financial advisors. Book topics range from portfolio management to e-commerce, risk management, financial engineering, valuation and financial instrument analysis, as well as much more.

For a list of available titles, visit our website at www.WileyFinance.com.

Commercial Property Valuation

Methods and Case studies

GIACOMO MORRI

PAOLO BENEDETTO

WILEY

This edition first published 2019
© 2019 John Wiley & Sons, Ltd

Registered office
John Wiley & Sons Ltd, The Atrium, Southern Gate, Chichester, West Sussex, PO19 8SQ, United
Kingdom

For details of our global editorial offices, for customer services and for information about how to apply
for permission to reuse the copyright material in this book please see our website at www.wiley.com.

Wiley publishes in a variety of print and electronic formats and by print-on-demand. Some material
included with standard print versions of this book may not be included in e-books or in
print-on-demand. If this book refers to media such as a CD or DVD that is not included in the version
you purchased, you may download this material at http://booksupport.wiley.com. For more information
about Wiley products, visit www.wiley.com.

Designations used by companies to distinguish their products are often claimed as trademarks. All
brand names and product names used in this book are trade names, service marks, trademarks or
registered trademarks of their respective owners. The publisher is not associated with any product or
vendor mentioned in this book.

Limit of Liability/Disclaimer of Warranty: While the publisher and author have used their best efforts
in preparing this book, they make no representations or warranties with respect to the accuracy or
completeness of the contents of this book and specifically disclaim any implied warranties of
merchantability or fitness for a particular purpose. It is sold on the understanding that the publisher is
not engaged in rendering professional services and neither the publisher nor the author shall be liable
for damages arising herefrom. If professional advice or other expert assistance is required, the services
of a competent professional should be sought.

Library of Congress Cataloging-in-Publication Data

Names: Morri, Giacomo, 1975- author. | Benedetto, Paolo, 1984- author.
Title: Commercial property valuation : methods and case studies / Giacomo
    Morri, Paolo Benedetto.
Description: Chichester, West Sussex, United Kingdom : John Wiley & Sons,
    2019. | Includes bibliographical references and index. |
Identifiers: LCCN 2019008189 (print) | LCCN 2019010227 (ebook) | ISBN
    9781119512134 (ePDF) | ISBN 9781119512158 (ePub) | ISBN 9781119512127
    (hardback)
Subjects: LCSH: Commercial real estate—Valuation.
Classification: LCC HD1393.55 (ebook) | LCC HD1393.55 .M67 2019 (print) | DDC
    333.33/872—dc23
LC record available at https://lccn.loc.gov/2019008189

Cover Design: Wiley
Cover Images: © onlyyouqj /Getty Images, © franckreporter /Getty Images

Set in 10/12pt and TimesLTStd by SPi Global, Chennai, India

Printed in Great Britain by TJ International Ltd, Padstow, Cornwall, UK

10 9 8 7 6 5 4 3 2 1

To Dani and her unusual travel ideas
Giacomo

To Silvia, Julian and Sofia Ann
Paolo

Contents

About the Authors

Giacomo Morri, PhD, MRICS, is Faculty Deputy and Associate Professor of Practice in Corporate Finance and Real Estate at SDA Bocconi School of Management (Milan, Italy) and a lecturer of Real Estate Finance at Bocconi University (Milan, Italy). He served as a Director of the Master in Real Estate and the Executive Master in Corporate Finance and Banking, and was in charge of real estate executive education. Giacomo is former President and a board member of the European Real Estate Society. He is a freelancing advisor for several real estate companies and asset managers, a non-executive director at UnipolSai Investimenti SGR and a RICS Registered Valuer. He is also on the advisory board of several real estate funds and a board member of various real estate companies.

Paolo Benedetto, MRICS, is Advisory & Valuation Director at Agire – IPI Group, an Italian real estate service company. His specialization is in real estate valuations. He is an Academic Fellow of Real Estate Finance at Bocconi University (Milan, Italy) and a Fellow of Corporate Finance and Real Estate at SDA Bocconi School of Management (Milan, Italy). Paolo is a member of the Italian board of the Royal Institution of Chartered Surveyors (RICS) and a RICS Registered Valuer.

Foreword

Property valuation is a field of professional practice that has been consistently challenged by academics over the last fifty years. The UK, in particular, has seen a continuing battle between proponents of simple income capitalization methods, which are perfectly appropriate in simple cases, and critics of these methods, who have observed the mathematical and logical errors which creep in when the case becomes less simple. The complications which have kept us busy include leasehold interests, over-rented property and reversionary (under-rented) assets.

In 2019, there are a lot more complications to be dealt with. The simplest of simple cases that gives comfort to the traditional valuer is a property let to a single tenant at a market triple net rent on a long lease. The cash flow begins immediately: there are no deductions to be made, there are no upward or downward shocks to be anticipated for a long time. The relationship between the cap rate, the required return and a simple rent growth rate is complicated only by the periodicity of rent reviews – and not complicated at all if they are annual. In such cases the "implicit" cap rate approach – while relatively useless in providing information – does a perfectly good job as a measure of value, and there is no need for a laborious explicit DCF approach.

But such cases have become rarer. Leases have become shorter. Buildings have become bigger and are more likely to be multi-let. There are more likely to be irrecoverable expenses. There are likely to be fitting out contributions or free-rent periods to support supposed "market" rent levels. Shorter leases increase the chances of a rent re-set within reasonable hold or analysis period. Retail rents may be turnover-based. The co-working generation has pushed the underlying revenue model for business space closer to the hotel revenue model, which is much less predictable. "Space as a service" implies a more complex EBITDA model for real estate, which starts to look more like a business than a bond.

The result is that explicit DCF-based valuations are now essential in the majority of cases. Computer-based valuation packages remove much of the labour needed to build such models, and we can observe a significant switch in the issues which underlie any debate or instruction about valuation.

First, black boxes are inevitable but dangerous. As property occupation becomes more short-term and more service based, the variations to a standard model become greater in number and risk, and it is essential that students and practitioners of valuation understand the theory and practice of building a solid, explicit cash flow model without reverting to an off-the-shelf package. Second, data is essential. If leases are shorter and space is a service, what is the likelihood of re-letting the space? And at what cost? After what period of vacancy?

This book is a very welcome and timely contribution to this switch. It is focused on a thorough understanding of the inputs into both implicit and explicit valuation methods and uses a set of highly practical examples for readers to follow. An examination of hedonic pricing prepares us for a world of automated valuation models in the residential for sale market, and it is great to see examples focused not on New York or London but in continental Europe.

Oxford, May 2019
Andrew Baum
Professor of Practice, Saïd Business School – University of Oxford

Foreword

For any real estate market player, landlord, investor, or lender, knowing the probable value of a real estate asset is fundamental. Why is it so crucial? It is of such importance as it enables quick move for arbitrages, reduces decision-making bias, avoids mistakes, and better manages and mitigates investment risks. In the end, understanding the true value of the assets we have in our hands makes all the difference between a profitable and losing investment – this is also the reason why I deeply believe valuation is an instrumental part of any real estate asset risk assessment.

Thanks to a didactic approach, the authors, in the first part of the book, provide all the keys related to the real estate valuation theory. Whilst they primarily focus on commercial real estate, they also include some colour on residential properties. This book being well balanced about delivering concepts and examples, its second part encompass rich and detailed case studies (office building, high street retail, hotel and residential development) that are presented as a concrete application of the theory.

After a reminder of the main standards of our industry, the economic characteristics of the real estate assets, and the various risk factors inherent to real estate investments, the authors focus on property valuation. They introduce a simple and well-structured framework for the analysis and valuation of real estate assets – both in a rigorous academic approach and at the same time in business logic, resulting from long experience with key stakeholders of the real estate business sector.

This book also offers a new classification of the valuation methods. The authors provide deep and meaningful insights on each of them, with reminders when necessary of the specifics of the real estate market (and the uniqueness of each asset) vs. that of the securities market. They ensure always to clarify the central notions, illustrating them with many concrete examples of application that help to better apprehend the valuation concepts, the methods, their characteristics and uses, their advantages and limitations.

Rather than providing the reader with lots of formulas, the book concentrates on giving the reader the right inputs to choose the best valuation approach to be applied in each specific case. While the authors make it clear "why the choice of a valuation method is fundamental to making a correct estimate of the market value", they also explain the reasons why applying different models at the same time, for other purposes than those of control, may not be relevant and "would only contribute to deviating from the correct value" in the case of significant differences emerging in the estimated value. It is also worth noting that the authors place more emphasis on the economic and financial valuation methods than on the other ones made less efficient in view of the evolution of the markets – these latter being used rather as tools for verifying the results of the former. Furthermore, the authors pay particular attention to key but somewhat grey concepts, such as the discount and cap rates. They remind us that, amongst the many variables to consider, the paramount importance of understanding and setting these metrics properly when using them as small changes up or down on these assumptions can lead to a great impact on the value.

In the end, this book will interest, of course, every real estate professional who wishes to deepen their knowledge on real estate valuations. But beyond that, this book brings for sure a welcome and worthwhile contribution to our industry and, more broadly, to the economy, as it shows the way to raise the bar of valuation practices thanks to a sophisticated and rigorous but always pragmatic approach. This can only reinforce trust in the real estate business sector; a fundamental aspect in the ever turbulent markets.

Paris, May 2019
Vincent Vinit
Chief Risk Officer, Generali Real Estate S.p.A.

Preface

Real estate accounts for a large portion of overall wealth, and it is a means of production and consumption, as well as an investment asset. For the reasonable conduct of these activities, it is essential to know their value, even when they are not the subject of a sale. While the most frequent reason for obtaining a Property Valuation is an impending sale, during which usually both the seller and the buyer make their valuation of the asset to get an idea of its "true" value, there are many other situations where it is still necessary to make an estimate.

Banks, for example, systematically resort to an asset valuation that will act as collateral for the loan granted and, on that basis, will be able to determine the amount of the loan. Again, in the case of successions or spin-off, the value of properties must often be determined. The International Financial Reporting Standards (IFRS) themselves require a regular valuation of properties at their Market Value. Other cases in which valuation is necessary are to determine the value of a property for insurance coverage purposes or as a basis for the calculation of property taxes.

However, unlike securities, each property is unique, and there is no equivalent sold on a regulated market for which the actual dealing price is known with certainty. The fact that the valuation is based on a prediction of more or less uncertain future events shows why the valuation process is so important and why it has to ensure generality (it has to ignore the characteristics of the parties involved in the negotiation and their respective contractual strengths and the valuer must avoid or use with care any data and parameters vitiated by anomalous or unusual situations, which may boost or reduce the value of the property), rationality (it has to determine the value using a logical, clear and mutually agreeable system) and demonstrability (the data used must be credible and objective).

The value is therefore different from the price as the former is an estimated *ex-ante* amount, based on future forecasts, and therefore by definition uncertain, while the latter is an ascertainable *ex-post* and therefore specific amount. If the market accepts an estimated value, it may become a potential exchange value, and therefore a sale price, assuming that market players consider the value fair and complete the transaction.

It is also appropriate, however, to distinguish between value and cost, where cost means either the price paid for a given asset or the total expenses necessary to develop such an asset. While in the first case, in certain circumstances, price, cost, and value may coincide (e.g. a transaction that is concluded between the parties at a price corresponding to the estimated Market Value, and which therefore becomes the purchase cost of the asset for the buyer), in the second case an alignment between them is unlikely. For example, consider the case of a Development Project, where the production cost of the Building should theoretically be lower than the selling price of the same, at least in the case of a transaction that guarantees a positive margin for the developer; or the case of a property with specific characteristics not suitable for alternative use whose Market Value will therefore presumably be lower than the cost of constructing it.

Property Valuation is, therefore, a fundamental activity in the modern economy and, as such, there is an extensive literature on the topic. However, as academics and professionals, we have always found that many of them mostly focus on the technicalities providing complex and lengthy formulas which, if on one side are irreproachable from a mathematical point of view, on the other leave vast space to the discretionary choice of inputs.

At this point, the reader will be asking himself what he/she will be able to find innovative in the book and what instead he/she will not find at all.

Provided that there is nothing new to be created in Property Valuation, even though valuation techniques are on a continuous evolution, let's think about the impact of artificial intelligence or the use of big data among the others, why or where should this book be different from many others? The book differentiates in providing a new perspective of Property Valuation. It does not start from formulas where it might be hard to identify the right data to input, but rather from reasonings which might guide the reader in identifying, with a higher degree of awareness, the right methods and the best parameters to apply in different circumstances.

The aim of this book, therefore, is to provide the reader with an easy to understand and clear introduction to Property Valuation, with a well-defined approach to the topic, a description of the different valuation methods and an application to some typical cases. Not having the ambition to cover all the issues related to Property Valuation, the book focuses in particular on:

1. The Market Value estimation, the objective perspective of an external appraiser and not the subjective one of a specific investor (as in the estimate of the Investment Value).
2. The Commercial Properties, which represent the primary real estate investment category, even though Residential is an essential part of the property market.
3. The Income Capitalisation Methods. The methods based on the Market Approach and those based on the Cost Approach, even if briefly described, will not be analysed in-depth because they are both very well explained in other textbooks and their application in the valuation of Commercial Properties is limited. On the other side, the Book will analyse rigorously the topic of real estate cap and discount rates, which often represent a grey area not only in practice but also in some textbooks. What exactly do Property Return Rates represent? What are the parameters to take into account in their construction? What is the relationship between the cap rate and the discount rate? The book tries to provide answers to these and other questions, even if there is the awareness that there is not a unique solution and that the primary reference regarding actual or expected returns should always be represented by market players.

In this perspective, the authors suggest that the reader should look at each property as a company, whose value directly depends on the product offered to the market, the use of Space, whose measurement and economic quantification of costs and benefits require technical, economic and financial competences and tools.

Property Valuation does not represent at all an exact science, and often there is not even an absolute agreement on the best approach in order to value a specific property; therefore, a conscious, reasoned and justified choice allows to minimise the margin of error and to strengthen the Property Valuation.

The reader will also find a straightforward description of the economic characteristics of properties and of their risks, in order to assess which are the fundamental parameters to take into account in valuation and how to estimate them, together with practical support on how to prepare a valuation report.

The book is based on the professional and academic experience of the authors. In their professional experience as advisors, risk managers and board members, the authors have been involved in hundreds of real estate valuations, either directly as valuers or indirectly as users of valuation reports written by other valuers. This experience has allowed the authors to acquire expertise in the elements of strength and weakness. Their academic activity, based on research and teaching in masters and executive programmes, recently led to the publication of an Italian language textbook[1] on real estate valuations, from which this book has partially taken inspiration.

The experience of the authors will guide the reader in distinguishing what is suggested by the theory from what is necessary or effectively possible to apply in practice, in an ideal comparison between "classroom" and "real world". In contrast to textbooks full of formulas that forget to help the reader on how to find "data" on the market, this book instead puts much effort on the underlying reasoning. Some evidence will also be provided on the most common mistakes in Property Valuation, in order to allow those who are not professional valuers to be able to read a valuation report critically. To this end, we highlight the importance of the selection of data, in their interpretation and in their processing.

Conversely, the book does not aim to debate around methods, definitions and classifications, but proposes some simplifications of all these in order to help the reader in understanding the principles and techniques to estimate the value of properties in a modern economic perspective, which finds its foundation in the market. The use of capital letters is not, therefore, oriented to give more importance to particular terms, which might not be so "strict" from a legal or economic point of view, but rather, as it is commonly used in contracts, to simplify the reading and to specify univocally certain concepts that will always be used in the book with the same meaning (and whose definitions will be found in the glossary at the end of the book).

Concerning the content,[2] the first eight chapters are mostly dedicated to theory and the different valuation "methods", while the last four chapters are dedicated to practise, with some case studies included. In order to balance theory and practice, but at the same time to keep the book effective in every country, some contents have been kept general on purpose. An outline of each chapter follows:

- *Chapter 1* provides an introduction to the subject of Property Valuation. A definition of the valuation requirement (i.e. the valuation subject, purpose and date, and the value basis to be estimated) is provided. Next, the chapter focuses on the different bases of value, in particular distinguishing between Market Value, Investment Value and other commonly used definitions. Finally, a brief description is given of the leading associations operating in the field of Property Valuation and which aim to raise operating standards and standardise international valuation practices.
- *Chapter 2* provides an interpretation of the economic features of properties, illustrating their characteristics and providing a preliminary classification for valuation purposes. In order to estimate the value of an asset correctly, it is essential to start by assessing the economic characteristics that determine the demand from potential users and buyers. These economic characteristics are also fundamental for choosing the correct valuation method, as they identify which market data is required to allow the value of the asset to be estimated. On the other side, it is also essential to identify the main types of risk involved

in the real estate sector so that the risk of property investment can in some way be adequately considered. The chapter will, therefore, also provide the reader with a description of the main elements of risk, although it is correct to refer to these as uncertainty, in order to identify an overall risk that can be associated with a specific property being valued, for which an expected return rate may need to be estimated.

- *Chapter 3* provides an overview of the economic and property market analysis which is the foundation of any Property Valuation.
- *Chapter 4* describes the valuation methods that will be analysed in-depth in the following chapters, proposing a new classification, not in order to introduce a new theory of Property Valuation or in order to impose new criteria, but rather to guide the reader in the estimate of properties value as a function of their economic characteristics. A brief description of the Depreciated Cost Approach Methods is provided in order to highlight their limits.
- *Chapter 5* presents the Sales Comparison Approach Methods, starting with the principles on which they are based, subsequently describing in greater detail the main application criteria – the Direct Comparison Approach and the Hedonic Pricing Model – showing how each one is used, and discussing their main advantages and limitations.
- *Chapter 6* provides a detailed description of the Income Capitalisation Comparison Approach Methods, of the two main application criteria – the Direct Capitalisation Approach and the Discounted Cash Flow Approach – and of the Residual Value Methods, which, based on the same models, allow for the estimation of the value of greenfields, brownfields and, more in general, all properties at the end of their life cycle.
- *Chapter 7* is dedicated to Property Return Rates (cap rate and discount rate), whose estimate is still one of the most critical aspects in the application of the Income Capitalisation Methods and which is often a source of mistakes or appraisals not sufficiently supported by empirical evidence.
- *Chapter 8* describes the main elements of what is known as a "valuation report", i.e. the document relating to the appraisal of a property.

The book is also enriched with examples and in-depth analysis, which are enclosed in boxes named respectively "Example" and "A Closer Look" which can be easily identified.

Needless to say, although the book aims at outlining factors common to any real estate valuation, and – hence – sets out principles, rules, and techniques applicable internationally, as a matter of convention, the examples are presented in euros. Of course, nothing would change were the pound sterling, US dollar, Lao kip or any other currency to be used. The choice to refer to the euro in the examples appeared the best way to express the international outreach of this book, as it is a symbol of internationalisation, having brought together a range of countries within a single currency.

As previously mentioned, the last four chapters are dedicated to several case studies representative of the methods previously described, in order to allow the reader to verify how they can be practically applied. These chapters focus in particular on the application of the Income Capitalisation Methods with the valuation of an office building, a high street retail unit, a hotel, and, through the application of the Multiple Periods Residual Value Approach, a mixed-use condominium development.

The case studies, even if all adapted from real valuation reports, are presented in an exemplifying and didactic form, which allows for reflection more on the identification of the economic characteristics of the properties, the choice of the valuation method, and on the right inputs to use, rather than on the technical criticalities or the mathematical calculations to apply. At the same time, the case studies presented do not complete the entire possible spectrum of potential properties to be valued, even though they represent a sample that, with the right adaptations, might be applied to a pretty wide array of properties.

Moreover, it must be taken into account the fact that the practical application of different methods by different valuers might lead to the choice of different solutions. As mentioned before, Property Valuation is not an exact science and therefore, as in any estimate, there is a certain degree of uncertainty. In this sense, the choice of writing different case studies jointly with different authors allows also having some examples of contrasting approaches used in the real estate industry.

In valuations aimed at determining the Market Value of properties, the logical and mathematical formulas are reduced to few calculations and, differently from investment analysis, the technicalities are pretty simple. It is, instead, crucial to underline everything that is behind the final calculation and therefore the identification of the economic characteristics of the properties, the choice of the proper valuation method, the market analysis, and the choice of the correct input data to use.

This is why all the case studies presented are simplified regarding property description, omitting all that information – technical, cadastral, urban planning, etc. – which is usually an essential part of valuation reports, while they focus on the choice of the valuation method, on the market analysis and, finally, on the application of the right criteria.

The book is combined with a dedicated website (www.cpv-mb.com) with:

- Microsoft Excel spreadsheet files with formulas of valuation examples, to assist the reader's understanding, and for instant pedagogical use.
- Microsoft PowerPoint presentations in order to synthesise for the reader the topics of each chapter and which represent a useful tool for teaching purposes.
- Links to websites mentioned in the text and to others of interest on related topics.
- An interactive bibliography with the ability to directly consult articles and documents mentioned, with links to the sources.

Any comments, critiques, suggestions, or information from readers are very welcome. Please feel free to contact the authors by email at info@propertyfinance.it.

Heartfelt thanks to all those who, at various times, have contributed in the realisation of this book. To Fabio Cristanziani (Generali Real Estate), Arianna Mazzanti (Milanosesto Development – Prelios Group), Ezio Poinelli and Pavlos Papadimitriou (HVS) who have written the case studies based on their professional experience. To professor Mihnea Constantinescu (University of Zurich and PrepayWay), Marco Denari (Partners Group), Stefano Farsura (Colonnade Group), Aldo Mazzocco (Generali Real Estate), Michele Monterosso (ING Bank), Fabrizio Trimarchi (Hotel Seeker), and Stefano Chierichetti for their invaluable support. Thanks also to all the students who have raised doubts and asked questions on issues related to the valuation topic, thus pushing the authors to never stop studying and learning!

Naturally, responsibility for all errors lies solely with the authors.

Finally, the authors strive always to sustain in the course of their work and research the fundamental principles of independence, integrity, objectivity, the respect of others and the profession, the assumption of responsibilities and the need to continually work to raise their own professional standards and to encourage the same in others.

Milan, Italy, June 2019
Giacomo Morri, MRICS & Paolo Benedetto, MRICS

NOTES

1. Morri G., Benedetto P. (2017), *Valutazione Immobiliare – Metodologie e casi*, EGEA, Milan (Italy).
2. The Book is the product of joint work of the Authors; however, Chapters 2, 4, 5, 6 and 7 are mostly attributable to Giacomo Morri, while Chapters 1, 3, 8 and 9 are mostly attributable to Paolo Benedetto.

Commercial Property Valuation

CHAPTER 1

Introduction to Property Valuation

This chapter provides an introduction to the subject of Property Valuation.[1] A definition of the valuation requirement (i.e. the valuation subject, purpose and date, and the value to be estimated) is provided. In the sections that follow, a focus is made on the several basis of value, in particular distinguishing between Market Value, Investment Value and other commonly used definitions. Finally, a brief description is given of the leading associations that operate in the field of Property Valuation and aim to raise operating standards and standardise international valuation practices.

DETERMINING THE VALUATION REQUIREMENT

The valuation process consists of a sequence of activities which can be defined as follows and will be examined in detail in this book:

1. Preliminary phase:
   a) Determining the valuation requirement, i.e. the nature of the property and the objectives of the valuation
   b) Gathering and analysing the documentation and information required.
2. Operational phase:
   a) Inspection of the property (unless it is exclusively a desktop valuation)
   b) Identification of the applicable method and criteria
   c) Gathering of market parameters
   d) Calculation of the value using the chosen method
   e) Writing of the valuation report.
3. Conclusion: checking of results.

Before considering the valuation methods and operational procedures to be used in carrying out the valuation, it is essential to identify all the elements that contribute to determine the valuation requirement unequivocally. Mostly, the valuer has to answer the following questions:

1. What is the subject of the valuation?
2. What is the purpose of the valuation?
3. What is the value definition to be estimated?
4. What is the valuation date?

The Subject of the Valuation

Without going into too much detail regarding the legal framework, which is outside the scope of this book, and even though the subject of the Property Valuation might also be security rights and limited use rights (*iura in re aliena*, such as surface rights or usufruct), throughout this book we shall refer exclusively to the full and exclusive right of ownership over a property, without going into the valuation of other cases, even though they are relatively frequent in professional practice.

We would also refer the reader to Chapter 2 for a detailed consideration of the economic characteristics and the classification of properties, as proposed by the authors.

Purpose of the Valuation

Concerning the purpose of the valuation, there are many circumstances that could result in a need (for regulatory compliance) or interest (for the client's reasons) in knowing the value of a property. Typically, however, the reasons stem from decisions of a financial nature which, being based on rational choices, require knowledge of the value of the asset itself. The most common purposes include, for example:

- Transfer purposes: M&A, inheritance transfers, court proceedings, sale and purchase of companies, transfer of companies and business branches, IPOs, and expropriation procedures.
- Strategic purposes: financing transactions, valuations for insurance purposes, tax compliance, statutory compliance, and compensation disputes.
- Economic feasibility: feasibility analysis, purchase or leasing decisions, and investment decisions.

In reality, as we shall see further on, where the Market Value is being determined, the purpose of the valuation has no impact on the value itself, which has to be unequivocal regardless of the client/Owner and his/her specific reasons.

Value to Be Estimated

The 'value to be estimated' is simply the 'basis of value' to be used for the valuation, details of which are given in the Section 'Definitions of Value' below. As stated in the Preface, this book focuses on valuations of the Market Value, but there are many 'types' of values to be estimated, including Investment Value or insurable value.

Valuation Date

Regarding the 'valuation date', a distinction should be made between:

- Report date: 'the date on which the valuer signs the report'[2]
- Valuation date (or 'date of valuation'): 'the date on which the opinion of value applies'[3]
- Date on which the investigations were carried out or were completed.

The valuation date is of particular interest as it can be in the present (at the time the valuation is requested) or in the past, but also in the future (in the hypothesis that, e.g. certain conditions will be satisfied).

While on the one hand a retrospective (or *ex-post*) valuation, i.e. referring to a past date, may seem easier, as there is typically a greater amount of information available to the valuer, on the other it is important to point out that the valuation has to be carried out as if one were living in the past and, therefore, without being aware of events that may have subsequently modified the value of the asset. A typical case in which a retrospective assessment may be required is that of tax, administrative or judicial litigations.

Conversely, a prospective (or *ex-ante*) valuation, referring to a future date, requires the valuer to base the estimate not just on current market expectations (as in the case of a valuation referring to the present), but also by incorporating events that have not yet occurred into its own forecasts. A typical case in which a prospective assessment may be required is that of a Development Project, where the value of the asset once completed needs to be appraised with reasonable accuracy, even though at present the development has not yet been completed. In fact, as detailed later on, valuations carried out with the Income Capitalisation Methods, for estimating the Present Value of a property, require an appraisal of the prospective value of the same (the so-called 'Terminal Value'), which is one of the main limitations of the same criterion.

It is particularly important to identify the valuation date correctly because it allows the valuer and users of the valuation to support and justify adequately the result achieved. In a broader sense, identifying the date can be viewed as an analysis of the conditions of the relevant market for the property and therefore of all the factors that positively or negatively influence its value. An accurate and comprehensive description of the contingent situation of the market in which the asset is located is an essential condition for correctly determining the estimated value.

Only after having answered these questions fully will it be possible to identify the most appropriate valuation method, apply the most appropriate approach for estimating the value, and, finally, verify the results of the valuation.

DEFINITIONS OF VALUE

The objective of the valuation activity is to estimate the value of an asset. In the broadest sense, the term 'valuation' involves a judgement on the equivalence between a property (the one being valued) and an amount of money (unit of measurement), given certain conditions and within a specified period. Valuing a property, therefore, means expressing its value in an amount of money, which is why choosing the right definition of value is of primary importance.

Market Value

There is currently no unequivocal definition of Market Value. There are as many definitions as there are national and international associations, entities or bodies (see also Section 'Valuation Associations, Codes, and Standards') determining the standards for Property Valuation. Among the most frequently used are the definitions adopted by the Appraisal Institute, Royal Institution of Chartered Surveyors (RICS) and The European Group of Valuers' Assocations (TEGoVA).

- Appraisal Institute (2002): 'The most probable price, as of a specified date, in cash, or in terms equivalent to cash, or in other precisely revealed terms, for which the specified property rights should sell after reasonable exposure in a competitive market under all conditions requisite to a fair sale, with the buyer and seller each acting prudently, knowledgeably, and for self-interest, and assuming that neither is under undue duress'.
- RICS (2017): 'The estimated amount for which an asset or liability should exchange on the valuation date between a willing buyer and a willing seller in an arm's length transaction,

after proper marketing and where the parties had each acted knowledgeably, prudently and without compulsion'.

■ TEGoVA[4]: 'The estimated amount for which the property should exchange on the date of valuation between a willing buyer and a willing seller in an arm's length transaction after proper marketing wherein the parties had each acted knowledgeably, prudently and without being under compulsion'.

Albeit with a few different nuances, all the definitions include the same basic concepts:

1. A certain amount of money has to be estimated by a competent person as being the consideration payable for the sale of the property.
2. The date as of which this consideration must be estimated is the valuation date.
3. There must be two distinct and independent players: a seller willing to sell at the best price achievable on the market and a buyer willing to buy, but without paying a higher price than he/she could pay for a similar asset.
4. The transaction must only take place following adequate marketing, i.e. the property must remain on sale for a sufficient time to ensure that it can be assessed by a sufficient number of potential buyers.
5. Both the seller and the buyer must act with full knowledge of all the information concerning the property, and both must be willing, and not obliged or forced, to complete the transaction.

Furthermore, according to the authors, the Market Value implicitly considers in its definition the Highest and Best Use (HBU), namely any use of the property that is physically possible (i.e. technically achievable), financially sustainable, legally permitted (or allowed by town planning regulations), economically convenient (which offers the best profitability) and which therefore allows the value itself to be maximised. Therefore, according to the authors, there is a single Market Value for each property, not a Market Value 'as is' and a Market Value in the event of it being used in a way that maximises its value. This better use of the asset should not be viewed in absolute terms. It has to be the best reasonable use attributed to the property by a typical player on the market. There may be a particular use that only some players are able to identify and achieve, the value of which (in this case the Investment Value, as defined in greater detail in the next section) is greater. In other words, one assumes that if there is a better use than the current one, which all players can reasonably identify, the asset should be valued with this prospect in mind.

To give an example, imagine a property located in the centre of a large city, the ground floor of which is currently used as a car park but could be converted for retail use. Presumably, in the event of a conversion, a higher rent[5] could be achieved and, therefore, a higher sale price for the property. If the capital gain achieved is higher than the conversion cost, the Market Value of the property will not be the value of the property in its current state, but the value resulting from the conversion of the ground floor, as it is reasonable to believe that the best offer will be made by someone who intends to pursue such a strategy. In other words, in the second case, in order to achieve a higher value, an investment has to be made. However, it is reasonable to assume that, if this investment is profitable, most of potential buyers will value the asset with this in mind. Conversely, if there was another particular use which only some players were able to identify, and which created a higher value (e.g. the Owner of a property that stands beside a hotel which might be interested in acquiring this property to create a restaurant), this use would not necessarily have to be considered in the valuation scenarios.

In summary, therefore, without wanting to give a new definition, one can reasonably say that Market Value is understood to be 'the estimated amount of money, or equivalent means, for which a property should be sold or purchased, as of the valuation date, by a seller and a buyer with no particular ties and both interested in the transaction, on a competitive basis, following an appropriate marketing activity in which both have acted in an informed, conscious and unrestricted way. This amount, subject to certain limits, must reflect the Highest and Best Use of the asset which is physically possible, financially sustainable, legally permitted and economically convenient for ordinary players.

Finally, it is worth mentioning that:

- The concept of Market Value is similar, but does not necessarily coincide with that of fair value, which is understood to be 'The price that would be received to sell an asset, or paid to transfer a liability, in an orderly transaction between market participants at the measurement date (IFRS 13)'.
- Equivalently to the definition of Market Value, there is also a definition of Market Rent. For simplicity, only the following definition is provided: 'The estimated amount for which an interest in real property should be leased on the valuation date between a willing lessor and willing lessee on appropriate lease terms in an arm's length transaction, after proper marketing and where the parties had each acted knowledgeably, prudently and without compulsion'.[6]

Investment Value

A second very frequently used basis of value is the Investment Value. Again, we have provided below the definitions adopted respectively by the Appraisal Institute, RICS and TEGoVA.

- Appraisal Institute (2002): 'The specific value of an investment to a particular investor or class of investors based on individual investment requirements; distinguished from Market Value, which is impersonal and detached'.
- RICS (2017): 'The value of an asset to the owner or a prospective owner for individual investment or operational objectives (may also be known as worth)'.
- TEGoVA (2016): 'Value of a property to a particular identified party for investment, owner-occupation or operational purposes'.

While the focus of this book on Market Value, given that the assessment investments and their respective financial convenience, in addition to relying on different principles, also requires the use of other criteria not detailed here, it is worth highlighting the main differences between the two definitions previously given.

In seeking a Market Value, the valuer takes an objective approach: in other words, his task is not to determine a value for a particular person or entity, but the value which the market is prepared to attribute to the asset, given that the Market Value is the highest price one could reasonably expect to achieve on the market, taking all the potential types of buyers into account. Consequently, the data used to determine a Market Value must be the most probable data you can get from the market, without referring to a specific person or entity. Conversely, when determining an Investment Value, one has to identify a specific person or entity and look at the asset from the latter's point of view, given that the Investment Value is the highest price a specific buyer may offer considering his investment requirements, his knowledge and his strategy.

VALUATION ASSOCIATIONS, CODES AND STANDARDS

As previously stated, there are numerous associations which, at international or national level, have been created and have developed with the primary objective of providing the real estate sector and, in particular, all those operating in the field of Property Valuation, with ethical and professional standards (rules of professional conduct and skills) to increase market transparency and objectivity in the valuation process to ensure, ultimately, greater protection of the various players involved (from simple savers and citizens to professional investors and lending institutions). The following passage is an example:

> *Consistency, objectivity and transparency are fundamental to building and sustaining public confidence and trust in valuation. In turn their achievement depends crucially on valuation providers possessing and deploying the appropriate skills, knowledge, experience and ethical behaviour, both to form sound judgments and to report opinions of value clearly and unambiguously to clients and other valuation users in accordance with globally recognised norms.*[7]

The most important international associations undoubtedly include the Appraisal Institute, RICS and TEGoVA.

- Appraisal Institute[8]: founded in 1932, this is a global organisation of property valuers that includes more than 18,000 professionals in nearly 50 countries around the world. Its mission is to advance professionalism and ethics, global standards, methods and practices in the field of property.
- Royal Institution of Chartered Surveyors[9]: established in 1868, this 'is the global professional body promoting and enforcing the highest international standards in the valuation, management and development of Land, real estate, construction and infrastructure'. Currently, there are 125,000 qualified and trainee property professionals around the world accredited with RICS. Based in London, RICS has regional offices in Brussels, Dubai, Hong Kong, Delhi, New York and Sydney and is currently present in 46 countries.
- TEGoVA[10]: created in June 1997 from the previous EUROVAL, The European Group of Valuers' Associations is a non-profit association currently consisting of 72 associations of property valuers in 37 countries, representing over 70,000 valuers in Europe. The primary purpose of the association is to create and disseminate harmonised standards for valuation practice, education and certification, as well as for corporate governance and ethics among valuers. TEGoVA supports its members in introducing and implementing these standards, particularly through the publication of the European Valuation Standards (EVS) since the early 1980s.

Although they are not always necessarily implemented by the jurisdictions of the individual countries, the professional assessment standards drawn up by these associations are indeed one of their most significant contributions, with which all members working both individually and through valuation firms are required to conform. Of particular interest are the RICS Professional Valuation Standards, better known as the 'Red Book', which comply fully with the International Valuation Standards (IVS) published by the International Valuation Standards Council[11] (IVSC) and the 'Blue Book' of the European Group of Valuers' Associations (TEGoVA), which instead contains the European Valuation Standards[12] (EVS).

NOTES

1. In the book, the words 'valuation' and 'valuer' are sometimes substituted by the words 'appraisal' and 'appraiser'. Similarly, many other specific terms may often be identified synonymously. The theory relating to real estate valuation is indeed pretty wide and sometimes different words are used to express the same concepts (simply think about different terms in British English and American English).
2. RICS (2017).
3. RICS (2017).
4. EVS1 referring to Regulation 575/2013/EU, art. 4, paragraph 1, point 76.
5. The terms 'rent', 'rental' and 'lease' are often used as synonyms in common practice. However, they refer to different things and they might assume different definitions in different countries due to different legislative frameworks. Indeed 'rental' might refer to 'an arrangement to rent something for a period of time, or the act of renting something' as well as to 'the amount of money that you pay to rent something for a period of time' (online Cambridge Dictionary). Moreover, a 'rental agreement' is usually referred to a tenancy of a short period (less than 30 days), that is automatically renewed at its end unless the tenant or the Owner (who has the right of changing the terms of the agreement with proper written notice) ends it by giving written notice, while a 'lease agreement' is usually referred to a set term (6 months, 1 year or even longer periods), where the tenant pays the 'rent', the amount of which cannot be raised by the Owner (who cannot change the conditions), unless the tenant agrees. For the sake of simplicity, in the book the term 'rent' has been used to indicate the amount of money corresponded for the Use of Space, the term 'rental' has been used as an adjective (such as 'rental market', 'rental sector', 'rental level', etc.) and, finally, the term 'lease' has been used to identify the contractual relationship between the tenant and the Owner ('lease agreement').
6. Definition adopted by RICS (2017).
7. RICS (2017).
8. www.appraisalinstitute.org
9. www.rics.org
10. www.tegova.org
11. www.ivsc.org
12. www.tegova.org/en/p4912ae3909e49

CHAPTER 2

Economic Characteristics and Elements of Risks of Properties

This chapter provides an economic interpretation of properties, illustrating their characteristics and providing a preliminary classification for valuation purposes. In order to estimate the value of an asset correctly, it is essential to start by assessing the economic characteristics that determine the demand from potential users and buyers. These economic characteristics are also fundamental for choosing the correct valuation method, as they identify which market data is required to allow the value of the asset to be estimated.

Property Valuations or investment analyses based on Income Capitalisation Methods rely on the expected yield to be identified which, in a nutshell, depends on the risk associated with the asset being analysed. For this reason, it is fundamental to give the reader some food for thought on the subject of real estate risk. As we shall see, no definitive answer is given to the problem of quantifying risk. Despite a large amount of financial literature on the subject, measuring the risk involved in direct real estate investment presents specific implementation difficulties.[1] Furthermore, even though it would be more correct to distinguish between the concepts of risk, where the likelihood of an event can be measured statistically, and uncertainty, which cannot be measured,[2] in this book the two terms will be used synonymously. Finally, despite the fact that the term 'risk' is often interpreted with a negative connotation, and this is how the factors that can impact on the value of a property will be presented in this chapter, one must not forget that the *ex-post* return might actually be lesser or higher than expected.

Real estate investment decisions are often taken with a 'fundamental uncertainty about the future'.[3] The problem, in fact, is that often there is not enough information and the available data are not normally distributed,[4] which means that statistical models and probability analysis are not very useful, although they have been used in research for many years.[5]

Furthermore, the property market is characterised by relatively long cycles, with periods of price contraction followed by periods of price rise. This cyclical behaviour can be explained by the lengthy production process, which leads to periods of excess supply alternating with periods of scarcity (availability of Space) and consequent variations in income (rent), and by rate variations in the capital market and consequent variations in the expected cap rates.[6] Periods of increasing values, which may last several years, can lead some Investors to underestimate the risk of property investment: in almost all real estate markets, in fact, there have been prolonged periods of sustained growth in value, albeit followed by periods of negative performance. Given this dynamic, many Investors, primarily private individuals, believe that the current yield is the 'basic' return, which will be further increased by a 'definite' capital gain return in the medium- to long-term.

Even though the myth of bricks and mortar being a safe investment may have waned recently, it is worth describing the main types of risk involved in the real estate sector so that the risk of property investment can in some way be adequately considered. In this chapter an attempt will be made to provide the reader with a description of the main elements of risk, although it would be better to refer to these as uncertainty, in order to identify an overall risk that can be associated with a particular subject property, for which an expected return rate may need to be estimated.

CHARACTERISTICS OF PROPERTY INVESTMENTS

The value of properties, particularly according to the specific definition of Market Value, depends strictly on economic characteristics, which must inevitably also take into account physical characteristics, such as location and the technical features of the Building.

In order to estimate the value correctly, it is important to outline some of these economic characteristics, in order to gain a better understanding, particularly in the following chapters, of the elements that determine it. The following is not intended to coin new definitions but, for the sole purpose of improving their understanding, only to assign precise meanings to frequently used terms.

Building and Land

For simplicity, the property is defined as an asset consisting of two elements: the Land and the Building on which it stands. This definition and distinction is obviously an extreme simplification, but it is a handy way of understanding the economic dynamics, as it allows the two elements to be analysed separately and the value relationships between them to be more clearly understood.

All real estate properties are built on Land. This term, therefore, broadly refers not only to the area on which the Building stands but also to the building rights and location. The Land component is, therefore, a feature of all properties, including any portions in which there is no direct correspondence between the real estate unit and the Land, such as an apartment within a residential condominium.

In physical terms, Land has unlimited duration and its utility does not decrease over time.[7] However, in some cases, from an economic point of view, where a leasehold or a concession exist, for example, Land may have a limited life. This second scenario is less frequent and arises from a legal constraint.

The Building is the structure built on the Land and is the component of the Property that loses its utility over time. In fact, every Building has a useful life which, albeit long, is nonetheless limited, as it is subject to natural senescence and technical/functional obsolescence. Old age means that, after a certain number of years, it is no longer economically convenient to use the building in its existing condition, but it is more advantageous to demolish it and rebuild it, or proceed with refurbishing.

In certain markets (such as in European countries), due to regulatory restrictions imposed to protect artistic heritage, owing to the different construction techniques and for cultural reasons, there is a tendency to renovate old Buildings rather than to demolish and rebuild them. In other markets (the United States being an extreme example), where different regulations and cultures exist, refurbishment is rarely carried out and often the demolition and reconstruction of the Building are more common, as it is seen as more cost-effective. For the purposes of this analysis, demolition and subsequent reconstruction can be considered to be radical forms of refurbishing.

For greater clarity, there are two different elements that determine the ageing of a Building:

- Physical senescence (technical resistance), i.e. loss of value resulting from:
  - Past use and maintenance carried out
  - Environmental effects
  - Effects of accidents
  - Failures caused by vibrations and stresses.
- Functional obsolescence (efficiency in use), i.e. loss of value resulting from:
  - Inability to perform the functions assigned
  - Technological progress in the sector
  - Change in User requirements
  - Operating costs becoming excessive.

Physical senescence can be prevented or reduced with adequate maintenance, which will keep the building in a suitable condition even for a very long time, or at least for as long as remains economically convenient. Functional obsolescence, however, depends on market factors rather than physical ones and is, therefore, more complex. First of all, it depends on demand, i.e. on the needs of the Space Users, which can change over time. Secondly, it depends on the supply of new Buildings with features that are more responsive to the new requirements. Since market changes (demand and supply) are harder to predict than the uncertainty associated with a maintenance plan, this element is the main risk factor associated with the age of a Building.

Dividing a Property into its two components of Land and Building, albeit more theoretical than applicable, allows one to draw useful conclusions for valuation purposes and to understand the market dynamics:

- The relationship between the Property and its components
- The different value dynamics of Land and Building
- The different possibility of intervention
- The case of Properties without Buildings

First of all, it is essential to point out that the value of a property does not depend on the value[8] of its Land and Building components, given that they, or at least the latter, are unlikely to have an independent value that can be estimated separately.[9] In this respect, while it is clear that Land has a value, its quantification is associated with the value of the property (existing or realisable) and with the construction cost of the Building. Clearly, a Building seldom has an independent value of its own, given that, other than in a few cases, it cannot be 'moved' to a different piece of Land to constitute a new property. See Chapter 6, Section 'Residual Value Methods' for a discussion of Land valuation.

If the value of a property were equal to the value of its component parts, with the value of the Building being determined based on its construction cost, the value of a modern office park in the middle of nowhere that very few Users would be interested in, would be at least equal to its construction cost. However, it is quite evident that in this extreme example of an almost vacant property, which is not generating any income, net operating income will continuously be negative and consequently it would have a very low or even negative value (representing a series of negative cash flows without any particular reconversion potential due to the poor location).

Secondly, still assuming that there is a theoretical possibility of assigning a separate value to the two components, it is useful to note that their dynamics are very different. The value of a property can vary over time based on many factors we shall discuss in greater detail, and it can either increase or decrease. Similarly, the value of the Land component will follow the same dynamic, while that of the Building component, due to ageing, will only fall (obviously ignoring any extraordinary maintenance or refurbishment work that may be carried out).

It could be argued that the value of some Buildings of historical importance can increase over time; however, apart from the fact that these are limited in number, it is worth remembering that every Building undergoes constant changes over time. For example, if you imagine a property built in the eighteenth century, which is still in use today, it is clear that little of the original Building will remain (e.g. the external façade, the structure and some of the common areas), but most of it (the doors and windows, internal areas, systems etc.) will have been 'replaced' over time. Furthermore, the utility of the spaces changes: the functionality (e.g. the efficiency of the layout) decreases while its prestige increases (e.g. allowing the Building to be used for prestigious retail Space).

The different value dynamics of the two components should suggest that, in the long term, the properties cannot increase in value, unless the value of the Land increases more than proportionately compared to the loss of value of the Building over time. This apparently strong statement may suggest that investing in real estate is not convenient, given that a loss would be suffered in the absence of a more than proportional increase in the value of the Land. It is worth pointing out, however, that the return on an investment essentially consists of the capital gain (the so-called 'capital gain return') and the current return (in the case of a property the return depending on the Net Operating Income). The importance of an effective asset management activity in achieving a current return that will offset the capital loss resulting from the loss of value of the Building component is therefore evident.

Thirdly, while the property owner can intervene on the Building, there is a limited amount of work that can be done on the Land. The owner, in fact, may decide to improve the Building, refurbish it or, in extreme cases, replace it by demolishing and rebuilding. It is therefore possible, subject to certain regulatory, technical and economic limits, to modify the features of the Building, adapting it to the new requirements in the Space Market. There is virtually no possibility of intervening on the Land; its characteristics (location, connectivity, the presence of other attractions) do not depend on factors that are easily controlled by the owner, but they are external factors which are beyond his control. Imagine that a new underground station is going to be built close to the property: the impact, in this case positive, on the value of the property results from a relative improvement in the location (Land) due to the better connectivity and the consequent increase in demand. Conversely, imagine the opposite effect that the closure of a large firm close to the property might have, considering that many tenants were suppliers to the firm.

In some cases, the owner may also intervene on the Land, e.g. by starting improvement work in the surrounding areas, but clearly, this can only happen above specific dimensions for it to be economically viable. For example, in the case of a Residential Development Project with fifty apartments intended for sale, even redevelopment of the surrounding public spaces would make it hard to ensure economic viability. However, in the case of an urban regeneration project, where the scale of real estate development scheme is considerable, the developer could have an economic advantage in carrying out several public works to improve the overall quality of the area (Land) on which the property stands and the surroundings.

Fourthly, there are also properties without Buildings which, nevertheless, generate Highest and Best Use (HBU) usable Space. An example of this could be an agricultural plot of Land located far from a town on which, regardless of whether it could be built upon, it would not be viable to build any kind of property. For example, along the lines of the previous example, a vineyard producing premium wine (i.e. Champagne or Brunello di Montalcino) is a property whose Space is used in a way which would be hard to improve by constructing any kind of Building.[10]

Use of Space and Investment Asset

From an economic point of view, properties are both goods which are physically used and also investment assets. Properties may be used either by their Owners or by third parties, in the latter case creating a Space Market by means of a lease agreement. Where the Owners are also the Users of the property (i.e. homeowner), given that no money (rent) changes hands for the availability of the Use of Space, an opportunity cost can be considered, i.e. the cost of renouncing the opportunity to obtain a quantity of money as rent from a third party.

In the first case, where physical use is made of the property, it produces the 'Use of Space', the utility of which depends on many factors associated with the Building (e.g. size, shape, quality, efficiency) and the location (e.g. centrality, connection, accessibility); in other words, the Land. The demand for the Use of Space for a specific property, therefore, depends on how sought-after and appreciated the previous characteristics are among Users (demand for the Use of Space) and on the availability of these goods in the same market (supply of Use of Space). Therefore, in view of this, a property is comparable to a business that produces the specific Use of Space product, the reference market of which is local, and the price of which is the rent.

In the second case, where the property is in the perspective of an investment asset, the Owner receives some utility not from direct use but from the income resulting from the sale of the Use of Space, i.e. the rent. In this case, therefore, the property has a value based on the future income it may generate and its risk. Furthermore, any sale of the asset involves selling the rights to receive future income, as with any other investment asset (such as a bond, the value of which depends on future coupons and the risk associated with this payment).

It is therefore essential to consider properties not only based on their size (surface area) but also – or perhaps above all – as assets capable of generating income, although it is evident that the former often assumes a fundamental role in generating value.

Owners and Users

The choice between being both Owners and Users of the property (i.e. homeowner), or exclusively Users (i.e. buyers of the Use of Space or tenants), is based on many subjective factors, mainly financial (e.g. constraints on the availability of capital, cost of capital, taxation) and strategic (e.g. intention to control the property, the opportunity to modify it, guarantee of long-term use, flexibility). In the Residential sector, where Space is a consumer good, families prefer to retain ownership of the property that generates the Space they use, thus favouring strategic control over it. Moreover, in some markets, due to regulations, Investors have no incentive to allocate capital to the Residential sector, which presents low returns and high legal risks, leading to the Space Market being limited to a few niches.[11] In the Residential sector there is, in fact, usually a well-developed market of homeowners[12] (Owners/Users), with no real separation between the Space Market and Investment Market.

In Commercial real estate, however, where businesses for which Space is a means of production needed to make other goods and services operate, strategic control is often of less value, while financial reasons are prevalent. Furthermore, in many countries, lower legal protection for the tenant compared to Residential reduces the risk for the Owner; consequently, in the Commercial segments, there are developed Space and Investment Markets .

To conclude, in the Residential[13] sector it is more straightforward and more realistic to estimate a value linked to the property transaction (Sales Comparison Methods) because Owners and Users often coincide and there is a less developed Space Market. Differently, in the Commercial sector, one can more easily calculate the income generated by the properties (i.e. the Space Market rent) and determine the expected yield[14] for Investors (based on the price that future tenants are prepared to pay, which obviously depends on the respective risk) by analysing the Investment Market.

Business Perspective

Where there is a separation between the Use of Space and ownership of the property, the value of the latter will evidently depend on the former, which is obviously associated with the respective risk. Consequently, although the analogy may seem a little 'stretched', a property can be compared to a business: the good produced by the property business is the Use of Space which the business Owner offers to the User, i.e. the tenant, who is an end client. Consequently, the value of the property depends solely on its capacity to generate income, which derives from a profit and loss account with a variable income component, the Use of Space (rent), and a series of fixed costs, independent of the actual production and/or sale of the product (e.g. taxes on the property or the insurance premium).

While it is intentionally simplified, the profit and loss account of an Income-producing Property (Table 2.1) presents only one major income component and several expense components which require some elaboration.

The 'Maintenance' item includes both extraordinary maintenance, usually the duty of the Owner, and current maintenance, usually the duty of the tenant.[15] The insurance premium is an easily identifiable item, but in this simplification it is considered a maintenance expense

TABLE 2.1 Simplified profit and loss account of an Income-producing Property

+	**Revenues**
	Rents (Use of Space)
−	**Costs**
	Maintenance
	Real estate taxes
	Management
=	**Net Operating Income**

as it is intended, through the insurance reimbursement, to recover the extraordinary expense of repairing any damage to the Building.

The 'Real Estate Taxes' item only includes fixed taxes paid because of the ownership of the property and not due to income. They vary in different countries but, in most of them, they are charged regardless of its actual use or income generation.

Finally, the 'Management' cost item, which is associated with all the management activities (marketing expenses and asset, property and facility management expenses) needed to operate the property.

It is worth pointing out that the cost structure is fixed as the expenses do not depend on the actual sale of the Use of Space, i.e. on the productivity of the asset that manifests itself through the lease. In fact, these expenses must be borne regardless of any actual use of the property (with the exception of part of the property expenses linked to the actual rents). On this point it is interesting to note that these are variable inverse costs, since if the property is not used (let), the Owner will bear higher costs, not only for planned maintenance costs, usually borne by the tenant, but also for the necessary restoration of the Building after a period of prolonged inactivity (e.g. damage to air conditioning system resulting from prolonged inactivity).

Therefore, the property is a business with a profit and loss account that has a dual peculiarity: its income derives from a single product (Use of Space), and the cost structure is independent of its production. Indeed, the costs increase if the asset does not produce, i.e. if the property is not used.

Location

The property is thus a business characterised by offering only one product, the Use of Space, but with a single reference market, the local one, i.e. where the property is located.[16] For this reason, the price of the Use of Space, i.e. the rent, is closely connected with the dynamics of supply and demand at the local level. The location has a dual meaning: the geographical market in which the property is located (macro level, i.e. the country or the economical region) and its exact location (micro level, i.e. the city area or even the single part of a specific street).

At the macro level, one needs to look at general trends in the relevant market, paying particular attention to the dynamics of demand, which are closely linked to the type of property. For example, in the Residential sector it is essential to analyse demographic dynamics, while in the Commercial sector, such as in the case of an office park, economic trends become essential, i.e. the demand for Space Use among businesses. Moreover, in the case of retail properties, the turnover they might generate, and therefore the spending capacity of the population living in the catchment area, are significant factors.

At the micro level, consideration must be given to the specific location of the property. Again, the interpretation will differ enormously depending on the specific type. In the Residential sector, for example, the availability of services, quietness and security are essential, while in the Commercial sector, in the case of office properties, connectivity and ease of access are more important. Furthermore, in the case of Trade-Related Properties, such as retail properties, the number of potential clients visiting the specific micro-area – and therefore its accessibility, visibility or presence of attractions which can make the individual location attractive – are important: its value may vary significantly within few meters according to the actual number of visitors.

CATEGORIES OF PROPERTY INVESTMENTS

For the sake of simplicity, property investment operations can be divided into three main categories:

1. Development Projects
2. Income-producing Properties
3. Trading Operations.

The three investment categories, which for simplicity are often classified as macro categories, are not actually easy to isolate, as intermediate situations exist, such as Income-producing Properties to be redeveloped, Income-producing Properties completed but not yet leased and Income-producing Properties already leased, where a further distinction can be made according to the residual length of the lease, the quality of the properties themselves, and obviously the phase they have reached in their Building life cycle. A further distinction can be made in Development Projects between different phases of zoning, construction, and marketing, which affect the level of risk and expected return.

In addition to these two common cases, Income-producing Property and Development Projects, there is a third category represented by Trading Operations. Usually, the latter derives from the acquisition of property portfolios which are then sold individually, benefiting from a price differential resulting from the different liquidity ('wholesale vs. retail'). Trading Operations also includes investments in Income-producing Properties and Development Projects initially defined as such but which, due to changed market conditions, are sold before the initial investment horizon because an opportunity to achieve a capital gain arises or because of a change in the Investor's strategy.

The structural characteristics of the three forms of investments mentioned above are presented below to provide a brief outlinse of their essential features.

Development Projects

A Development Project is very similar to any industrial production activity which involves acquisition of the area (purchase of raw materials) and construction (production process) as a real industrial process in which the raw materials (Land and Building) are used to obtain a final product (the property, i.e. the Space available for use) which will be sold to the end client (direct User or Investor).

Note that, just like any industrial activity, there is a considerable operational risk stemming from many uncertainties: time needed to complete the entire operation, actual costs of construction, price dynamics and sales volumes. Furthermore, due to the particular nature of the product, which has a very long life cycle and is hard to modify after it has been built, there is a higher degree of complexity. Finally, it is essential to consider that some types of property, such as shopping or leisure centres, present a further risk arising from the uniqueness of the product which, albeit conventional, presents a high degree of uncertainty regarding actual success in each specific case.

Due to these uncertainties, there is a high level of risk which is equal to, if not higher than, that of many industrial activities. Unlike the production of other goods, in the case of real estate Development Projects it is important to note that once the construction phase has started, one is faced with a considerable degree of rigidity if changes to the product are required, and with a high probability for the need to complete the product in order to sell it.

The risks are clearly outlined in the literature.

Developers are essentially subject to three macro-categories of risk in their activity:

Zoning: the more the initial intended use of the property differs from the target use, the greater this risk;

Industrial: this is the macro category of risks inherent in the construction activity. These include increases in the cost of raw materials (e.g. iron and steel) and in the cost of labour, leading to an uncontrollable rise in construction costs or unforeseen circumstances of various kinds which, as they could not be estimated in advance, were not included among the costs;

Market: this is the risk to which an operator is exposed and is represented by the fact that in drawing up the business plan certain assumptions were made about the sale price which are not then achieved during the marketing phase.[17]

Income-Producing Properties

Unlike Development Projects, investment in Income-producing Properties presents a much lower operating risk, since they are as companies already existing selling a good (Use of Space) to already existing clients (tenants) with a supply agreement already in place (lease agreement).[18]

It is interesting to note that the cost structure of a property, in terms of maintenance, management, insurance and taxes payable by the Owner, is quite constant over time and easily predictable.

The economic benefits consist of the future rents, net of the operating expenses borne by the Owner. The volatility of its cash flow is obviously lower than that of a Development Project, as there is less uncertainty: the rent is relatively constant, both because of the existence of lease contracts and of the relative stability of Market Rents over time.

Given the low volatility of the revenues and costs, the final income expected is stable and also, therefore, its volatility is lower. Consequently, the risk, and therefore also the expected return, are lower than in a Development Project.

Trading Operations

In Trading Operations (of single properties or portfolios), properties are sold in a short period of time, either as a result of an initial strategic decision or because market conditions have changed, i.e. leading to an unexpected capital gain. The former includes acquisitions of real estate portfolios where the Investor benefits from a price difference by buying 'wholesale' in a segment where there is a reduced competition due to the large size of investment (there is a limited number of potential investors due to the considerable capital required) and reselling on a 'retail' basis to other Investors with a lower investment capacity (e.g. private individuals). In other cases, a real estate investment becomes a Trading Operation when, because of changes in market conditions, it may have become convenient to sell the property before the initially forecasted period. This may happen if a high return is already achieved, higher than the one initially expected, because of an increase in the Market Value of the properties. It is more likely therefore in the case of Land, where there is higher volatility than in the case of Income-producing Properties.

SKILLS IN ASSET AND INVESTMENT MANAGEMENT

Real estate investment in a broad sense is often compared with other asset classes such as stocks, bonds or other forms of investment. It is important to point out here that the analogy is not entirely correct because, unlike securities, properties (which are actual businesses) require active management and a specific investment process.

The skills required for real estate investment differ considerably in the case of Development Projects from investments in Income-producing Properties and Trading Operations.

In the first case, as already mentioned, it is a real industrial processing activity, with many variables to be considered and, when a project is started, many players to coordinate for years. Furthermore, even if the value increases over time, as a result of the proper execution of the development phase, it is not a straight increase. In other words, the value of a Development Project is not directly proportional to the stage it has reached, but only to the achievement of certain stages when it might be negotiable. During the construction phase, for example, it is quite difficult to find a potential buyer, given the considerable valuation and technical complexity. However, once the construction permits have been obtained, the construction phases have been completed, or a tenant has been identified, the asset will be more marketable. Because of that, during the valuation process, it may not be realistic to assume that the value will increase straight over time just because the construction work is taking place.

In the case of Income-producing Properties, while efficient asset and property management activities may have a considerable impact on the financial result, the operator has less discretion than in the case of a Development Project.

Once the property is built, the Owner has limited impact on its performance: efficient maintenance must be ensured, but improvement work can only take place over long periods of time in order to avoid being uneconomical and, once a lease agreement is in place, there is no significant opportunity to make changes. Obviously, the actual conditions of the Building must be considered: if it has been recently built and leased, the Owner's influence over the performance will be reasonably limited. However, if a Property is only partially leased or the Building component presents an opportunity for improvement, the Owner may impact more on the performance, making it more similar to a Development Project.

Finally, Trading Operations, when they are defined as such from the start rather than having turned into them as a result of changes in market conditions, require considerable commercial skills (during the sale) and ability to execute the transaction (due diligence, contract drafting, financing, etc.).

Real estate investments are classified according to a risk/return profile in Core, Valued Added and Opportunistic. To match the simple classification used in this book, Core investments are Income-producing Properties, while Valued-Added investments are existing properties with a potential value increase achievable with Building refurbishment. Opportunistic investments are those with the highest risk/return profile as Development Projects and Trading Operations.

Generally speaking, transaction costs associated with seeking investment opportunities, analysing them and carrying out due diligence work make convenient investments in properties with minimum dimensions proportionate to the capital available. For this reason, some Investors, particularly institutional ones, tend to acquire entire portfolios, especially when they are homogenous in terms of property type, quality or geographical area. In addition to individual properties, therefore, whole portfolios are also available for purchase on the market. Given that the total cost of a portfolio is higher than that of individual properties, its liquidity is lower, because of the smaller number of potential buyers.[19] For this reason, a positive margin can be achieved between the purchase cost of a portfolio and the income from selling the individual properties which, given their lower unit value, present greater liquidity.[20] Consequently, when estimating the value of multiple properties, the subject of the valuation must be correctly defined. If the value of individual properties is being determined, single estimates will need to be carried out, but where the value of the entire portfolio is being determined as the subject of the sale, one has to consider the different liquidity of the same and consequently the different (usually lower) value (compared to the sum of the value of individual properties).

ECONOMIC CLASSIFICATION OF PROPERTIES

Properties can be classified according to different criteria. The most well-known classification is the one used by the land registries, which identifies different categories based on the use of urban property units. This classification is based on a number of primarily physical criteria, without analysing the economic characteristics of the properties, as is instead proposed in this section to gain a better understanding of elements generating value and the valuation methods to be adopted in each case.

Property Classification Criteria

In determining the right way to estimate the value of an asset it is useful to classify properties according to an economic logic based on the criteria described below:

- Capacity to generate usable Space
- Space as an end consumer good or as a raw material for the production of other goods and services
- Type of User of the Space: family/individual or business
- Durable consumer good or means of production
- Flexibility for Users
- Income-earning potential resulting from the activity carried out in the specific property.

Capacity to Generate Usable Space Properties, particularly those consisting of Land and Buildings,[21] can generate potentially usable Space for various purposes. Examples include apartments, which generate Space usable by families, or office properties, which generate Space usable by a company's workers. Broadly speaking, these properties generate usable Space (Use of Space), which can be sold by the Owner in the Space Market (i.e. leased to third parties) or used directly (bearing the opportunity cost of not receiving any rent).

Other properties, even if they consist of Land and Buildings, do not, however, generate usable space, such as in the case of old Buildings for which there are even potentially no Users at all. One example of this could be an abandoned industrial property, whose Building conditions are such as to prevent anyone from using it in its current state: renovation works are necessary because in its current condition it cannot produce usable Space. This situation can also arise if the Building is in a good physical condition but there are no potential Users in the area where it is located; for example, an office property adjacent to an industrial property outside an urban area. In this case, the property is used by a specific User, the business which uses the whole property complex, but when this User leaves, perhaps as a result of the business closing down, there may be no other Users in the market for the same property. These last few cases can be defined as Brownfield sites, i.e. properties which, in order to generate a utility (Space for which there is an actual demand) require a Residual Value Method (i.e. replacement or refurbishment of the Building by improving its quality or changing its use).

Finally, one has to consider properties without a Building, i.e. Land, some of which are Commercial Properties with a specific purpose, as in the case of agricultural Land. There is no scope to build on these, neither legally nor in financial terms. The Land has already achieved its maximum capacity to generate a utility through the agricultural use; in other words, its value depends on its capacity to generate income through the potential cultivation, rather than any potential future opportunity to build. For example, the value of farming Land far away from an urban area does not depend on the building potentiality but only on its agricultural productivity.

In other cases, however, plots of Land may currently generate no or limited amount of utility which does not represent their HBU. One example is a buildable plot of Land temporarily used as a car park: its current use can generate an income, but its value is not depending only on this income, since it will be predominantly related to its potential future use (the opportunity to build a property).

In all these cases, the value of the asset (Land) is closely linked to the value of the Building that could potentially be erected on it. Consequently, in this respect, Brownfield sites are in every respect comparable to Greenfield sites, except for demolition and cleaning costs, and risk profile.

Based on the above criteria, properties can be classified as illustrated in Figure 2.1 below and as better described in Subsection 'Macro Categories of Properties'.

The assets at the top of Figure 2.1, defined as *(1) Residential* and *(2) Commercial*, differ from the ones lower down, described as *(3) Land*, as they are able to produce some utility (usable Space) in their current state, while the latter are only a raw material for producing the former and are not currently generating their maximum utility (except partially and in the limited cases described above).

Users and Different Purpose of Space Asset Use   Properties can be divided into two categories according to their purpose:

1. Consumer goods (Residential Space)
2. Means of production (Commercial Space)

The first of these is Residential Space, i.e. property in which Space is a consumer good. The end consumers, individuals and/or families, use the Residential Space as an end consumer good, without it being used directly to produce other goods or services. This is clearly the case with Residential Properties, where the end User makes use of the asset, drawing a direct utility from it without using it for other productive purposes. The classification is not directly linked with regulations; there is no particular difference between an apartment, a cellar, a garage or a parking space.

Choosing a Residential Space is therefore similar to choosing any other consumer good, being based on personal preference and financial constraints, i.e. disposable income. For example, a dwelling may be chosen based on its proximity to a place of work or the quality of the schools or other services in the area.

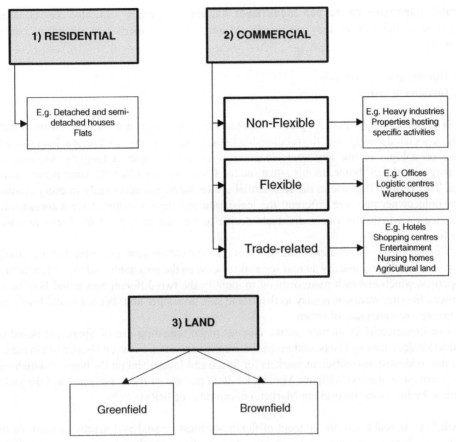

FIGURE 2.1   Economic classification of properties

The second category, where Space constitutes a means of production (Commercial Space), meaning that it is used in a production process by Users, covers businesses in a broad sense, both private and public. In this case, Commercial Space is a necessary means of production, on a par with the raw material needed to produce other goods and services. One can easily see, therefore, how the raw material of 'Space' exists in all goods and services, including the seemingly most intangible ones. Think of the production of any goods (e.g. this book) in which the Space in an industrial unit, warehouse, administration office, or a retail store is used; similarly, think of any service for which offices or other premises are used for production and supply. In view of the above, therefore, the choice of use of Commercial Space is not dictated by the direct consumption of Space, but by the utility it generates in the context of the production activity.

To conclude, according to this criterion, the Space pertaining to the assets described in Figure 2.1 as *(1) Residential*, is a consumer good used by families/individuals, the purchase of which is dictated by the direct utility derived from its use, while the Space of properties included in *(2) Commercial* is a raw material for the production of other goods and services by firms, whose choice of Use of Space is therefore dictated by production needs.

Durable Consumer Goods and Investment Assets Properties can also be classified according to the reasons they are purchased and, in this respect, two categories can be identified:

1. Durable consumer goods
2. Investment assets.

The first category includes properties which are not chosen according to an investment logic, associated mostly with the relationship between risk and expected return, but primarily based on a logic of use and strategic control, as, for example, a family's decisions on the purchase of their home. In this situation, the Owner is very often the same person as the User. This is often the case in the Residential sector, albeit not necessarily in every country, since homeowner rates are different: the legislation and the tax system have a considerable influence on whether private individuals decide to become owners of the home in which they live.

Control of the ownership of the home is an outstanding strategic value for the family. In these cases, there is usually no real separation between the ownership and use of Residential Properties, which makes it more difficult to identify the two different Space and Investment Markets. In other words, it is easy to determine sale prices per unit, but not rental levels nor the Investor required rate of return.

For Commercial Properties, as the choices made regarding use of Space are based on production decisions by Users, and given the greater separation between Users and Owners, it is easier to identify two different markets for Space and Investment on the basis of which one can determine rental levels (Space Market, i.e. Rent per square metre per year) and the yields required by Investors (Investment Market, i.e. cap rates or IRRs).

Flexibility In real estate the concept of flexibility must be analysed mainly in terms of the User/client because in physical terms any change of use involves carrying out significant amounts of work on the Building, often comparable to a new construction. This work can, of course, be limited (i.e. implementing a marginal change of use from residential to office use for small premises in central locations) or radical (i.e. transforming a property from an office building into a hotel). In other cases, the Building will have to be completely demolished and rebuilt, such as where an industrial Building is converted into a residential complex.

Residential Properties are highly flexible for the User as families have similar needs and there are many of them. Commercial Properties, however, need to be classified further based on this criterion because they present different levels of flexibility depending on the client.

It is important to consider flexibility on at least two levels:

1. Building
2. Use.

With regard to the Building, one has to determine whether it was built for a specific User and/or for a specific use. An example of this might be a property built for a specific production process which cannot be used for other purposes, such as in the case of a steelworks.

With regard to use, there may be a limit even where there are no limits associated with the Building in itself, such as in the case of properties with multiple potential Users, such as warehouses or offices. The flexibility of the property may also depend on its location and dimension, even if the Building itself is flexible. An example of this might be a property which has a flexible Building (e.g. a warehouse) but is located in an area where there is only one User (such as in the case where a company has developed over time in an area where there are no other companies). In this instance, the property could, theoretically, have a new User. However, although a warehouse (the Building) is flexible, in this case it becomes non-flexible because of a lack of potential new clients if the current User – realistically the only potential User – decides to vacate.

Another example might be that of a business park of considerable size located in a secondary office market. For example, a large property leased to a public authority in a small secondary city where there are only a handful of other companies: if the Space were vacated, there might not be sufficient demand and therefore no actual new Users.

Properties for which it is easy to identify a new User are, however, very flexible; for example, in city centre offices or warehouses in industrial areas, when the existing User leaves, a new client will easily be found.

Business and the Specific Property   The category of Flexible Properties includes those defined as Trade-Related Properties, in which the tenant's activity coincides with the product/service offered, such as in the case of hotels or retailers. In these cases, the activity of the company that uses the Space depends on the characteristics of the Space itself, in terms of both location (Land) and physical structure (Building). For this particular kind of asset, the operating margin generated by the activity performed in it must be sufficient to pay the price of the Use of Space, i.e. the rent or business branch lease.

Unlike other flexible assets, such as offices, the activity carried out in the property becomes fundamental. In the case of Flexible Commercial Properties, the price of the Space is not dependent in any way on the economic margin of the activity carried out within it, but only depends on its demand and supply. For example, in a leased office, where tenants may be banks or industrial companies, the rental level does not depend on the margin achieved by the two different businesses or on the specific activity they actually perform in the property, but solely on the demand and supply of Space in a specific geographical market.

Differently from the previous example, the price of the Use of Space of Trade-Related Properties not only depends on demand and supply, but is also linked to the economic result of the activity performed in them and may potentially be proportional to it.[22] For example, the better the quality of the Building and the more attractive the location, the higher will be the turnover for a hotel business carried out in the property. Consequently, a fixed price for the Space exposes the Owner to the risk that if the company using the property (the tenant) achieves a higher margin, the Owner may potentially lose a portion of the income that he would have achieved if the lease agreement were proportional to the tenant's income. Conversely, if the fixed price of the Space is too high (flat rent with a fixed amount), the User might not be able to afford the cost, leading to the closure of the business; a new User will require a lower rent to ensure that the cost is sustainable in the performance of the specific activity.

In other words, for Trade-Related Properties, it is essential to analyse the sustainability of the cost of Space, which will require an analysis of how economically sustainable[23] it is for the business that may be performed in them. Given that in this case (e.g. a hotel or a shop), the flexibility is limited to several companies in the same sector, the price of the Space will depend both on the demand and supply and on the sustainability for the business carried out. For this reason, the price of the Space will depend first and foremost on the business actually or potentially carried out. Obviously, demand and supply also plays a significant role, but always in relation to the business itself: a surplus of hotel rooms in a specific location will reduce the turnover of the hotels in the area, resulting in a lower margin for the hotel business and, consequently, less ability to pay rent for the Use of Space.

Macro Categories of Properties

Based on the criteria stated above, for explanatory purposes we shall classify properties into the macro categories illustrated in Figure 2.1:

■ Residential Properties
■ Non-Flexible Commercial Properties
■ Flexible Commercial Properties
■ Trade-Related Commercial Properties
■ Land.

Residential Properties   Residential Properties are used by end consumers, who often want to have strategic control over them. The use and purchase decisions are primarily dictated by the needs of the family (e.g. consumption decisions) rather than by investment logics (e.g. the relationship between risk and return).

In many countries,[24] the separation between Owners and Users is quite limited because families want to have strategic control (ownership) of the assets themselves, because of tax incentives or because of a lack of good rental properties, owing to a regulatory system that penalises residential investments. Therefore, these are primarily long-lasting consumer goods rather than investment assets, despite often representing the main asset of many families. Where the majority of the market is made by homeowners and the rental market is not well developed, it is very likely that the value of Residential Properties is lower when they are occupied/leased and therefore not ready for immediate consumption by the new home Owner.

Residential Properties are more flexible for Users compared to Commercial, with a higher uniformity (many families with similar needs). In this respect, there are no particular problems in identifying new Users within the same local market and for qualitatively similar properties.

Finally, Residential Properties are the most widespread real estate typology and therefore they are bought and sold frequently, representing the highest number of transactions in any market. For this reason, it is often possible to collect samples of data of comparable transactions[25] for each asset (to this purpose see Chapter 3, Subsection 'Characteristics of the Comparative Factors and Information Sources') which have recently taken place on the market, and which, for valuation purposes, can then be used to determine an average transaction value.

Non-Flexible Commercial Properties   Non-Flexible Commercial Properties are used and usable only by a specific User which, either for reasons associated with the Building or because of the absence of demand in a particular geographical market, are unlikely to be used by a different company. This category mainly includes non-flexible Buildings developed for the purpose of hosting specific activities (e.g. refineries, smelting furnaces, steelworks).

In this case, a separation between Owners and Users is unlikely because few real estate Investors are interested in taking a risk linked to the solvency of a specific User. This would be similar to investing in the business carried out in the property, i.e. the company itself. Consequently, there are no real Investment and Space Markets for these types of property and the User is forced to be the Owner as well. From a different perspective, Users may not want to lose strategic control where the property has been built for their own specific requirements or where any transfer could have a significant impact on their activity (e.g. if it contains equipment which is worth much more than the property itself). This is often the case with industrial sheds, properties where particular kinds of manufacturing take place or specific properties for which, mainly because of the size of the local market, it is hard to find a new User.

To conclude, Non-Flexible Commercial Properties are rarely bought and sold and are extremely different from each other. For this reason, it is very hard to get samples of comparable transactions which have recently taken place in the market.

Flexible Commercial Properties Flexible Commercial Properties are used by companies that produce other goods and services, whose choices regarding the Use of Space, therefore, depend on their choices of production. These are flexible assets, which means that, for the User, using a specific property is not central to their decisions. What is important is to have the availability to use a certain amount of Space with some specific characteristics.

For many companies, having strategic control of the property (as in the case of an administration office or warehouse) is not essential, as Space is easily flexible for the User and, from the property owner's point of view, the client is easily replaceable. Consequently, there is separation between Owners and Users, which gives rise to both a Space Market and an Investment Market.

For non-User Owners (Investors), the decision to purchase such properties is very much dictated by investment purposes, such as the relationship between risk and the expected return, while the consumer logics typically applied by families when buying homes are not relevant. It is worth noticing that, as opposed to home owned residential, the value of Commercial assets decreases when they are not leased (vacant Space). More generally, the value is also lower when they are temporarily vacant and they are not generating an actual income because, even if this is temporary, the risk is higher as the income is only potential.

For valuation purposes, there is little uniformity between these assets because very often, in addition to the features of the property itself (location and quality of the Building), the value also depends on the actual rental situation. Factors like the type of lease agreement, the rental level compared to the Market Rent, the residual life of the contract and the creditworthiness of the tenant all have a bearing.

Finally, the price of the Space depends essentially on its supply and demand. This is the case with offices, logistics premises, industrial sheds and some generally small retail units.

To conclude, as these properties are flexible for the User, but do not always present a high degree of uniformity, it is easier to conduct a search for Comparables in the two different markets: in the Space Market one can determine the Market Rent by analysing comparable properties, in terms of rent and the lease agreement (i.e. rent per square metre), while in the Investment Market one can determine the rate of return for assets comparable in terms of investment risk (i.e. yield).

Trade-Related Commercial Properties Trade-Related Commercial Properties, also defined only as 'Trade-Related Properties',[26] present a number of similar features to Flexible Commercial Properties in terms of separation between Owners and Users, but they are distinguished by the fact that the price of the Use of Space depends directly on the activity performed within the properties themselves, as better described in Subsubsection 'Business and the Specific Property'.

While Owners will apply investment logics to their purchase decisions here as well, when analysing the Space Market, it is not enough to look at demand and supply, but it is fundamental to analyse the sustainability of the rent paid by the business which can actually be performed in the property. This is the case with hotels, leisure properties, cinemas and retail establishments, mainly shopping centres, retail boxes and factory outlets.

Land Without the presence of the Building component, Land does not generate any utility for the User, except in limited cases where the property consists exclusively of the Land,[27] which is classified under the category of Commercial Properties. For this reason, from an economic point of view, Land is comparable to the raw material needed to create all the other types of properties through a real estate development process.

As discussed in greater detail later on, in the section regarding the Residual Value Methods, the value of a plot of Land is influenced by the Development Project that could be realised on it, and therefore by the value of the property that could be built on it, net of the total cost required to produce it (Building).

Even though applying a Residual Value Method requires many elements to be estimated, very briefly the value of a plot of Land is influenced by the difference (considering the risk that impacts on the cost of capital) between the value of the property that could be built and the actual cost of constructing the Building (including all the elements required to complete the Development Project and its sale). A simple simulation helps to understand why the value of the Land is so volatile.

The example shown in Table 2.2 simulates the variation in the value of the Land that accompanies a variation in the Market Value of the property that can be built on it, assuming that the full cost of constructing[28] the Building remains constant.

This scenario is entirely plausible as the price changes of some of the cost components (such as the direct costs of construction like labour, materials, energy, etc.) are not strictly correlated with the performance of the property market, while other changes, such as the cost of capital, present higher correlations. In fact, while the price of raw materials (e.g. steel) is also linked to the demand from other industrial sectors, the performance of which does not directly affect the value of properties, other costs, such as capital costs, caused by changes in rates (cost of debt and government bonds) have a direct effect on the performance of the entire real estate market and therefore on the value of the property.

This simple example shows how a change, however small (+/− 10% and 20%), in the Market Value of the property can have a considerable effect on the value of the Land (+/− 40% and 80%).

TABLE 2.2 Example of Land and property values volatility

	Worst	Negative	Base	Positive	Best
Property value	€ 80	€ 90	**€ 100**	€ 110	€ 120
Δ Property value	*−20%*	*−10%*		*10%*	*20%*
Building cost	€ 75	€ 75	€ 75	€ 75	€ 75
Land value	€ 5	€ 15	€ 25	€ 35	€ 45
Δ Land value	*−80%*	*−40%*		*40%*	*80%*

The value of Land, therefore, varies more intensely than the value of property. Consequently, during real estate market expansionary phases, even if the value of properties increases, the value of the Land will increase more than proportionally. It is worth pointing out, however, that there is a lack of empirical evidence of the sale prices of Land because they are extremely diverse properties; in fact, apart from the surface area, there are other elements that determine its value, such as the building rights and the stage of the planning process.

A plot of Land is therefore comparable to a call option with the underlying asset being the property and with an exercise price equal to the cost of construction of the Building, with reference to the real options theory.[29] Apart from the obvious differences, however, unlike a call option on a security, Land has no expiry date but is burdened by the recurring cost of overheads, including in particular property taxes, even when it generates no income. For this reason, the higher volatility in the value of a plot of Land, and the risk compared to the underlying asset (property), should not come as a surprise. Some Investors believe, mistakenly, that Land is a low-risk investment because of the low unit value, ignoring the fact that its value variation is more than proportional to changes in the value of the properties that could be built on it. Finally, the lower liquidity of these assets compared to Income-producing Properties, which are more appealing to the majority of Investors, is often given no consideration.

For explanatory purposes, Land can also be divided into the following categories:

- Buildable and Non-Buildable Land
- Brownfield and Greenfield.

Buildable Land fulfils all the legal and economic requirements for building. Legal 'buildability' is commonly understood to be an appropriate intended use according to current legislation and zoning which authorises construction of a Building.

The concept of economic 'buildability' is less obvious and refers to the economic feasibility of developing a property on the Land by incurring the cost of constructing the Building. Given that the value of the property does not depend on the construction cost of the Building, economic 'buildability' can only be ascertained when its value is higher than the construction cost. Consider, for example, a Buildable Land for residential units located dozens of kilometres from the nearest town, in an geographic area where there is no demand to use Residential Space. In this case, even though theoretically the Land could be developed from a legal point of view, it is not economically 'buildable'; furthermore, the value of that Land might even be reduced by the legal 'buildability' as it may be associated with a higher operating cost due to the higher property taxes charged on a Buildable Area compared to one where nothing can be built.

Particular attention also needs to be paid to the seemingly opposite case: Land where currently nothing can be built because of the current zoning rules and the lack of legal permits, but located near a major crossroads and ideally suited for a retail property. Its value will be associated with the future opportunity to transform the Land into a property, once the legal 'buildability' has been granted, i.e. the actual opportunity to construct the Building. The Market Value will, therefore, depend on the probability of developing the property, the size of the Building, and by the expected timescales, rather than on the current profit-making capacity (e.g. the income may be produced by the agricultural activity).

Conversely, Non-Buildable Land does not satisfy the previous legal and economic 'buildability' requirements.

The term Brownfield indicates an area that was used in the past for other Buildings, the Space of which is now no longer usable, and that could now be used for a new development project. These are often decommissioned properties where the Building requires major redevelopment work or, even more evidently, complete demolition and reconstruction.

In economic terms, there are no significant differences with Greenfield Land, on which no Building has ever been constructed before.[30] The two additional elements to consider are the costs associated with the demolition and the decontamination costs. In other words, when estimating the value of Brownfield Land, compared to Greenfield Land, we need to consider the two previous cost elements. They are very different. In the case of a demolition, there is a high degree of certainty about this element, being easily quantifiable in terms of amount and timescale; in the case of a reclamation both elements are extremely random, thus making Brownfield Land riskier than Greenfield Land. For completeness, it is worth pointing out in favour of Brownfield Land that often its legal 'buildability' is more certain (i.e. zoning and building rights), which has the opposite effect on the level of risk.

A SIMPLE DEFINITION OF RISK

In literature, there are several ways of quantifying risk based on statistical measurements such as the variance and correlation of returns, which are based on a distinction between diversifiable and non-diversifiable risk. It is therefore essential to define the concept of real estate risk based on prospective use of Space for properties.

Non-diversifiable risks are linked to sources of systematic risk, such as the main macroeconomic or financial variables, the general economic trend, the trend in market interest rates, and inflation. These sources are often summarised in a single systematic risk factor, known as market risk, and cannot be eliminated through diversification.

Conversely, diversifiable risks (also known as specific or residual risks) are understood to be risk factors that are not linked to sources of systematic risk: the term diversifiable refers to the fact that they can be eliminated through the diversification process, which consists of investing in assets whose return depends on unrelated variables, in order to reduce overall variability by offsetting risk. In other words, it is about investing in a portfolio of assets in which part of the return is linked to negatively correlated factors, so when one generates a negative return, the other generates a positive return that offsets some or all of the loss on the first.

Although many risks are diversifiable, creating truly diversified property portfolios is quite a complex operation. The main limitations include the need for active management, which can become problematic where there are many different types of properties in different geographical markets. In short, there is a trade-off between the benefits of diversification and management complexity. It is estimated[31] that around 30% of the risk associated with a real estate investment can be eliminated with a portfolio of five properties and that minimal reduction of risk is achieved above the threshold of thirty properties: the risk that remains is around 60% of a non-diversified portfolio.

In estimating the cost of capital, it is often assumed that the investor is perfectly diversified and, consequently, that the return is solely a function of the non-diversifiable risk. When one is valuing a single property investment, or the Market Value of a specific asset, this assumption seems challenging to satisfy. It is, therefore, preferable to estimate the risk in an overall logic, i.e. assuming that risk is a concept more similar to variance, specifically the likelihood of future deviation in future income compared to the expected value.

The various elements of risk are illustrated below without necessarily taking into account whether they are actually diversifiable, i.e. whether they are risks that are also incurred by holding a diversified portfolio. Without claiming to be exhaustive, an attempt is made below to provide the reader with some guidance on the various risk factors that characterise real estate investment throughout the life cycle of a property. Even though this book focuses only on estimating Market Value rather than valuing investments, it is necessary to understand how an Investor – in a broad sense the market participants – judges economic convenience based on risk and the expected return. Risk elements serve ideally to estimate an expected return with a Build-Up Approach, but they can also be useful for the purpose of assessing adjustments to the rates extracted from the market.[32]

It is worth noting, very briefly, that operational risk is primarily associated with the absence of positive cash flow and, in the case of a property, with the likelihood that there is no User willing to buy the Use of Space. Consequently, the quality of the property in a broad sense, with its various constituent parts (Land and Building), will be the central element to be assessed in estimating the investment risk and therefore the expected return.

Although the following classification cannot be exact, as some factors could fall into various types, to simplify the illustration we shall start by describing the common risk elements always present in each type of property and then focus on the most typical in each of the two phases of life, firstly, Development Projects, and secondly, Income-producing Properties.

COMMON RISK ELEMENTS IN REAL ESTATE INVESTMENT

Capital Market

In the capital market all investments are competing to attract capital. Asset prices are determined by the collective judgement of Investors based on the overall characteristics of each investment, such as current performance, total return, risk, liquidity, volatility, taxation, etc. For this reason, bonds, equities and real estate investments compete with each other, as well as other forms of investment, such as commodity futures, stock options, precious metals, etc. There is, therefore, a 'communicating vessel' effect that correlates the returns of the different asset classes, because, all risks being equal, Investors will shift capital allocation to investments that offer the higher expected return. Consequently, there is an exogenous financial component which has an impact on the real estate market, whose size depends on the general performance of the capital market and the perception of risk that the Investors attribute to a specific asset class.

In this respect, several studies[33] note that the rate of growth of real consumption per inhabitant, the real short-term interest rate, the term structure of interest rates, and unexpected inflation systematically affect the returns on Commercial Properties. The diversifiable nature of these risks will depend on the size of the investment considered; some risks can be reduced by merely increasing the number of tenants within a Building or, again, diversification across several cities or regions will significantly reduce the risk elements related to the local economy. However, even if local elements of risk are mitigated when a portfolio is diversified geographically, national macroeconomic risks will persist. For example, in the case of a national economic crisis that leads to an increase in property taxes, some elements of risk at the national level can only be reduced by an international diversification strategy.

To conclude, the capital market risk is associated with a change in capital market rates, both in relation to the risk-free rate and in relation to the incremental risk premium associated with the real estate investment.

Liquidity

Real estate assets are highly diverse and are traded in a private market, so matching supply to demand is more difficult than it is with the homogeneous securities traded on stock exchanges. The direct consequence is the lower liquidity of assets, whose level depends on many factors. It is evident that the liquidity of a property with standard characteristics (e.g. a three-room apartment in a semi-central area of a large city) is more likely to find a potential buyer than a less common property (e.g. a luxury villa located in a secondary area). Consequently, the level of liquidity of properties, in addition to being lower than listed securities, depends on the specific characteristics, the most relevant ones definitely being the intended use, location, and size.

The liquidity risk factor generates a trade-off between selling the property and its price. There is no definition of the 'normal' time needed to sell a property at its Market Value as it varies according to the liquidity of the asset and the phase of the market.[34] In general, the liquidity of a property will be higher in an expansive phase market than in a recessionary phase.

It is useful to note that this risk is remunerated by the market with a higher return compared to assets traded on regulated markets. This *a priori* unfavourable characteristic for real estate investments is an opportunity for an Investor with a long time horizon who will suffer less from lower asset liquidity and benefit from higher returns.

The lower liquidity also derives from the high transaction costs and, consequently, from a lower rotation of the properties in the Investors' portfolios compared to securities.

To conclude, the liquidity risk is associated with the difficulty of selling the asset, both because of time required and because of the differential between the value and the price achievable.

Financial Structure

Financial structure risk[35] is linked to recourse to debt and, consequently, to the possibility of insolvency and bankruptcy. Given that debt[36] takes priority over equity, the cash available to remunerate the latter is residual, with a leverage effect that becomes greater the higher the debt incurred.

While operational risk, in a broad sense, is associated with the volatility of operating cash flows, financial risk will lead to increased volatility of final Free Cash Flows to Equity, i.e. cash flows after the effect of the financial structure.

Financial structure risk is associated both with the quantity of debt and with the level and potential change in the interest rate over time. On this point, it is worth noting that even though a hedging instrument is not always used to hedge the risk of rate fluctuations, it is advisable to assume fixed rates when valuing a property, as this risk factor should not be included in the asset valuation.

Typically, properties are financed with higher leverage than that used in other business sectors, as the property – thanks to the mortgage guarantee – represents excellent collateral.

Not only that, but especially in the case of Income-producing Properties, relatively stable operating cash flows ensure good debt servicing coverage. Conversely, in a Development Project, owing to the greater volatility of cash flows, due to the greater uncertainty about the timing and price of the sale of the assets, as well as the higher risk caused by the need to complete the asset before receiving the positive cash flows, recourse to a lower leverage is advisable.

To conclude, financial risk derives from the higher volatility of Free Cash Flows to Equity available to the Investor, resulting from the presence of a fixed negative flow for servicing the debt.

Regulatory

While the problem is the same for other business sectors, without wanting to go into the many relevant aspects (e.g. administrative, fiscal, authorisation-related, contractual), it is worth pointing out that regulations have a considerable impact on real estate investments as they govern every stage of the asset's life and impose restrictions on its use. We shall merely point out here that from the point of view of Investors, and consequently of the risk, the following elements have a significant bearing:

- Unpredictability of change in the regulatory framework
- Number of entities responsible for issuing authorisations
- Uncertainty about the interpretation of regulations
- Duration of authorisation processes and resolution of disputes.

Regulatory risk, from the Investor's point of view, is associated not so much with the presence of more or less restrictive legislation than with the possibility that this may change more or less frequently, that it may be subject to different interpretations, that it may include decisions made by different entities or, finally, that it may lead to uncertainty in the authorisation processes. Changes to legislation can make real estate investments more or less appealing; for example, an increase in real estate transfer tax has an adverse effect on the market.

To conclude, this is the risk associated with the uncertainties about the time required to obtain the necessary permits and potential changes to the regulatory framework.

Location

By definition, properties cannot be moved and, consequently, their value is associated with the economic performance of the market in which they are located, i.e. the market in which the Use of Space will be sold to Users in return for rent. Location-related risks are fundamentally associated with the appeal of an asset and are for the most part exogenous, as the Owner of the property only has a limited power to intervene.

'Location, location, location!' is undoubtedly the most well-known real estate mantra and, in terms of risk as well, it is definitely the main element to consider, as well as probably the first question asked when gathering information about a property. This subject is discussed in detail in Subsubsection 'Business and the specific property', so we shall simply reiterate here that location can be considered at different levels.

Great importance must be attributed to the economic development prospects of the region where the property is located. Regions with high growth economic potential will attract new production sites, consequently driving the entire property market (new demand for offices, shopping centres, homes, etc.) due to the higher demand for Space use.

The second distinction is based on the micro-location of the property within a specific economic area. While it is clear that there are significant differences in value between two properties with the same physical characteristics but placed in different neighbourhoods of the same city (centre, semi-centre, periphery), the same consideration is also valid within the same neighbourhood: numerous elements modify the perception of risk (presence of noisy roads, public transport stops, social services, commercial activities, etc.). Likewise, it is essential to analyse the opportunity for future variations of these elements; among others, the expectations of environmental change or the possibility of new settlements that change the characteristics of the area, such as forecasts of infrastructure projects or community facilities (e.g. roads, schools, markets) that would improve the environment in future.

Property markets are conventionally divided according to specific criteria into central, semi-central and peripheral areas for the Residential sector; central business district, semi-centre, periphery or hinterland for the office sector; high street, premium and mainstream for the retail sector, etc. But even within the same city, values (and the risk connected to the asset) will vary considerably and there will be differences at a micro-zone level too. The value of retail property can vary according to which side of the same street it is located and, in extreme cases, even its position on the same side of the street, a few metres away from another, depending on the actual flow of visitors.

To conclude, this is the risk of the lack of Use of Space demand in a specific market, that is strictly linked to the economic cycle.

Intended Use and Type of Properties

The flexibility of properties depends on the variety of potential uses and on the number of potential Users.[37] The opportunity to change the intended use of the property without a significant investment amount gives the asset greater versatility, which allows its easier relocation in the Space Market as the characteristics of demand change. The opportunity for a higher number of entities to use the property, both in absolute terms and in terms of categories, reduces the risk of vacancy – one of the most critical real estate risk factors.

The flexibility of properties, however, is minimal. In fact, although it is theoretically possible to convert an existing Building for different uses, basically this possibility is often uneconomical or requires a complete replacement of the same, i.e. a total refurbishment of the Building.

As an extreme example, an industrial Building such as a steel plant or a chemical plant has no possibility of being used differently (only one use) and it will be difficult to find another User (there are only few steel producers operating in that area); in other words, it is very close to a technical plant. At the opposite extreme, a property that consists of Land alone has multiple possibilities for future use (and multiple potential Users), limited mainly by location and zoning constraints. Between the two extremes, there are various types of properties, each with its own level of flexibility according to the possible uses and the number of potential Users.

An increasing risk differential can be identified from the most flexible sector, the Residential one, to sectors such as offices and retail up to scarcely flexible properties, such as hotels and multiplexes.

Finally, the current use of a property may not coincide with the HBU under existing regulations, which means one needs to consider the potential for future development and, therefore, a smaller potential risk. For example, if a Building may be converted into a property that can generate a higher income (and therefore a higher value), the lower level of risk generated by these expectations should be considered.[38] For example, consider the case of an old office property, currently still in use and therefore classifiable as an Income-producing Property: due to its location and physical structure, in the future it may be transformed into Residential Property (assuming that this is the HBU). In this case, a lower level of risk will be attributed to this asset because of the potential of transforming it into a higher value asset.

To conclude, this is the risk associated with a lack of demand for the Use of Space for a particular purpose, owing to the specific nature of the asset in relation to the potential Users.

DEVELOPMENT PROJECTS

In a Development Project, the risk tends to decrease over time from the initial plot of Land without building permits, to the completion of the Building. For this reason, and for greater clarity, the risk factors 'encountered' in a Development Project are set out and described below.

Authorisation

Authorisation risk, which is a form of Regulatory risk[39] to a certain extent, is associated with the uncertainty about when and if all the permits required for the property to be built will be obtained. A plot of Non-Buildable Land presents a high degree of uncertainty, not only about when and if it can be transformed into a Buildable Area, but also about the actual building rights and restrictions. Therefore, depending on the stage at which the Development Project is analysed, the associated risk will be different (and potentially decreasing). There is no need to point out that the level of return required will be higher in the earlier phases. For example, a developer may purchase a plot of Land with no building rights and go through the authorisation process, or purchase the same Land with a building permit already issued. Clearly, in the second case, the higher cost of the Land will make the investment less profitable, but the risk profile will be lower.

To conclude, this is the risk associated with uncertainty about the timescale to get all the Building permits and features (i.e. intended use and size) of the property that can be built on the Land.

Environmental

Broadly speaking, environmental risk[40] is associated with the presence of polluting substances either in the Land or in the Building. Although we are talking about a Development Project here, where greater attention is therefore paid to the Land, this risk exists even in the case of Income-producing Properties, in particular when the Building is quite old and therefore built at a time when regulations were different, and less attention was paid to environmental issues. For example, the Building might contain asbestos or the Land might be contaminated by oil or other liquid leaking. There may also be negative external factors such as sources of electromagnetic contamination from other properties close by.[41]

Note that, in the case of Land, the risk associated with potential environmental pollution is a critical factor, because it is difficult to quantify the cost and time needed for proper environmental decontamination, which will also have negative repercussions on the time needed to complete the Development Project.

To conclude, this is the risk associated with uncertainty about the cost and timescale of any reclamation work.

Construction-Related

The Building construction phase presents risks of proper execution, i.e. the risk that the complete property might not conform to the original plan, that the overall costs might be higher, and that delays might arise for different reasons. While in the first two cases, a good project manager and a proper construction contract with a reliable general contractor which provides compensation in such an event can be sound mitigation methods and are currently applied; the risk associated with potential delays not attributable to suppliers remains and depends to the complexity of the project itself. The construction risk, mainly with reference to the timing, therefore leads to two immediate consequences: on the one hand a higher overall cost of the Building (i.e. the cost of capital invested for a longer period), and on the other hand a higher Market risk (i.e. the units for sale will be available on the market later than the original forecast). This second aspect exposes developers to greater uncertainty because, as the time within which the asset will be sold becomes longer, it will be more exposed to market value fluctuations[42] and changes in preferences.[43] Moreover, in the meanwhile, other development schemes may be finished with new real estate supply available in the market that will satisfy needs of Users and buyers.

To conclude, this is the risk associated with uncertainty about the cost and timescale for completing the property.

Market

The Development Project is intended to create a new property, so it ends with the identification of a User and, often, an Investor who buys the asset based on the income generated. Consequently, the market risk of the Development Project is connected with uncertainty about future interest among Users and Investors, who sometimes, as in the Residential sector, coincide. Furthermore, the value of the asset will also depend on the income generated and the return required by the market in the future when it will be sold.

Consequently, the Development Project is exposed to the Space Market and Investment Market risks. In order to reduce the first element, some developers prefer to start new projects only after they have identified tenants interested in the Use of Space (having entered into so-called pre-lease agreements); other more cautious developers also choose to lessen the Investment Market risk by immediately looking for a buyer (entering into a so-called pre-sale contract). In the Residential sector, this is quite a common practice (known as an 'off-plan sale'), at least during expansive phases of the real estate market. It has the dual benefit of being self-financing (thanks to advance payments made as the work progresses) and reducing the market risk, in exchange for the buyer having a greater opportunity to personalise the unit or some price reduction. For completeness, we should point out that where a Development Project takes place that does not fulfil the two conditions stated above, the term 'speculative' is typically used. In this case, obviously, given the greater risk, the return will have to be higher.

In the pre-let and pre-sale cases, clearly, the tenant or buyer will require a lower price for bearing part of the risk.

To conclude, this is the risk of not finding a User or an Investor, or more specifically, of not achieving the rental and price levels initially expected.

INCOME-PRODUCING PROPERTIES

Once the Development Project has been completed, the Income-producing Property, albeit characterised by less volatility of income and costs, is nevertheless subject to several risk factors.

Physical and Technical Features

The physical features of the Building contribute to the appeal of the Use of Space and are important elements for determining the risk. In other words, the 'better' the quality of the physical Space, and therefore, broadly speaking, the better the features of the Building, the lower the risk that a User will not be found. Purely for the reader's consideration, without any claim to this being comprehensive, the following is an indicative list of elements that must be considered, not necessarily in order of importance:

- Construction quality
- The degree of technical and functional obsolescence
- The technological standard of the systems and structure
- Any outstanding architectural features
- Physical conditions and upkeep
- Design
- Size (e.g. floor map and Space efficiency)
- Quality of the materials and systems
- Flexibility based on the Users requirements
- Environmental sustainability
- Age and stage of life
- Compliance with any standards and regulations
- Historical building
- Architectural and artistic covenants
- Availability of public or private parking areas in the building.

In particular, the risk linked to the level of technical and functional obsolescence, also definable as Technical Risk, refers to any unforeseen problems of a Building, resulting both from wear and tear and from incorrect design. Basically, they are unforeseen costs that lead to a lower actual level of profitability. This risk, which during the acquisition phase can be mitigated by carrying out an accurate technical due diligence, rises with the age of the Building, increasing the possibility of unexpected costs (e.g., leaks from the roof, other infiltrations, air conditioning system breakdowns). In summary, other things being equal, the older the Building, the greater the technical risk.

The physical characteristics have an impact on the specific flexibility, i.e. the possibility of easily remodelling or adapting the space to fulfil the changing requirements of the market or of a new User. An example of low specific flexibility might be a large single-tenant office property where a costly refurbishment operation is required to adapt it to different Users (e.g. a requirement for smaller units), whereas a Building designed to be more flexible could be adapted for use by several tenants with less effort.

To conclude, this is the risk associated, in a broader sense, with the quality of the Space, which is inversely linked to the ease of finding a User.

Management and Market

Market risk in the case of an Income-producing Property is merely the uncertainty about selling the Use of Space, i.e. the possibility that an income will not be achieved because of the absence of a User prepared to pay a satisfactory rent. In other words, it is the actual attractiveness of the property Space, both as a result of the Land component, i.e. the Location, and the effect of the Building component, i.e., broadly speaking, all the other Physical Characteristics, as previously described.

However, a property, unlike financial securities, is a firm, which, even in the simplest cases, requires management activity, with a consequent risk connected to its correct performance.

In this respect, there are properties which are relatively simple to manage (e.g. an office leased to a leading multinational company with a thirty-year lease agreement and with maintenance charges wholly paid by the tenant), while others, as in case of Trade-Related Properties, are extremely complex (e.g. a hotel, where the sale of Space, i.e. the room, takes place on a daily basis, and there are multiple operating costs, both variable and fixed). Consequently, although all properties require asset and property management activities to be carried out correctly, it is evident that the risks will vary depending on the different types of properties and their complexity.

Returning to the example of a hotel, from a management point of view, the Owner could obtain income either through direct management or through a lease with a third party. In the first case, by using a specialised manager under a hotel management service agreement, even if mitigated by the support of a specialised operator, the operating risk would remain entirely on the Owner. To put it simply, the income would be the difference between the revenue from the sale of the rooms and the cost of managing the hotel. In the second case, when a lease agreement is in place the income would be the rent, with the market and hotel management risk transferring to the tenant, a hotel manager. In this situation the risk would be reduced: even in the theoretical and extreme case of no clients at all, the rent would still be paid by the tenant. In reality, however, contracts with a variable rent are common; moreover, the sustainability of the rent also becomes a central element in order to assess whether in the long-term the tenant will be able to pay rent.

To conclude, this is the risk associated with managing the property as a business, i.e. with clients who buy the Use of Space (generating income) and bearing their own operating costs.

Rental and Contractual Situation

This element of risk could be considered a subset of the previous one. In fact, another real estate sector mantra, which is often repeated during economic recessionary phases, is 'Tenant, tenant, tenant!'. For properties, as well as for any other business, the first and most important line of the profit and loss account is income, so the client, and the respective contract that binds him, become fundamental in assessing the risk associated to the property. To put it simply, one could correctly say that a leased property presents a lower level of risk than a vacant one, since its revenues are actual and not only potential. However, the importance of this element deserves a closer analysis of the agreement in place between the property and the client.

In order to simplify, two main forms of contracts are commonly used in real estate: property leases and business branch leases, the latter in particular for Trade-Related Properties such as retail properties and hotels. However, in every country there are a variety of contractual formulas and some of them can be extraordinarily complex and not always unambiguously interpretable. Therefore, a careful legal analysis is needed to assess the actual risks.

The client (tenant) is an element of risk: the higher his creditworthiness, the more the income it will guarantee. However, careful analysis is required of contract clauses that allow the tenant to 'free himself' of the commitment when certain conditions occur; moreover, in the case of a corporate group it is important to analyse the relationships and the guarantees existing between the subsidiary and the mother company.

The duration is another essential element, because the longer it is, especially in relation to the previous point, the higher the certainty of future income. To give an extreme example, one could compare an old property for which a residual twenty-year contract exists with a primary tenant, with a property which only has a short residual period to run. To be more precise, the important element is not the whole life of the lease agreement but the remaining duration, i.e. the break option available to the tenant.[44]

The actual rental level (known as the 'passing rent') in relation to the Market Rent (known as the 'Estimated Rental Value' – ERV) is an element of risk because if it is higher (known as 'over rent') there is a greater likelihood that the tenant will refuse to renew the contract on expiry or will terminate it when a break option is available. Conversely, in the opposite case (known as 'under rent'), the certainty of future income increases, and so does the incentive for the tenant, *ceteris paribus*, not to vacate the property during the lease term.

In some cases, lease agreements also provide for an adjustment over time, which is usually linked to the official inflation rate, but in different percentages. Consequently, inflation itself becomes an element of risk, since it conditions the actual contractual rent.

Other elements that lead to a different level of certainty of income are any charges transferred to the tenant.[45] However, while the uncertainties of their variability are reduced for the Owner, direct control over the quality of maintenance can often be an element of risk for the quality of the Building in the future if it is not managed directly.

Finally, any guarantees on lease payments, in particular sureties granted by third parties, including banks and insurance companies, are elements that contribute to reducing the risk.

In conclusion, the actual rental status represents the risk associated with actual income and is an essential element for valuation purposes.

NOTES

1. The 'direct property investment' specification is required as, unlike indirect property investments, i.e. investments in securities representing property portfolios, such as property companies, REITs and property funds, the problem does not exist, and the conventional securities finance models can be used.
2. Keynes (1921) and Knight (1921).
3. Akerlof and Shiller (2009), p. 144.
4. Understood as Gaussian distribution, it represents the distribution, or rather the family of distributions most commonly known and used in statistics.

5. Wyman et al. (2011).
6. Di Pasquale and Wheaton (1992).
7. Even in accounting and tax calculations, no depreciation is entered for Land as there is no impairment to consider. There may however be special cases, such as in quarries, where the Land itself loses value as a result of use.
8. The definition of value is very broad, please refer to Chapter 1, Section 'Definitions of Value'. In this case we are referring to the Market Value.
9. Sometimes it is required to the valuer to divide the value of the property into the value of its Land and Building components. Among the other particular cases, this might be the case for accounting or fiscal purposes (e.g. Land is not depreciable, while the Building is) or due to the fact that the Building is on a leasehold. In those cases the Land component will be typically estimated using a Residual Value Method (please refer to Chapter 6, Section 'Residual Value Methods', while the Building component will be estimated as the difference between the value of the property and the value of the Land. When Building and Land ownership are separated and a lease agreement is in place, the Land value may also be estimated based on the rent using Income Capitalisation Comparison Approach Methods.
10. We are referring here to the concept of Highest and Best Used (HBU), described in Chapter 1, Sub-section 'Market Value'.
11. Examples include leasing to students, workers temporarily working away from their office or ageing apartments for which there is a lack of interested buyers.
12. See tradingeconomics.com/country-list/home-ownership-rate for a detailed analysis of the home ownership rate of countries worldwide.
13. It is worth remembering that in some countries there is also a well-developed residential rental sector (e.g. USA, Germany, Switzerland), where some Residential Properties are created for the specific purpose of leasing (so they can be included in the Commercial definition), while other Residential Properties are created for sale to families, the final Users. So in this book, Residential is considered a different sector from Commercial when related to homeowner of single homes or apartments in properties with fragmented ownership.
14. Unless otherwise specified, it is always understood to be the expected return.
15. Planned maintenance, the cost of which is charged to the User, should really be considered a loss of income as it is not recovered in the event of the Space being sold (i.e. if the Property is not let).
16. For a more detailed examination, see Di Pasquale and Wheaton (1992).
17. Authors' translation from Borghi (2009), page 19.
18. In a broader view also a Residential Property can be considered as an Income-producing Property even if directly used by the Owner. In this case, even if there is not a rent, it must be taken into account the opportunity cost of renouncing to obtain it from a third subject.
19. Except for certain market phases in which, due to a strong demand for investment, some Investors may be prepared to pay a premium for greater value assets, such as portfolios, which allow the capital allocated to the sector to be invested more quickly.
20. Liquidity has an impact on the investment risk and consequently on the expected return. The lower the liquidity of an asset, the greater the risk associated with it and consequently the lower its value.
21. As previously stated, some Properties without a Building can also generate usable space, the classic example being agricultural Land. However, the value of a Property without a Building, namely consisting only of Land, is not based on the usable space: one example being a Buildable Area, where the value derives not so much from the actual use but from the potential use (the future possibility of using the Building built in the future).
22. The higher the economic result of the activity performed in the Property, the higher the demand for Use of Space.
23. Also referred to as 'effort rate', as better described in the retail appraisal example in Chapter 10.
24. In the Euro Area 66.4% of the population live in a home they own (as of December 2016), with respect to 64.4% of the United States (as of September 2018) and 63.4% of the United Kingdom (as of December 2016), source: tradingeconomics.com/country-list/home-ownership-rate.

25. The word 'Comparable' as a noun is often used in this book to describe 'transaction' or 'Comparable data'.
26. 'Any kind of property intended for a specific kind of company, where the value of the property reflects the commercial potential of the company', RICS (2017). Also see 'VPGA 4 – Valuation of individual trade related properties', RICS (2017).
27. For example, agricultural Land, which is still Property but has no Building, nonetheless generates some utility for the Space User resulting from the potential cultivation. Another example might be an open-air short-stay car park temporarily operated on a buildable plot of Land.
28. This includes all the cost of capital, both Equity and Debt.
29. The theory and applications of real options were developed from 1977 onwards by Stewart C. Myers, based on financial options and the well-known Black-Scholes formula. A real option is understood to be an opportunity to delay one or more decisions to a time in the future when new information will be available. For further details on this subject see Lucius (2001), Capozza and Li (2002), Copeland and Tufano (2004), Hui and Fung (2009), Pomykacz and Olmsted (2013) and Brealey et al. (2016).
30. This can apply to both Buildable and Non-Buildable Land.
31. Brown and Matysiak (2000).
32. Both the Build-Up Approach and Property Return Rates are described in Chapter 7.
33. Amongst others, Ling and Naranjo (1997) on the US market.
34. A study carried out in the UK showed that the average time needed to sell a Commercial Property is ten months and that to shorten this period a price reduction is necessary (Crosby and McAllister, 2004).
35. The subject is widely discussed in literature and there are various financial manuals that provide a complete description of the phenomenon. For the purposes of this book, we shall provide a very brief description of the leverage effect of the debt, which is that it multiplies the expected risk and return. For further details on property financing in general, see Morri and Mazza (2015).
36. This term refers to all the forms of financing against payment provided by third parties to the Investor, that is, the owner of the equity. This form of capital is characterised by having an explicit, tax-deductible cost, with antedated repayment compared to the equity. Unlike equity, it does not benefit from the actual result of the investment but is exposed to a lower risk of loss in the event of a negative scenario.
37. Sirota and Barel (2003).
38. As will be clarified further on, this will correspond to a reduction of the rate in the valuation model used in the Economic and Financial Method.
39. Already discussed in Subsection 'Regulatory' but dealt with separately here because of its relevance and specificity in Development Projects.
40. See Boyle and Kiel (2001) for an in-depth analysis of the environmental risk impact on the value of a Property.
41. Bond and Wang (2005) analyse the impact of mobile telephone masts on the prices of Properties, while Theebe (2004) studies the influence of aircraft, train and motor vehicle noise on prices. Finally, Des Rosiers (2002) examines the impact of high voltage power lines on property values.
42. In theory it may also have a positive effect, as the selling price may rise in an expanding market.
43. Obsolescence risk is related to different preferences of Users or buyers, especially for Residential.
44. A commonly used metric is the Weighted Average Lease Term (WALT). The WALT may be calculated at property or portfolio level weighting the remaining lease duration of every real estate unit by its rent.
45. Although in some countries there are regulatory limits to such transfers, in double or triple net contracts certain charges such as insurance premiums, taxes and extraordinary maintenance costs are transferred from the Owner to the tenant. More in detail, a double net lease stipulates that the tenant is responsible for paying insurance premiums and property taxes along with the rent, while in a triple net lease he is also responsible for paying for maintenance costs.

CHAPTER 3

Market Analysis

This chapter provides an overview of the economic and property market analysis, which is the foundation of any Property Valuation. The more rigorous the market analysis, the more robust the valuation will be. Furthermore, as will be illustrated in Chapter 4, all valuation methods are based on a comparison, so the choice of comparative factors is a fundamental aspect of the valuation process.

ECONOMIC ANALYSIS

Market analysis must begin with an economic overview. Firstly, this allows the existing and prospective overall scenario to be defined, in order to gain a better understanding of the dynamics of demand and supply of properties based on the economic trend. Secondly, especially when the Discounted Cash Flow Approach is taken, it allows the choice of variables, including the inflation rate, the rate of growth of market rates and the risk-free rate (in this respect, see the case described in Chapter 9 for a detailed discussion of the choice of the main factors) to be justified. Finally, it provides a better understanding of the dynamics of supply and demand of properties based on economic trends.

The economic analysis must, therefore, highlight the dynamics of the main factors, such as Gross Domestic Product, expected economic growth rate, inflation rate, unemployment level, etc. By its nature, the data required for the economic analysis is usually drawn from reports published by the main institutional, economic and political sources (including the World Bank and International Monetary Fund globally, the European Central Bank (ECB) and the European Commission at European level). Considering the reliability of all these sources, the choice between them is arbitrary, but it is essential, particularly with the Income Capitalisation Methods, to use consistent data (e.g. if the valuation concerns a portfolio of properties, the inflation rate used must be identical for all the properties).

ANALYSIS OF THE PROPERTY MARKET

The next step in the analysis is on the property market, both globally/nationally and locally, a process which has a few peculiarities.

Unlike securities markets, where stock exchange transactions are registered and all the data are immediately available to the market participants, in the property market there is a delay required for them to be processed, as well as some difficulties in collecting the data themselves, including price trends and volumes of sales.

To begin with, the data became publicly available after a much greater delay than in the securities markets, where prices and volumes are available in real time. In the property market, data collection usually takes place over a relatively long period (depending on the data, the type of property and the market transparency, it ranges from a month to a year) and this leads to a delay in the availability of official information. The market reports produced by research organisations and real estate brokers therefore always refer to a previous period, with delays of a few weeks to a few months to allow the information collected to be processed.

Secondly, the complexity is increased by the specific nature of each property, which, unlike securities, is unique. The difficulty of measuring property market trends is well known (translation from original Italian language):

> *Analysing the evolution of the price of securities (shares and bonds) does not pose particular problems, as they are the subject of numerous transactions in organised markets (Stock Exchanges) and information about how prices are evolving is available in real time. [. . .] Determining the evolution of property values is considerably more difficult because of the features of the assets and markets. Properties are relatively rarely exchanged, so there is very little information available on the prices of properties, a situation which is exacerbated by a lack of transparency in the property market. Most often, transactions are characterised by a certain level of confidentiality, which makes it difficult to obtain information. Finally, the information that can be gathered on property transactions is not always reliable, because in some cases the published prices may not be the same as the ones paid (quid pro quos, exchanges of Land, transfers of costs or even undeclared payments). The limited number of property transactions would not be such a thorny problem, however, if the properties involved were easy to compare to one another. This comparison is difficult because of the very different features of properties, i.e. their significant degree of diversity.*[1]

The reliability of reports from the property market depends on existing and available data including, for example, the number of property transactions[2] or the method by which they are collected, and therefore the transparency of the market in a broad sense.

Furthermore, the quality of the information varies depending on the market cycle: typically, during expansionary phases, when the demand for real estate investment increases, there is an initial increase in volume followed by a rise in property sale prices. The opposite occurs when the market contracts. This cyclical behaviour is known in the literature as the 'honeycomb cycle',[3] whereby a change in market conditions has a different effect on sale prices and volumes, with the latter presenting a higher reactivity to changes than the former. For this reason, in order to determine the market cycle phase, it is important to analyse the number of transactions or the volume of investment rather than the price level alone, as, given the uniqueness of the assets, the latter is less reliable due to the aforesaid measurement difficulties. It is also important to note that there is a certain seasonality in transactions, with a prevalence of transactions during the latter part of the year, due primarily to financial years coming to an end, and mainly affecting Commercial Properties.

In order to determine the trend in the property market, it is useful to analyse the transaction activity because the price dynamics, albeit important, suffers from a delay in the time, since prices tend to adjust slower.

Comparative Data and Valuation Method

Without wishing to pre-empt matters that will be addressed in greater detail in the coming chapters, it is important to point out how the choice of the typologies of Comparables to be sought and applied depends on the valuation method the valuer intends to adopt:

- If the Sales Comparison Methods are used (see Chapter 5), the comparative data, at the property level, are the sale prices of transactions involving properties that are comparable to the asset being valued.
- If the Income Capitalisation Methods are used (see Chapter 6), however, the comparative data, at the property level, are the yield rates[4] of comparable assets to the one being valued and recently sold (Investment Market) and the rents (Space Market).

It is worth remembering that comparisons must also be made of property costs and, therefore operating expenses or, in the case of Development Projects or redevelopment, the direct and indirect construction costs (and the respective timings) and the market's absorption capacity.

Finally, in the case of Trade-Related Properties, it is essential to carry out market analysis of the activity performed in the properties themselves in order to verify the sustainability of the rents for tenants (effort rate).

Characteristics of the Comparative Factors and Information Sources

Information can be collected in several ways (direct and indirect sources, as it will be discussed below) and at different times (e.g. during a site visit, through discussion with local players or consulting institutional sources, online etc.), depending on the type of valuation performed (i.e. desktop, drive-by or full) and the sources of information available. Regardless of all this, however, the comparative factors must fulfil the following requirements:

- Reliability: they must be drawn from reliable information sources, whether direct or indirect.
- Recentness: they must relate to a period during which the relevant markets (i.e. the macroeconomic conditions and the property markets) have not undergone significant changes compared to the valuation date. Obviously, a trade-off exists between the length of the period in which comparative data are sought, and therefore the amount of comparative data themselves, and their potential usefulness: the longer the period (and therefore, presumably, the higher the amount of comparative data available), the less they are likely to be reliable because of time passing.
- Uniformity: they must be as uniform as possible, regarding the methods by which they have been collected and processed.
- Specificity: because each property is unique and that its uniqueness is the sum of a series of complex characteristics, the data must be as specific as possible to allow the significant characteristics of the property to be identified.

The data collection phase is naturally affected by the selection of information sources. The fact that the property market lacks a central and organized structure like a stock exchange, which would allow data to be collected, is partly overcome by the existence of many information providers whose activity consists of processing information on the market.

The information they supply is a useful aid to decision-making for players; however, due to the particular nature of the market, it must be carefully analysed to determine how it was obtained, analysing the data collection and processing methods.

A distinction can be made in this respect between direct and indirect sources.

- Direct sources, also known as primary sources, consist of players who participate directly in the process of exchanging data, including buyers, sellers, real estate brokers and advisors. Direct sources have data available on individual property units, such as sale prices, rents and yield rates.
- Indirect sources, also known as secondary sources, include all the players who, while not participating directly in the transaction process, collect and process information available on the market. These include Revenue Agency offices, specialised companies, valuers, research centres and associations. Indirect sources are beneficial in the valuation process because one also needs the quotations, i.e. the average prices and rents, minimum or maximum, obtained by sounding out property market experts, asking for their opinions and processing them. Secondary information is usually supplied by indirect information sources and it complements the specific research and analysis focused on the direct collection of transaction data.

The primary indirect sources generally consist of databases and observatories that collect and process economic data systematically to map property values geographically. The final output consists of regular market reports which differ from direct sources because they provide aggregate information by property segment, resulting from the processing of elementary economic data (prices, rents and yields on individual property units). For example, quotations may state the average value of new/refurbished or used dwellings located in a central, semi-central or peripheral area (or, in the case of the main cities, by individual street) or even the minimum and maximum prices of industrial sheds of a certain size located in a peripheral area with good accessibility to major trunk roads, etc.

Data collection is particularly arduous and delicate because there is no accurate data: often one has to rely on transaction values which could be recorded at prices that do not consider all the elements of the transaction (e.g. payment terms, correlated parties, guarantees, etc.). A second problem is the relative low number of transactions, particularly in the Commercial segment, where the average size and value of properties are larger, and the properties themselves are heterogeneous. Also because of that, in the Commercial sector researches are more focused on Expected Rental Value (ERV), vacancy rates, investment volumes, yields and new supply rather than selling price for unit.

In order to reduce the problems connected with the use of transaction prices, additional information from market players is also used. Research is typically carried out among a sample of real estate brokers to gather the opinions of players who have better visibility of the market, with information on actual sales and negotiations taking place, or who are willing to perform certain operations under particular conditions. For example, even in the absence of actual transactions finding out through interviews that a certain number of Investors are interested in investing in a particular asset class, in a specific location, for a 7% yield, makes this an undoubtedly useful market parameter (survey approach method).[5]

The raw data thus collected and processed, alongside statistical methods, provides a general opinion. The process begins by eliminating abnormal values – often the result of data collection errors – by using corrective parameters that allow results to be normalised. The resulting sample, depending on the quality and quantity of the raw data collected, should be more or less representative of the population as a whole (i.e. of the specific market considered).

This sample is then used to generate various kinds of information. The output from observatories is relatively diverse and varies by source, although typically information is produced on the average price and time of sales, rents, vacancy rates, leasing time and yields.

There is no minimum or maximum number of Comparable Properties a valuer can use as a reference, although this will depend on the availability of data regarding market transactions. While, ideally, one should choose at least three or four transactions, it is important to state how difficult, if not impossible, it can sometimes be, particularly in the case of secondary markets or in relatively stagnant periods, to obtain even only one usable item of data. In these cases, valuers are forced to use asking prices and to apply a reduction factor to account for the average discount between asking price and actual price at which transactions are closed. Some secondary sources elaborate and publish data on the average difference between the asking price and actual price paid (average discount on the price) for the various typologies of properties. Needless to point out that in such situations the valuer must be extremely careful, because some sales ads may have been published months before (and therefore they might not be explanatory of the current market scenario) or may show values only 'in the eye of the seller', that are far from the actual prices at which transactions are actually closed.

NOTES

1. Hoesli and Morri (2010), p. 236.
2. Property transactions are typically expressed in terms of the number of unit sold in the case of Residential Properties and are recorded periodically with a high degree of geographical detail. In the Commercial sector, in order to measure the volume of sales in the market, preference is given to measuring the actual volumes of investment in monetary amounts, as published by the leading real estate brokers specialised in the Commercial Properties.
3. Janssen et al. (1994).
4. These will be fully discussed in Chapter 7.
5. Damodaran (2012), Chapter 26 'Valuing Real Estate'.

CHAPTER 4

A New Simple Classification of Valuation Methods

Theory[1] and practice usually agree on identifying three different approaches to Property Valuation, which have been summarised as follows by RICS (2017):

1. A market approach, 'based on comparing the subject asset with identical or similar assets (or liabilities) for which price information is available, such as a comparison with market transactions in the same, or closely similar, type of asset (or liability) within an appropriate time horizon.'
2. A cost approach, 'based on the economic principle that a purchaser will pay no more for an asset than the cost to obtain one of equal utility[2] whether by purchase or construction.'
3. An income approach, 'based on capitalisation or conversion of present and predicted income (cash flows), which may take a number of different forms, to produce a single current capital value.[3] Among the forms taken, capitalisation of a conventional market-based income or discounting of a specific income projection can both be considered appropriate depending on the type of asset and whether such an approach would be adopted by market participants.'

Each approach has its methods with different application criteria:

1. Market Approach Methods[4]:
    a) Direct Comparison Approach[5]
    b) Hedonic Pricing Model
    c) Multipliers and Rules of Thumb.[6]
2. (Depreciated) Cost Approach Methods:
    a) Replacement Cost Approach[7]
    b) Reproduction Cost Approach[8]
3. Income (Capitalisation) Approach Methods:
    a) Direct Capitalisation Approach
    b) Discounted Cash Flow Approach[9] (DCFA).

The traditional repartition above, although widely used in practice and literature, has at least two limitations:

1. The (Depreciated) Cost Approach Methods,[10] which are not only severely limited in their applicability but often also fail to provide a Market Value, resulting instead, in some cases, in the maximum price obtainable from a potential sale of the property.

2. Both the Market Approach and the Income Approach Methods are based on market data, so both should be defined as 'comparative', with the sole difference being the subject of comparison.

On this last point, Lind and Nordlund (2014) argue – and this is their proposed vision – that there is no substantial difference between the Sales Comparison Methods and the Income Capitalisation Methods.

Assume to estimate the Market Value of a property and that data (prices and characteristics) are available regarding a certain number of comparable assets recently sold. Assume also that there is a stable relationship between the sale price of the Comparables and their size. A valuer applying the Direct Comparison Approach, could easily estimate the value of the property by multiplying the price per unit extracted from the market analysis ($€/m^2$) by the surface area of the subject property.

Assuming that there is a stable relationship between the Net Operating Income (or rent) of the Comparables and their sale price (i.e. there is a *de facto* stable relationship in the yield), it would be more correct to estimate the value of the property using a Direct Capitalisation Approach, by dividing its Net Operating Income by the yield extracted from the market.

It is worth pointing out that

comparing historical circumstances that have already taken place with existing ones is the basis for any valuation method. The logical reason for the valuation, as a likely consequence of known causes stemming from experience, is in fact based on an inductive process of comparison. It can, therefore, be said that the valuation method is unique and based on a comparison.[11]

It is easy to see, therefore, that there is no significant difference between the two approaches since in both cases the starting point is a piece of information (the price or yield) derived from recent transactions. Subsequently, the surface or the Net Operating Income are used respectively as a normalising factor. Finally, assuming that a stable relationship can be found between the Cost Approach Method and the value of a property, one can reasonably conclude that the former is also based on a comparison and that, therefore, all the methods are based on a comparison.

Furthermore, as also pointed out by Lind and Nordlund (2014), the Income Capitalisation Methods are also believed not to present such significant differences between the two application criteria (Direct and Discounted Cash Flow), as the former is a 'compression' of the latter (from several periods to a single one) or, vice versa, the latter is an 'extension' of the former (from the analysis of a single standardised period to the detail for multiple periods). This subject will be discussed in greater detail in Chapter 6, Section 'Approach and Application Criteria'.

While there is no intention here to propose a new classification, we believe that, given the above, it is more straightforward (and easier!) to classify Market Value valuation methods as follows:

1. Sales Comparison Approach Methods:[12]
   a) Direct Comparison Approach
   b) Hedonic Pricing Model.

2. Income Capitalisation Comparison Approach Methods[13]:
   a) Direct Capitalisation Approach
   b) Discounted Cash Flow Approach.

For the sake of simplicity, Multipliers and Rules of Thumb have not been included in the new classification and are not discussed herein. Traditionally, being based on direct sales comparison, they are included in the Sales Comparison Methods, but since they rely on economic parameters such as Net Income or Earnings Before Interest, Taxes, Depreciation, and Amortisation (EBITDA), they should also be considered as belonging to the Income Capitalisation Methods.

Multipliers are market parameters which, applied to economic quantities, allow the value of an asset to be determined. While there is no scientific basis for them, in practice they are used because they are easy, quick to apply, and mainly based on market evidence. They are generally employed to determine the value of a business activity[14] rather than a property. It is impossible to identify a uniform and identifiable range of multipliers *a priori*; generally, each type of business has its own parameters applicable to different levels of income. The most widespread are the multipliers for potential revenue, actual revenue, Gross Operating Profit, Net Operating Income (NOI), Earnings Before Taxes, Net Income and cash flow. Even if algorithms are different, Multipliers are based on the same principles of the Income Capitalisation Methods.

The Depreciated Cost Approach Methods[15] have been excluded from the new classification proposal because they are often inapplicable and misleading when estimating the Market Value. However, for completeness, a brief description is given in Section 'Depreciated Cost Approach Methods', mainly in order to explain their limitations. Note that in some cases they could be used to estimate the Market Value when the other methods are inapplicable. In these cases, the reader is asked to reflect on why they do not work! When there is no market of Owner-Users, nor a dual market of Users and Investors, one might be faced with assets for which there is no market at all (and for which, consequently, it is impossible to estimate a Market Value!), as sometimes in the case of Non-Flexible Properties. In these situations, consideration may be given to applying a Residual Value Method, which, even if based on the cost of construction, is however different from the Depreciated Cost Methods.

Note that the Residual Value Methods are not mentioned in the previous classification either. In this case, even though they are considered extremely useful, they are viewed merely as a different way of applying the Income Capitalisation Methods and they will be described in Chapter 6, Section 'Residual Value Methods'.

CHOICE OF VALUATION METHOD

The valuation method choice is fundamental to estimate Market Value correctly. It is essential to be aware from the beginning that, while in some cases several criteria can be applied at the same time, one of them generally indicated as the main one and the others for control purposes, in other situations some models may not work appropriately and may contribute to deviating from the correct value. Care should therefore be taken if, when applying different models at the same time, significant differences emerge in the estimated value. In these cases, it is likely that (at least) one of the models is not suitable because it does not reflect the operation of a specific market or because the data required to apply it are not easily and correctly obtainable. In these situations, the application of several models does not improve the quality of the estimate; on the contrary, the use of an average value[16] would only contribute to deviating from the correct value because of unsuitable models being applied.

In the case of Residential Properties, particularly in markets with a high homeownership rate, the Sales Comparison Methods are recommended. Houses indeed are properties whose space is a final consumer good usable by families/individuals as well as a durable consumer good over which, very often, Users want to have strategic control (i.e. to be Owners) which allows them to improve its usefulness resulting from use. In this case, it is simpler to collect reliable data in the sales market (price), rather than in the rental market. Furthermore, as the percentage of Owners/Investors is limited in most of markets, it may be difficult to find information on the expected yields. Of course, Residential Buildings developed and managed for lease only, should be treated as Commercial real estate.

Additionally, these are often relatively uniform properties with a high number of transactions,[17] so comparison factors can be identified by segmentation based on location, size, quality, and other typical parameters of the housing market. Otherwise, application of the Income Capitalisation Methods would encounter difficulties in determining the income and expected yield. In most countries, if we exclude specific niche markets, such as big cities or university areas, there are no sufficiently large rental markets, and it is even harder to determine the expected yields.

In the case of Commercial Properties, it should be immediately noted that the number of transactions is lower than in the Residential segment. Moreover, Commercial Properties are more diverse and heterogeneous. Additionally, in many cases, there is a separation between the Owner and the User, which, for valuation purposes, makes the lease agreement and its terms also important (e.g. the different levels of tenant's rating or the duration of the lease agreement). Finally, generally speaking, identifying comparison transactions based on physical factors is more difficult and less significant for these properties (e.g. the extreme case of shopping centres, where the number of clients in the catchment area and their spending power can be more relevant than the Net Lettable Area).

For these reasons, the Income Capitalisation Methods are often preferred for Commercial Properties, although in some cases, where the characteristics outlined above for Residential Properties exist, the Sales Comparison Methods could also be used; these include, for example, small size shops and offices, manufacturing sheds, garages, parking spaces, and other assets with a high number of transactions and where the Owner coincides with the User.

It is important to point out a few facts about Commercial Properties based on how flexible they are for the User. In the case of Non-Flexible Commercial Properties, it becomes challenging to find information about the sale price of similar assets as there could be virtually no Comparable Properties. Again, because of the difficulty of identifying a new User, any estimate of rental income may be unrealistic. Furthermore, it is hard to find real estate investors interested in Non-Flexible Commercial Properties, because the low level of flexibility would expose them to the risk connected with the current tenant, rather than to the general demand risk for the real estate market, i.e. the typical risk of real estate investment.

For these reasons, estimating Non-Flexible Commercial Properties is very hard and, *a priori*, as there is no Space Market nor Investment Market, none of the methods listed above seems suitable. In these circumstances, some valuers resort to the Depreciated Cost Methods, the main limitations of which are described in the Subsection 'Use, Advantages, and Limitations of the Depreciated Cost Approach'.

In some cases, the asset could be valued based on the rent that could be earned during the period in which the current User could continue its activity and, subsequently, assuming that there are no new Users, using a Residual Value Method to assess the Terminal Value.

Note, however, that in many cases estimating a period of use for the current User can be quite random. For example, in the case of a company operating in a growing sector, which would not benefit from being moved to another location, this rental period could be fairly unlimited. Note, furthermore, that in many cases the possibility of property reconversion could be merely theoretical, as in the case of a property located in a rural area where there is no demand for Space of any kind.

Flexible Commercial Properties are rarely easy to compare, because of their physical features, and they frequently present a separation between Owners and Users (different lease agreement terms). The decision to base the value estimation on a physical feature is not, therefore, the best, particularly if the lease agreement has a significant impact. In practice, it is simpler to gather information about the income (passing rent and ERV in the Space Market) and expected yield (yields based on trading values in the Investment Market) rather than to search for the sale price of properties that are not really comparable. Consequently, the best choice is often represented by the Income Capitalisation Methods that base the comparison on economic elements rather than on physical features.

This choice is even more appropriate for Trade-Related Properties. In these cases, it is also essential to perform a careful analysis of the economic sustainability of the rent for the User. The margin generated by the User is the reference parameter for estimating the income generated by the property and its sustainability: this is also called EBITDAR (Earnings Before Interest, Taxes, Depreciation, Amortisation and Rent). The choice of other methods, notably the Direct Comparison Approach, may, however, be acceptable when there are comparable standardised properties: returning to the example of the hotel, searching for a value per room may work for standardised facilities like 'business hotels' in medium to large cities. Where hotels only open seasonally, this comparison would not, however, be significant; needless to say, using a value per square metre, which is acceptable and correct in the Residential sector, would be inappropriate, as the amount of surface area is not the central element that generates profits/income/utility for the User.

Finally, in the case of Land and Brownfield sites, the valuer is faced by the problem of enormous diversity, given that in its current state the asset is not generating any income, but its value depends on the future utility (i.e. the intended use of the property that may be developed). The use of Sales Comparison Methods can work when there are some Comparables, not based on the asset in its current state, but on what can be achieved in terms of size and intended use; for example, a Land where Residential units may be developed may be valued using as Comparables other Residential areas recently sold considering the building rights, i.e. using a value per square metre of the Buildable Area that can be developed.

Otherwise, in most cases in which there are no comparable areas with similar physical factors, Income Capitalisation Methods are recommended as they estimate the Land value based on the economic factors that contribute to determining the value of the property that may be developed and the respective costs. In this case, reference is made to the so-called Multiple Periods Residual Value Approach, which was not indicated separately in the above classification but is one of the ways of applying the Discounted Cash Flow Approach (for the relevance of which see Chapter 6, 'Residual Value Methods').

Another category of existing assets worth mentioning is the property portfolio, where the subject of the analysis has to be defined correctly, determining whether an individual unit (e.g. an apartment) or the whole portfolio (e.g. the whole residential complex) will be valued. In the latter case, the sum of the value of the individual units (each correctly estimated with a Comparison Approach Method) is not the value of the portfolio (Residential complex), as this will have a different level of liquidity and different potential buyers. An example will clarify: in the valuation of a property portfolio made of a few dozen apartments, the value of every single unit can be estimated correctly using the Direct Comparison Approach, as the potential buyers of single apartments will likely be families. But it would not be correct to state that the Market Value of the whole property portfolio is equal to the sum of the estimated Market Value of the individual units. In this case, the buyer would no longer be a family, i.e. a User, but an Investor, who would value the portfolio based on the future income from the sale of the individual units to end clients, net of the costs of managing the portfolio and the cost of divestment (e.g. brokerage fees, due diligence costs).

In this case, two paths may be followed. The first, which is more simplistic, consists of applying a discount to the sum of the values of the individual units. This solution, albeit simple, presents the insurmountable problem of objectively estimating the discount parameter, unless there is a robust portfolio market to get it from. The second, which is methodologically more correct, consists of using the Discounted Cash Flow Approach; albeit apparently more complex, the option of making assumptions on how long it will take to sell all the units (the selling price of each of them could be estimated with the Direct Comparison Approach) and of estimating the required rate of return more easily, makes the analysis more objective.

The same consideration also applies to the valuation of a development scheme, already built but in which some of the units remain unsold. At this stage, some valuers will apply the Direct Comparison Approach and estimate the value of the asset as the sum of the values of the individual units. There are cases of valuers who, having been instructed to value a Development Project on a periodic basis, change their valuation method according to the stage of completion: initially, while the complex is under construction they (correctly) rely on a Residual Value Method, but subsequently, at the end of the construction phase, they (incorrectly) apply a Direct Comparison Approach summing up the value of all the property units built. This way they fail to consider the time and risk necessary to sell the properties and the relative profit expected by a potential buyer of the Development scheme. This method is incorrect, however, as a potential buyer of the asset (a development scheme nearing completion) would consider not only on the sale price of the individual units but also the time needed to make a sale and the profit achievable, including a risk factor. In this case, as for the portfolio case, it is better to proceed with a Discounted Cash Flow Approach, which already correctly includes both elements.

The reader will have realised that combinations of different valuation models are often appropriate: going back to the example of valuing a Residential Development Project, it is clear that in order to apply the Discounted Cash Flow Approach, the Direct Comparison Approach will be used to estimate the future sale prices of the individual units for cash flows estimation. The Discounted Cash Flow Approach, when applied to value an existing asset with a very long residual life, also requires the use of the Direct Capitalisation Approach to determine the Terminal Value.

Therefore, while for educational and communicative purposes it is useful to classify methods and models, for application purposes it is equally useful to maintain flexibility in combining them. Note, however, that combining these approaches does not necessarily mean performing different valuations with different models but, as illustrated earlier, using one model within another.

DEPRECIATED COST APPROACH METHODS

Introduction

In many cases, the Depreciated Cost Approach Methods, also referred to, for simplicity, as the Depreciated Cost Methods, are not appropriate for estimating the Market Value of a property because there is not always a direct relationship between the cost incurred for the construction and the utility the market attributes to the asset. In particular, if 'wrong' properties have been built, i.e. properties for which there is little or no demand of use, the Depreciated Cost Approach is unlikely to be even close to their (actual low) Market Value. It is, however, useful to describe the method because in a few limited cases it could be applied, but above all, it is useful to help the reader understanding its limitations and avoid unwary use when it would be inappropriate.

Description

The Depreciated Cost Methods are based on the principle that in most cases an Investor will not pay the price for a property that is above the value of the Land on which it was built and the cost of constructing the Building, net of any depreciation.[18] These methods are therefore based on a substitution principle, where the potential buyer chooses between buying a property and constructing a Building with the same features on a similar plot of Land, considering the depreciation of the existing asset.

The transaction price may deviate from the equilibrium price, which consists of the substitution cost if, for example, certain features of the asset do not correspond to what the buyer is looking for or if the buyer decides he can immediately make use of the asset. In the first case, there would be an undervaluation, in the second case an overvaluation.

The methods will be described for the sake of completeness, but they are not considered entirely appropriate for the purpose of determining specific values, such as the Market Value.

In summary, the Depreciated Cost Methods consist of the sum of the following elements:

1. The cost of constructing the Building from new, including the cost of capital (positive sign)
2. The depreciation of the Building (negative sign)
3. The cost of the Land (positive sign).

In the first step, various approaches can be taken to determine the cost of constructing a new Building, but the solution most frequently adopted is to value the surface area created at the cost of constructing a single unit. Given that the cost per square metre (or square foot) is the unit of reference generally used in construction, analytical information in this respect is readily available on the market.

Estimating the cost of the Building by multiplying the number of square metres (surface) by the average cost of construction per square metre is a relatively simple operation. The various components of a property do not have the same cost per square metre and to avoid excessive distortions, the total square metres of the main elements (garage, office areas, commercial premises, etc.) can be subdivided and each one multiplied by the respective construction cost.

Another cost element to be included is the cost of capital, including both the amount of equity used by the developer and the amount of debt borrowed from banks.

In the second step, in order to quantify the depreciation of the subject property compared to a new Building, three main factors need to be estimated:

- Material wear and tear
- Functional obsolescence
- Economic obsolescence.

The degree of material wear and tear of the property depends on the age of the Building, the quality of construction, the ordinary and extraordinary maintenance and the actual use of the property. This final element, for example, is dependent on who uses the asset: some evidences have shown that a property occupied by the Owner, all other factors being equal, is often in a better physical condition than a leased property. The location can also affect its material wear and tear, with exposure to bad weather and pollution, for example, influencing the degree of wear.

A loss of value can also result from functional obsolescence, i.e. the lack of a particular function compared to a property built today that complies with modern building quality standards and fulfils market requirements. There are many examples of this, such as the number of bathrooms per dwelling, the presence of a lift or not, the type of heating system, the quality of the thermal insulation and soundproofing of the Building, the connection of office areas to computer technologies or, finally and more commonly, energy efficiency. All these elements have undergone significant changes over time, which are reflected in current regulations. For example, an apartment in a Building without a lift or with an antiquated and inefficient heating system will be affected by functional obsolescence.

Economic obsolescence is perhaps more complicated to quantify, since it refers whether there is a real demand for a particular type of property or whether there is no demand for its characteristics or even its current use. There is no lack of examples[19]: a luxury villa for which there is no demand because it is situated in an area that is now economically depressed, or a hotel in a region that no longer attracts visitors. Some very luxurious finishes, such as gold taps, may be very expensive to install but their value will depend on the real demand for this kind of feature. Moreover, the second example illustrates the impact of economic obsolescence, which can have an effect on the Building without necessarily having any impact on the value of the Land. If a hotel Building can be converted for a different use, e.g. Residential, the value of the Land on which it stands may not be affected, while the value of the Building will fall by the amount required to convert and adapt it to its new use. However, the dividing line between the impact of economic obsolescence on the Land and the Building is relatively hard to establish.

Quantifying the depreciation is relatively tricky, particularly if the Building is old. The simplest way to proceed is to consider a linear annual depreciation rate, e.g. a rate of 2% if the estimated useful life of the Building is 50 years. A non-linear depreciation of the Building can also be considered, choosing lower rates in the first few years of life and subsequently adopting higher rates.

These solutions are simple, but not very satisfactory. It would be more appropriate to consider the useful life (and therefore the real economic depreciation rate) of each component of a Building. These solutions are only valid in theory because, in the real world, there is no correspondence with the real depreciation attributed by the market participants.

The following variant, which is often easier to use, would be more appropriate: rather than trying to determine the useful life of an old Building, or of each component, in order to calculate an ageing amount, one could estimate the refurbishing cost required to ensure the property is equivalent to a standard new property. As the reader may recognise, this is based on the same principles of the Residual Value Methods.

In the third step, finally and no less difficult, there is the value estimation of the Land. In theory, it could be determined using information on recent sales of comparable plots of Land, resorting to the Direct Comparison Approach. However, this approach has severe practical limitations because, particularly in urban areas, there is not an active market for Land, and each plot of Land has not only a different location but also different building rights (see example and explanation in the section 'Choice of Valuation Method').

An example will better illustrate the application of the Depreciated Cost Approach.

EXAMPLE 4.1: EXAMPLE OF APPLICATION OF THE DEPRECIATED COST APPROACH

The subject property is a 23-year-old warehouse in an industrial area on the outskirts of a medium-sized city, with a Net Lettable Area of $2,500\,m^2$ standing on a plot of Land measuring $5,000\,m^2$.

In order to value the Land, trades of areas used for the same purpose and with the same Buildable Land ratio $(0.5\,m^2/m^2)$[20] are analysed. The market analysis reveals an average Market Value of € $70/m^2$ of Land, based on which one can estimate a value/cost for the Land of € 350,000.

An estimate is then done of the cost of constructing a new warehouse. The parameters are determined as follows:

- Direct construction costs (also defined as 'hard costs'): € $500/m^2$
- Indirect construction costs (also defined as 'soft costs'): 15% of the hard costs
- Developer's margin (meaning the builder's profit on his equity): 12% of the hard costs
- Financial charges: 1 year of debt financing with an LTC (loan to cost) of 60% of the hard costs at an average cost of debt rate of 4.5%.

In total, therefore, the full construction cost of a new warehouse is estimated € $648.5/m^2$ or € 1,621,250, determined as follows:

- Hard costs: € $500/m^2$
- Soft costs: 15% * € $500/m^2$ = € $75/m^2$
- Developer's margin: 12% * € $500/m^2$ = € $60/m^2$
- Financial charges: 1 year * 60% * € $500/m^2$ * 4.5% = € $13.5/m^2$.

Subsequently, the depreciation is estimated: assuming a linear depreciation rate over time and a useful life of the warehouse of 50 years (1/50 = 2%), the depreciation is

(Continued)

calculated as being € 745,775 (23 years age * average annual depreciation rate of 2% * full construction cost).

Finally, the Market Value of the property is estimated as the sum of the value of the Land (€ 350,000) and the full construction cost of a new shed (€ 1,621,250), net of the estimated depreciation (€ 745,775), which gives a final value of € 1,225,475 (or € 1,230,000 if rounded to the nearest ten thousand euros as usually done in practice).

Use, Advantages, and Limitations of the Depreciated Cost Approach

With the right adjustments, the Depreciated Cost Approach can provide a basis for calculating the insurance value of a Building. In this case, it is not necessary to value the Land, and the depreciation is irrelevant. It is not, however, suitable for estimating the Market Value, as there is no direct relationship between the realisable cost of an asset and the usefulness attributed to it by Users and Investors.

This method, which is simple to apply in theory, presents two main problems in practice. Firstly, the value of the Land has to be determined, so other methods need to be used; secondly, the depreciation has to be quantified as the loss of economic value resulting from the obsolescence of the Building and its physical deterioration, which is difficult to measure objectively.

The limitations illustrated above mean that it is not recommended to value assets for which there is a market of Owners/Users (for which the Sales Comparison Methods are preferable) or Space (where the Income Capitalisation Methods are preferable). Some valuers sometimes use it to estimate the value of properties for which there are no comparable transactions nor information about rents, as the property is occupied by the Owner, such as luxury Residential Properties, or is unusable, such as abandoned industrial properties. This choice is somewhat questionable if you intend to estimate the Market Value: the absence of both a Space Market and an Investment Market should be taken as an indication that there is no market, so Market Value estimation is meaningless, regardless of the valuation method adopted.

NOTES

1. Brueggeman and Fisher (2010) and Pagourtzi et al. (2003).
2. 'Utility' is understood to mean the satisfaction deriving from the consumption of a certain quantity of product.
3. 'Current Value' is understood to mean the sum of money necessary today in order to have available a certain sum in the future, given a certain rate of return.
4. Also known as 'Sales Comparison Approach Methods'.
5. Also known as 'Comparable Transactions Approach'.
6. 'Rules of Thumb' is understood to mean general or approximate principles, procedures, or rules based on experience or practice.
7. 'A method that indicates value by calculating the cost of a similar asset offering equivalent utility', IVS 105 Valuation Approaches and Methods, IVS (2017) available at www.ivsc.org/standards/international-valuation-standards.

8. 'A method that indicates value by calculating the cost to recreating a replica of an asset', IVS 105 Valuation Approaches and Methods, IVS (2017) available at www.ivsc.org/standards/international-valuation-standards.
9. Also known as 'Yield Capitalisation Approach'.
10. Described in more detail in the section 'Depreciated Cost Approach Methods'.
11. Authors' translation from Ferrero (1996).
12. 'Sales Comparison Approach Methods' is preferable to 'Market Comparison Approach Methods' because, in order to estimate the Market Value, all criteria must use the market as a reference. Using the 'market' definition for a model, would imply that the other criteria do not refer to the market. For the remainder of this book they will be referred as, for simplicity, 'Sales Comparison Methods'.
13. For simplicity and to ensure greater consistency with the terms used in standard practice and the relevant literature, for the remainder of this book it will be referred to simply as the 'Income Capitalisation Methods', with a warning not to forget the implied term Comparison!
14. Cinemas, hotels, golf courses and fitness centres are some of the types of properties for which valuation practice also uses rules of thumb or multipliers derived from the market. Both the Property and the activity performed in it (film screening, sports activity, hotel activity, etc.) are therefore valued.
15. In the remainder of this book they will be referred as, for simplicity, 'Depreciated Cost Methods'.
16. Note in this case how, in practice, a simple average of the values calculated using the various valuation methods is sometimes used in addition to a weighted average, applying the weighting chosen by the valuer to the various values. Use of this approach is discouraged because, apart from having no scientific basis, it is random in its choice of weighting factors and therefore subject to a greater risk of error.
17. This does not always apply, such as in the case of detached homes of particular architectural value or other assets with unique features, including rental properties.
18. This is also referred to in literature as the Depreciated Replacement Cost, 'the current cost of replacing an asset with its modern equivalent asset less deductions for physical deterioration and all relevant forms of obsolescence and optimisation' (RICS, 2017).
19. These examples explain and remind the reader that the Market Value of an asset does not vary in proportion to its cost.
20. Which means that 0.5 m^2 of Building can be constructed per m^2 of Land.

Sales Comparison Approach Methods

This chapter presents the Sales Comparison Approach Methods, also referred to, for simplicity, as the Sales Comparison Methods, starting with the principles on which they are based, subsequently describing in greater detail the main application criteria – the Direct Comparison Approach and the Hedonic Pricing Model – showing how each one is used, and discussing their main advantages and limitations.

APPROACH AND APPLICATION CRITERIA

In the Sales Comparison Methods, the value of an asset is obtained based on the identified prices of comparable transactions. This method is based on the assumption that no rational buyer is willing to pay a price higher than the cost of purchasing similar assets that present the same degree of usefulness. This assumption stems from the two main principles of substitution and equilibrium between demand and supply:

- Substitution Principle: the value of an asset is related to the price that should be paid for a perfectly identical asset.
- Equilibrium Principle: the price of an asset depends directly on the market (demand and supply) and is, therefore, the synthesis of the negotiation process.

For the Sales Comparison Methods to be applied, one needs a sample of transactions[1] relating to identical assets. By definition, strictly speaking, there are no identical properties because they are all unique, at least in terms of location. However, in practical terms, the flexibility of an asset can be identified based on the main features that contribute to determining its attractiveness. The price of an asset always depends on the relationship between demand and supply and will tend to vary over time.

The Sales Comparison Methods can be divided into two main application criteria which will be illustrated separately,[2] both for greater clarity of explanation and because, while all of them are based on the same principles, their calculation algorithms and application methods differ:

1. Direct Comparison Approach
2. Hedonic Pricing Model.

With regard to the Direct Comparison Approach, there are many manuals that provide a clear and in-depth description with numerous examples of how it is used. The Hedonic Pricing

Model is rarely used because of the difficulty of obtaining a sufficient amount of information about transactions, but it is important since in the future, thanks to AI and the increasing amount of data available, could become of practical interest.[3] Despite this, knowledge of the Hedonic Pricing Model helps to gain a better understanding and ensure the more effective use of the more widespread Direct Comparison Approach. While the former, as illustrated in the Section 'Direct Comparison Approach', is based on multiple regression models, where several variables contribute to assigning a value to the unit of measurement used to determine the value of the property, the latter can be seen as a linear regression with a single variable, where the value depends solely on the Net Sellable Area. Later, this value is modified by making some adjustments based on the specific characteristics of the property being valued which differ from the comparable transactions.

DIRECT COMPARISON APPROACH

In order to estimate the value of a property, the Direct Comparison Approach uses the values of Comparables which have been recently sold. The real prices of Comparables can be used to estimate the value of the subject property by making some adjustments that take into account its specific features. There are three steps to using this model:

1. Selecting the Comparables
2. Standardising the transaction price of the Comparables
3. Estimating adjustments.[4]

To begin with, a valuer has to search for the Comparables for the subject property. Therefore, one has to analyse, assess and verify the existence of similar properties that have been recently sold and their prices, considering all the elements that affect the demand and the supply. Comparability is determined based on the physical features of the Building (age, condition, etc.) and the Land, i.e. the location.

The features of the Comparable Properties must be as similar as possible to those of the subject property and the comparable assets must have been the subject of a recent transaction at a market price.[5]

In this respect, there is no time frame that can be defined as valid in all cases. Its length depends on the type of property, the frequency with which it changes hands and the complexity of the transaction. For example, Residential Properties, such as apartments in an urban area, are relatively frequently traded and the transactions present a low level of complexity. Differently, Commercial Properties are not traded frequently, and present a higher complexity due to a series of contractual hurdles (such as leasing agreements or authorisation certificates and licences).

A variety of features need to be considered when defining transactions that are comparable to the subject property. Firstly, the physical features of the property, such as its intended use, location, accessibility and connections, size, age, condition, finish, and systems. Secondly, the regulatory features, whether legal (presence of third-party rights) or related to town planning or tax (amnesties, exemptions from income or wealth taxes, etc.). Finally, the economic and financial characteristics, such as the lease agreement,[6] overheads, maintenance, and profitability.

There is also no minimum or maximum number of Comparables, although this will obviously depend on the availability of data regarding market transactions. Ideally, at least three or four Comparables need to be chosen.

Finally, one must exclude all transactions that do not fulfil the normality requirement,[7] meaning those that are not open market transactions, such as prices resulting from auctions or buyers with a specific interest in the property (e.g. a neighbour who needs to extend his house).

The second step is to 'standardise' the transaction price of Comparable Properties by identifying a unit of comparison. As the surface area has a direct effect on the value of properties, in most cases the unit considered is the Net Lettable Area.[8]

For some property types, the unit considered can vary depending on the income 'generating' unit drawn from the sample of Comparables analysed. Different types of properties can, in fact, have their own units of measurement: price per square metre in the Residential or office sector, per parking space or mooring space, per seat in multiscreen cinemas, per hotel room, per bed in student residences, etc. It is worth pointing out, however, that for Commercial Properties in particular, but more generally for those where there is a separation between Owner and User, where the value of the property is driven by its income potential, it may not be appropriate to use this unit of measurement (or generally the Direct Comparison Approach). This depends on the cost and income structure: consider the economies of scale resulting from the size of a property, as in the case of a hotel, where some fixed costs have a different incidence depending on the number of rooms. In some cases, however, where the cost structure is relatively similar, the model does have some validity: going back to the hotel sector example, in the case of relatively similar properties like business hotels located in medium to large cities, the use of a value per room may be appropriate.

The value of the asset is obtained by multiplying the average value drawn from the market (expressed in the reference units of measurement) by the quantity of the asset to be valued.

The third and last step involves making adjustments because the subject property may not be exactly the same as the Comparables, owing to its age, condition, or accessibility. After having gathered all the information on the property and the market, the differences between the information obtained and the subject property need to be checked. For this reason, this model is never applicable to properties which, by their nature, are effectively unique in every respect. Even in properties which may apparently seem uniform, such as a building split into two semi-detached homes, there may be differences in orientation or noise level (e.g. if one half of the building is closer to a road). This final step is important because it directly relates to the choice of Comparables. In practice, it is often felt that two properties are not comparable if an adjustment needs to be made that exceeds a certain percentage[9] of the value of the unit of measurement. If this happens, other (better) Comparables must be chosen that are truly similar to the subject property.

EXAMPLE 5.1: EXAMPLE OF APPLICATION OF THE DIRECT COMPARISON APPROACH

The subject property is a two-bedroom apartment in good condition, situated on the second floor of a residential building, with no lift, in a semi-central area of the city, with good access to public and private services. The Net Sellable Area of the apartment, which has no garage or cellar,[10] is $80 \, m^2$.

(Continued)

The valuation process begins by seeking and selecting Comparables which have recently been sold on the market, determining the sale price and Net Sellable Area of each one (as shown in Table 5.1).

TABLE 5.1 Example of application of the direct comparison approach

Comparable Properties	1	2	3	4	5	6
Sale price	*€ 250,000*	*€ 240,000*	*€ 255,000*	*€ 237,000*	*€ 215,000*	*€ 223,000*
Garage	€ 18,000		€ 15,000		€ 16,000	€ 20,000
Cellar	€ 5,000		€ 7,000	€ 8,000		€ 8,000
Rectified price	€ 227,000	€ 240,000	€ 233,000	€ 229,000	€ 199,000	€ 195,000
Net Sellable Area (m²)	82.00	84.00	85.00	80.00	69.00	71.00
Price €/m²	€ 2,768.29	€ 2,857.14	€ 2,741.18	€ 2,862.50	€ 2,884.06	€ 2,746.48
Average price €/m²	*€ 2,809.94*					
Average price €/m² (rounded)	€ 2,800					
Net Sellable Aresa subject Property (m²)	80.00					
Asset value before adjustment	*€ 224,000*					
Reduction	5%					
Asset value post adjustment	*€ 212,800*					
Asset value (rounded)	**€ 213,000**					

The next step is to standardise the transaction prices of the Comparables found, eliminating ancillary elements which are not present in the asset being valued, carrying out a separate valuation of these elements and deducting them to obtain a rectified price.

Finally, a standardisation by a unit of measurement is carried out, in this case dividing the price obtained in the previous stage by the Net Sellable Area. The average value thus obtained, rounded to € 2,800/m² constitutes the unit of comparison.

Applying the average value per square metre to the Net Sellable Area of the subject property returns a gross value of € 224,000 (€ 2,800/m² per 80 m²). Subsequently, a reduction must be applied due to the absence of a lift (adjustment estimated at 5%), which reduces the Market Value of the subject property to € 212,800 (€ 224,000/1.05), or € 213,000 if rounded up.

The Direct Comparison Approach is particularly appropriate for valuing fairly uniform or 'standard' properties, i.e. standardised types in which there is an Investment Market with Owners who are also Users, rather than situations in which there are separate Investment and Space Markets. The most common are residential types – detached, semi-detached or terraced homes, apartments in condominiums – small size offices and shops, warehouses and light industrial. The model is sometimes used to estimate the value of Land, where buildability (a type of construction and whether it can be built) are considered in addition to the quality of the location when selecting Comparables.

This method works efficiently the more uniform the properties and the more frequent the transactions; for example, estimating a car park space is relatively simple since they are quite uniform and in the same location there may be many assets with the same features recently sold.

As specified in greater detail in Chapter 6, Section 'Residual Value Methods', however, comparing plots of Land is very difficult, as the value is influenced not only by the size of the plot and the area on which buildings can be erected, but also by the intended use and the actual size of the Building that may be developed.

In particular, in most countries the market for Residential Properties is a market of Owners who are also Users,[11] in which the ownership of relatively similar assets is exchanged with the aim of direct use[12] and, therefore, it is easy to determine the sale price per square metre of Net Sellable Area. It is not, however, appropriate for properties in which there is a separation between Owners and Users, i.e. where there is an Investment Market and a Space Market, and where consequently it is hard to identify Comparables based on the transaction price. Consider the office market, in which there is an increasing separation between Owners and Users and where, consequently, a large rental market is generated. In this market, Comparables can be identified in order to determine the ERV. Finally, this model cannot be used for property types in which there is no Investment Market nor Space Market, such as in the case of some special properties (e.g. publicly owned hospitals, bridges, or roads).

The attractiveness of this model derives from direct evidence from the market. However, the selection of Comparables is not easy, considering the great diversity of properties and the small number of transactions. Furthermore, given the frequently limited transparency of property markets, it can be difficult to obtain information on transaction prices and/or the features of the properties sold. Finally, the reliability of the information obtained must be considered carefully, because of the reliability of some direct sources (i.e. they may have no incentive to provide correct and complete information) or because of the approximation of indirect sources (i.e. they are based on average values of large samples).

HEDONIC PRICING MODEL

The Hedonic Pricing Model[13] is used to estimate the rental value of primarily Residential Properties, as well as to determine residential property market indexes. Over time, the Hedonic Pricing Model has also been used to estimate the value of many other types of assets, such as second-hand cars, works of art and vintage wines.

The Hedonic Pricing Model is based on the idea that the supply and demand for heterogeneous goods include supply and demand for each characteristic, or attribute, of such goods.[14] Generally speaking, the supply and demand for properties can be perceived quite easily: the supply of a certain kind of asset corresponds to the assets put on sale, while the demand consists of buyers interested in buying that kind of asset. Provided that these elements are observable, the supply and demand for properties as a whole can be defined as an explicit supply and demand. However, the supply and demand for each characteristic, or each unit of a characteristic for attributes measured on a continuous or discrete scale,[15] cannot be perceived directly and are therefore defined as an implicit supply and demand. Taking the classic example of the 'presence of a lift in a Residential Property', the supply consists of all the apartments for sale in properties with a lift, while the demand will consist of buyers wishing to buy an apartment equipped with a lift. In this respect, the 'satisfaction', hence the term 'hedonic', found by a buyer in acquiring a property, corresponds to the sum of the appreciations derived from its individual characteristics, such as the prestige, location, and quality. In other words, the property buyer is, in reality, buying all the various components and its price is the sum of the theoretical prices of its components.

There is, therefore, an implicit price in each characteristic which will emerge from a comparison between the supply and demand for each characteristic. This means that there is a price for the existence of a lift in a property, a price for a 'good' rather than 'less good' neighbourhood, a price for a Building in good condition, a price for a panoramic view, etc. Implicit prices are measured using multiple regression models; information on the price of the transaction and the values of the characteristics considered in the regression model need to be collected for a sample of properties sold in a specific period of analysis.

The Hedonic Pricing Model is used in mass appraisal[16] and presents two major advantages:

- Significant reduction in subjectivity
- Definition of the impact of every attribute on the value of the property.

First of all, it significantly reduces the subjectivity of the valuation. In fact, various qualitative characteristics, such as the quality of a district, can be measured through quantitative elements, such as the average income of the district's inhabitants. Subjectivity in the measurement of some parameters cannot, however, be eliminated entirely, because it arises from the fact that various attributes are qualitative, which is one of the peculiarities of the real estate sector. As they have an impact on living conditions and aspirations, decisions to buy a property, particularly a Residential one, are partly guided by emotions.

The model is sometimes criticised because a property would be valued without visiting the site, but this criticism is unfounded. Visiting the property is undoubtedly essential to define the quality of the location, the quality of the construction and the maintenance of the Building. Subjectivity is also reduced because the price of each attribute is determined based on the price of market transactions. The Hedonic Pricing Model is, therefore, in itself a valuation model strictly based on comparisons.

The other undeniable advantage is the opportunity to isolate the impact of an attribute on the value of a property. The Hedonic Pricing Model[17] can, however, also be used to isolate the impact of any characteristic on property prices,[18] such as in a study[19] in which the value of a sea view and distance from the city were valued in the city of Auckland, New Zealand.

The Hedonic Pricing Model does, however, have its limitations as it only provides reliable estimates if the subject property is relatively standard, and consequently, there is a sufficient number of transactions involving similar assets.

Notwithstanding the theoretical and practical limitations to its use, understanding the model is useful for a better application of the most commonly adopted Direct Comparison Approach. In fact, the latter is based on a major single element (i.e. the value per unit, e.g. €/m^2), but the valuation process is completed by adjustments. In other words, the Hedonic Price Model relies on the value of each characteristic of the property, while the Direct Comparison Approach is based only on less precise adjustments.

NOTES

1. Ideally, the transactions must be completed, but in practice potential transactions, i.e. asking prices in property sales ads, are commonly used after appropriate assessment.
2. A brief description of the two criteria will be given in the following sections without going into detail about how they are used, in keeping with the intention of the authors to focus the text on the Income Capitalisation Approach Methods.
3. It is principally used in mass appraisal where it is the basis for Automated Valuation Models (AVMs). One interesting application is presented in Schulz et al. (2014), according to which AVMs allow one to provide 'good appraisals for average properties based on a manageable, but sufficiently sophisticated, statistical model'.
4. In practice, this last step is often performed automatically when standardising the transaction price of the Comparable Properties mentioned in the previous point.
5. This means that it has to respect the conditions set out for the 'Market Value'.
6. Even if this feature should be considered, when there is a separation between the Owner and User of the subject Property, it might be better to use the Income Capitalisation Approach Methods. In some cases, for example when the subject Property (such as a residential unit) is leased, but the market mainly consists of buyers interested in the direct use of the Property, the existence of a lease agreement in place is a burden that may negatively affect its Market Value.
7. Similar to those stated for Market Value definition.
8. In the rest of this book, as it is not a technical manual, unless otherwise stated, the terms Gross Surface and Net Lettable Area will have the following meaning: Gross Surface Area: the sum of all the surface areas (covered and uncovered) of a Property, divided by purpose and floor, as well as by primary purpose and secondary purpose (lift shafts, corridors, utilities areas etc.); Net Lettable Area: the surface area of a Property that is currently rented or could be rented to one or more tenants; generally, this excludes the entrance hall, atrium, utilities area, lift shaft, etc., unless the Property is of particular monumental value or prime real estate. It is determined by applying weighting parameters to the various areas of the Gross Surface in order to obtain a single uniform piece of data for each use of the Property.
9. In practice, often a limit of 20% is applied, but there is no unanimity of opinion on this value.
10. Note that the absence or presence of certain ancillary elements could have an impact on the full value of the asset that differs in its extent from the value of the ancillary element alone. For example, the value of an apartment with a parking space within the same Building will naturally be greater than the value of the same apartment that lacks this ancillary element: in the former case, the usefulness for the User will be greater.
11. Especially in countries where there is a high propensity for families to own the home in which they live.
12. It is relatively easy to classify Residential Properties into uniform categories according to qualitative parameters, such as their condition or quality.
13. For further details, see section 3.3.2 of Hoesli and Morri (2010), originally written by Professor Martin Hoesli, from which this section is taken and adapted.
14. The theoretical basis of the hedonic approach can be found in Lancaster (1966) and Rosen (1974).
15. The surface area of the home is a continuous characteristic because it can assume any value within reasonable limits. On the other hand, the quality of the neighbourhood where the dwelling is located is often measured on a small scale (ranging from 'Excellent' to 'Good', 'Satisfactory', and 'Bad'). This is referred to as a discrete or categorical feature.

16. For a detailed discussion of this subject, see Kauko and D'Amato (2008).
17. Also see Bourassa et al. (2005).
18. For a review of the literature on the impact of environmental characteristics on the prices of Residential Properties, see Boyle and Kiel (2001).
19. Bourassa *et al.* (2004)

CHAPTER 6

Income Capitalisation Comparison Approach Methods

This chapter provides a detailed description of the Income Capitalisation Comparison Approach Methods (also referred to, for simplicity, as the Income Capitalisation Methods) and of its two main application criteria: the Direct Capitalisation Approach and the Discounted Cash Flow Approach (DCFA). It also includes the Residual Value Methods, based on the same criteria and which allows for the value Land and, in general, all properties at the end of their life cycle.

APPROACH AND APPLICATION CRITERIA

The Income Capitalisation Methods are based not only on the principles of substitution and equilibrium between supply and demand set out above, but also on the principle of anticipation, according to which a rational buyer will not pay a price higher than the Present Value of the economic benefits that the property will be able to generate during its lifetime, implicitly also suggesting that it will not be possible for this price to exceed the purchase cost of similar properties which present the same degree of usefulness.

They are often presented as economic and financial methods because they are based on principles that are applicable and applied to all other types of investment assets and therefore differ from the other methods introduced in the previous chapters, which are more common in real estate. The Income Capitalisation Methods allow to express the value of a property according to the same factors that determine the value of any other asset: the expected income and the risk associated with its achievement.

As previously mentioned, it would be even more correct to use the 'Income Capitalisation Comparison Approach Methods' definition, which is still a market comparison, although one that, unlike the Sales Comparison Methods (which analyse the Owners/Users market), is based on an indirect comparison of two economic variables in two different markets: the expected economic benefits (income or cash flow), derived from the Space Market, and a required (immediate or total) rate of return, derived from the Investment Market.

The Income Capitalisation Methods, therefore, assume to identify an economic benefit and a time adjusting factor (cap rate or discount rate) based on the risk of the previous economic benefit.

The economic benefit of an Income-producing Property is, primarily, its rent net of operating costs. The economic principle also remains valid if the User is also the Owner of the property: in this case, the economic benefit consists of the alternative cost of buying the Use of the Space in the market or the opportunity cost of choosing to use the property himself (rental expenses). In order to estimate the economic benefit, it is essential to identify the amount of income the Property can generate by analysing a sample of Comparables in the Space Market, while also considering the actual rent from the lease agreement currently in place.

The time correction factor based on the risk associated with the economic benefit (cap rate or discount rate) is instead a measure of the rate of return required by the potential buyers/Investors to invest in an asset whose expected return presents a specific level of risk. In order to identify this parameter, a valuer has therefore to analyse the Investment Market; in other words, the market in which Owners trade the ownership of properties (i.e. the right to receive their future economic benefits) based on their expected returns. This element is often hard to quantify due to the complexity of measuring risks and returns. This subject will be addressed in greater detail in Chapter 7.

Recently, the practice and theory of Property Valuation have quite rightly focused on the Income Capitalisation Methods, which are well-suited to the valuation of properties that generate a regular income (e.g. Income-producing Properties, such as shopping centres, hotels, offices). However, these methods, with the appropriate approaches described in the Section 'Residual Value Methods', are also applicable to the valuation of Land and Development Projects, giving rise to the Residual Value Methods.

The Income Capitalisation Methods provide two application models[1] based on different measurements of expected economic benefits and return:

- Direct Capitalisation Approach: This is used in order to convert the forecast of an expected income of a single period in an indication of value through a direct passage, by dividing the estimated income at an appropriate cap rate (one income and one rate).
- Discounted Cash Flow Approach (DCFA): This is used in order to convert all the future cash flows in a Present Value, by discounting all the expected economic benefits (several cash flows) at an appropriate discount rate.

However, in the case of a property, not only the useful life of the Building can be very long, often spanning many decades, but the Land component presents an infinite useful life. Consequently, as the future economic benefits cannot be estimated over a very long period of time, if not infinitely for the Land component, it becomes very important to choose the right time horizon and to estimate a Terminal Value, a theoretical price at which the property may be sold in the future. Given that, as it will be clearly shown further on, particularly in the case of an Income-producing Property, estimating the Terminal Value involves using the Direct Capitalisation Approach. The distinction between the two models stems more from a descriptive and applicative requirement than an economic principle, as the DCFA often requires the use of the Direct Capitalisation Approach to estimate the Terminal Value.

Even though they are the expression of the same method, there are significant differences in their application. In particular, the differences between the Direct Capitalisation Approach and the DCFA may be summarised as follows:

- The definition of economic benefit which the asset is able to produce:
  - The Direct Capitalisation Approach is based on finding an income (accounting measure).
  - The Discounted Cash Flow Approach identifies a cash flow (financial amount, which may only occasionally coincide with the equivalent income).

- The time horizon considered:
  - The Direct Capitalisation Approach determines the value of an asset over a single period of time by defining a stabilised periodic income (usually annual) and a rate (cap rate) relating to that single period of reference.
  - The Discounted Cash Flow Approach covers multiple periods of time over a time horizon divided into several periods.
- The calculation algorithm:
  - The Direct Capitalisation Approach is based on the capitalisation of the future benefit, transforming an existing estimation of income into an estimation of value.
  - The Discounted Cash Flow Approach uses the principle of anticipation to discount the value of future income flows.

Analysing both approaches is important to understand the strengths and weaknesses, as well as the conditions of applicability.

Finally, it is important to note at the outset that the Income Capitalisation Methods use two types of Property Return Rates:

- The cap rate, which relates the value of an asset to a single income amount over a period of time (Direct Capitalisation Approach). It is the expected market income yield.
- The discount rate, which is used to discount the cash flows of income generated by an asset and represents the yield required by the market for an investment with the same level of risk (Discounted Cash Flow Approach). It is the expected market Interest Rate of Return.

The rest of the chapter describes the two approaches, while, given the complexity and importance of the subject, the whole of Chapter 7 is dedicated to describing Property Return Rates.

DIRECT CAPITALISATION APPROACH

The Direct Capitalisation Approach refers to expressions based on quantifying a stabilised periodic income, generally on an annual basis, thus avoiding a precise estimate of the income expected throughout the whole economic life of the asset. The mathematical formulas used to determine the value of a property vary in their structure depending on the time horizon and methods by which the annual income is earned. Valuation theory and practice agree in mainly using a perpetuity, given that real estate assets have an extremely long life cycle and that the difference between the Present Value of a perpetual annuity and the value of a time-limited annuity becomes small within a few years.

A vast amount of literature does exist, in which various calculation formulas are given which consider any limitations on the life of the asset or on its capacity to generate income (e.g. a concession). The authors have chosen not to look at these aspects in detail because, on the one hand, they are dealt with in detail in numerous valuation textbooks[2] and, on the other, the difficulty, if not the objective impossibility, of determining specific parameters suggests that the Direct Capitalisation Approach should not be applied in some cases and the use of the DCFA is preferable.

The Direct Capitalisation Approach Calculation Algorithm

In order to perform the valuation, the expected economic benefit (income) and the respective cap rate need to be identified: as the calculation algorithm is very simple, and only requires two pieces of data, the slightest variation in the quantities used have a considerable impact. The basic calculation algorithm[3] is:

$$V = \frac{I}{r}$$

where:

- V = value
- I = income
- r = cap rate.

The Direct Capitalisation Approach stems from the Gordon model[4] to determine the value based on future monetary flows; initially used to value shares, it is also applicable to other asset classes. The Gordon formula for calculating the price of shares is:

$$V = \frac{D_1}{k - g}$$

where:

- D_1 = dividend (cash flow) expected in the subsequent period
- g = dividend growth rate
- k = cost of capital (discount rate).

The formula is the derivation of:

$$\sum_{t=1}^{\infty} D^* \frac{(1+g)^t}{(1+k)^t}$$

which represents the infinite series of dividends generated by a company, which grows at a constant rate g. Therefore, according to the first formula, the value of a company is dependent on its dividend capitalised at a rate of $(k - g)$; in other words, the expected rate of growth of dividends is subtracted from the discount rate.

This last relationship also indicates that, on a purely mathematical level, assuming the income is stabilised, the value of the asset would be equivalent to the discounted value of a perpetual annuity. In fact, an equivalent result is obtained with:

$$V = \sum_{t=1}^{\infty} \frac{I}{(1+k)^t} = \frac{I}{r}$$

The calculation algorithm is extremely simple and in this very simplicity lies the more significant limitation of the model, given that a precise estimation is required of both the income (I) and the cap rate (r). Given the importance of the latter, we refer you to Chapter 7, Section 'Cap Rate' for a detailed discussion. Purely for clarity of presentation, we shall define the cap rate as a income yield, i.e. the income return calculated as the ratio between the income and its price, for comparable assets which have recently changed hands in the market. The following paragraph describes how the income is determined.

Profit and Loss Account of an Income-Producing Property[5]

The Income Capitalisation Methods require different definitions of economic benefit based on the model actually applied. The Direct Capitalisation Approach uses an economic quantity based on accounting principles, aimed at identifying the average, or stabilised, income-generating capacity of the property. To this end, a number of adjustments need to be made in order to distribute the multiannual costs within the current income (see A Closer Look 6.2 for further details). Consider, for example, the extraordinary maintenance expenses: these are incurred in a specific period/year, and therefore not necessarily in the current one, but have to be distributed so that the average reduction in the income-generating capacity can also be considered in the current period as if it were a provision.

The DCFA resorts to a precise definition of cash flow, i.e. the liquidity actually produced in each period. For this reason, at least in theory, there is no need to resort to the multiannual distribution of costs that only actually occur in a single period, but one does have to identify precisely the period in which every cost occurs. For example, in the case of extraordinary maintenance expenses, rather than distributing these over multiple periods, an estimate can merely be made of the period in which this expenditure will have to be incurred. However, it is worth remembering that, in practice, this distinction is not always that clear, because, given the difficulty of estimating future values correctly, even when estimating the precise cash flow, an average periodic value is often used, in a similar way to a provision. This simplification is in many cases acceptable because it has no significant impact on the result.

There continues to be a lack of terminological uniformity in the economic definitions used in the real estate sector. In particular, the definition of income is affected by uncertainty both in the actual definition to be applied (at what level of the profit and loss account), and in its quantification (historical or prospective). Formulating a correct and unequivocal definition is vitally important in the field of valuation. Table 6.1 proposes a model of profit and loss account for an Income-producing Property according to the most common accounting principles.

With reference to Table 6.1, note that any definitions of income below the Net Operating Income, i.e. the Income Before Taxes and the Net Income, are meaningless for Market Value estimation purposes because they are dependent on the Owner of the asset.

The primary function of the depreciation is to determine the income according to accounting and fiscal rules, while the financial charges and taxes on income depend respectively on the financing strategies adopted by the Owner and his/her tax status.[6] In Market Value estimation, the major element is the capacity of the property to generate income, regardless of the form of financing or the tax status of the Owner.[7] One could argue that, at least as regards the financial charges, players could decide to adopt a very similar optimum financial structure,[8] but even if this argument were accepted, the decision would not increase the accuracy of the valuation.

A similar consideration could also apply to taxation, but the presence of players with tax exemptions (such as real estate investment funds and REITs in most of the countries) suggests that this extra complication, which, similarly, would not improve the quality of the valuation, should be avoided. In fact, using one of these definitions, the same property, i.e. with the same Price and the same Revenues, would reveal different yield rates if purchased exclusively with equity or using debt as well, or again if it belonged to a tax-exempt individual.[9]

TABLE 6.1 Profit and loss account for a property according to accounting principles[10]

		Revenues	
	a	+ Rents	
	b	+ Other revenues	
C = a + b		**Potential Gross Income**	
	d	− Effective vacancy	
	e	− Credit loss	
F = C − d − e		**Effective Gross Income**	
	g		Property taxes
	h		Property insurance
	i		Stamp duty
	j		Extraordinary maintenance
	k		Tenant improvements
	l		Property & Facility Management
	m		Leasing fees
	n		Other minor expenses
O = g + [...] + n		**− Total operating expenses**	
P = F − O		**Net Operating Income - NOI**	
	q	− Depreciation	
	r	− Interest expenses	
S = P − q − r		**Earnings Before Taxes - EBT**	
	t	− Taxes	
U = S − t		**Net Income - NI**	

Note: The table refers to a 'typical' year and does not include the initial investment and the final divestment.

In order to determine the amount of the income for the purpose of applying the Direct Capitalisation Approach, the typical template of profit and loss account shown in Table 6.1 requires a few changes. The template shown in Table 6.2, which considers the stabilisation of income by calculating a number of provisions, is recommended in this respect.[11]

The reader will have noticed a few minor differences. Firstly, Table 6.2 shows that it would be preferable to use an average amount for extraordinary maintenance, similar to a provision, as this item is variable over time and the use of an actual value may result in the wrong valuation of the income-generating capacity of the asset. Secondly, definitions of income below the Net Operating Income have not been considered; as previously discussed, financial and fiscal variables depend on the Owner of the asset rather than on its income-generating capacity.

Generally, it is also noticeable that, while it is presented here in a didactic form, the Effective Gross Income can also be determined by defining a simplified rent roll, which directly considers the leased and non-leased units. The same apply to the cash flow estimation.

TABLE 6.2 Profit and loss account for estimating income for the purpose of applying the Direct Capitalisation Approach

	Revenues	
a	*+ Rents*	
b	*+ Other revenues*	
C = a + b	***Potential Gross Income***	
d	*– Effective vacancy*	
e	*– Credit loss*	
F = C – d – e	***Effective Gross Income***	
g		*Property taxes*
h		*Property insurance*
i		*Stamp duty*
j		*Reserve for Extraordinary maintenance*
k		*Tenant improvements*
l		*Property & Facility Management*
m		*Leasing fees*
n		*Other minor expenses*
O = g + […] + n	*– **Total operating expenses***	
P = F – O	***Stabilised Net Operating Income***	

A CLOSER LOOK 6.1: RENT ROLL

A synoptic table which summarises the main details of the existing lease agreements for a particular property is commonly named 'rent roll'.[12] Ideally, for each agreement, there should be a clear indication of the following elements:

- Name of tenant, stating both the company name, as shown in the lease agreement, and any trading name (if different from the company name, as is often the case for retail properties). While it is not normally included among the information stated in a rent roll, it is, however, important to express a judgement on the tenant's creditworthiness or financial reliability, and ability to pay the existing rent, potentially using credit checking databases.
- Type and structure of the lease agreement in place.[13]
- Date of commencement, i.e. the effective date of the agreement, which usually differs from the date on which it is signed or registered.
- Duration, first (and others[14]) expiry date of the agreement.
- Presence of any early withdrawal clauses (known as a *break-option*) which, in particular, allow the tenant to interrupt the lease agreement before the natural expiry dates stated therein without incurring any penalties.

(Continued)

- Indexation of the rent to the inflation rate or any rent review clauses.[15]
- The surface of property leased to the tenant (Gross Surface Area and Net Lettable Area).
- Existing rent (so-called 'passing rent'), expressed as an absolute value and in €/m². of Net Lettable Area (so that it is immediately comparable to the expected rental value (ERV) determined by the market analysis).
- Headline rent (if different from the passing rent), also expressed as an absolute value and in €/m² of Net Lettable Area.
- Grant of any free-rent periods, i.e. periods during which the lease agreement is in force but no rent is payable.
- The incidence of the rent on the tenant's turnover (known as 'effort rate'), which is a fundamentally important element for Trade-Related Properties.
- Presence and number of guarantees.
- Presence of any other relevant clauses affecting the rent amount and the risk.

In particular, if the agreement has recently come into force, one may also include any extraordinary maintenance (TIs) paid for by the Owner, which, together with step-up rent formulas and free-rent periods, are typical forms of incentive and negotiation offered during the negotiation phase.

For valuation purposes, it is important to consider legal and contractual *break-options* because, if the passing rent exceeds the ERV, there is a greater likelihood of the tenant asking for a review of the existing lease agreement or deciding to vacate the property.

Due consideration should also be given to the operating expenses borne by the tenant which, particularly for certain types of retail properties (such as shopping centres or factory outlet centres), given that they include significant promotion and marketing expenses, can be high compared to rents. In these cases, it is worth checking that the incidence of the total amount paid by the tenant in the sum of rents and expenses is not too high compared to its turnover (the ratio between these two amounts is also known as 'effort rate'). More generally, it is also essential to assess how strategic the property is for the current User, how likely it will become vacant and when, and whether he has invested to fit the space according to his specific requirements.

In a property with multiple units available for rent to different tenants, some of them may be vacant, while some may have passing rents that are not at the same level of the ERV. For vacant units, one could simply resort to using the ERV. However, in this case, the greater risk perceived by the Investor will have to reflect the choice of cap rate. Where rents are not at the same level of the ERV, however, any cap rate correction is more difficult. In situations where the income expressed by the property is not stable, it is therefore preferable to use the DCFA rather than the Direct Capitalisation Approach. Finally, one must always check the actual sustainability of the existing rent[16] both in the case of Flexible Commercial Properties and, more importantly, in the case of Trade-Related Properties. In other words, if the tenant might not be able to sustain the existing rent, and there are no sufficient guarantees of this payment, it would be more realistic to use an ERV for valuation purposes. With Trade-Related Properties, it is fundamental to analyse the historical and prospective profit and loss account of the business operating the property to verify the actual sustainability of the rent (i.e. the 'effort rate'); otherwise, in this case, one could also opt to estimate a maximum rental amount sustainable by an ordinary player.

Operating Expenses are all costs borne by the Owner and can be classified into two main categories[17]:

- Fixed Expenses, which occur regardless of whether the property is used (including taxes on the property, maintenance costs and insurance premium)
- Variable Expenses, which depend on whether the property is leased (including property management and facility management costs, lease registration tax and other charges).

This distinction, however, is somewhat theoretical because some operating cost components are fixed, while others may be borne by the User.[18] It is also worth remembering that, in the case of unused properties, the maintenance expenses may even be higher because significant costs may have to be incurred to restore operations, particularly for technical systems and equipment if they are not operated for some time.

A CLOSER LOOK 6.2: OVERHEADS IN THE PROFIT AND LOSS ACCOUNT

In theory, and even more so in practice, there are considerable differences in the way some overheads that do not regularly arise in the operating cycle of a property (usually annual), should be considered for the purpose of calculating the stabilised Net Operating Income. These include so-called tenant improvements (TIs), extraordinary maintenance,[19] capital investment expenditures (CapEx) and leasing fees:

- TIs: the internal refurbishment costs of a property (e.g. floating floors, suspended ceilings, internal partitions, work on systems etc.), which usually are subject to negotiation between the Owner and the tenant when a new space is leased or re-leased.

- Extraordinary maintenance: construction works to make the changes required to renovate and replace structural parts of the Buildings, and install and supplement the systems without altering the volumes and surface areas of the individual property units and without changing the intended use. The aim is to maintain or restore optimum operation and economic management, particularly by undertaking preventive works which, while being of benefit over a quite long period of time (i.e. 3–5 years or more), will last less than the average economic life of the Building itself.

- CapEx: investments made to improve and increase usability, and therefore value, of the property, by maximising its capacity to generate income and increase the rent. Unlike extraordinary maintenance, which is intended exclusively to maintain the property in appropriate physical conditions, CapEx are aimed to increase its quality. An example of CapEx is the installation of an air conditioning system in a Building with no cooling system, to earn a higher rent or find tenants more easily

(Continued)

(discretional works); differently, replacing an existing air conditioner is a necessary extraordinary maintenance operation intended to maintain the physical efficiency of the asset. Both these operations will, therefore, have a duration that is potentially equal or longer than the average economic life of the property itself.

- Brokerage fees for renting the spaces (leasing fees): fees to be paid to brokers for searching for tenants, usually calculated as a percentage of the headline rent.

In practical terms, the TIs (exclusively for the part borne by the Owner) and the brokerage fees can be considered in the same way, as both arise exclusively at the time the spaces are leased (or re-leased). As regards these cost items,[20] for the purpose of calculating the Net Operating Income, they must be taken into account as an annual provision and estimated on the basis of the average duration of the existing lease agreements and the rate of rotation of the tenants.

As regards extraordinary maintenance and CapEx,[21] however, the former must be included among the cost items, considering the recurrent costs involved and, consequently, their annual incidence. When significant CapEx are required in a property, it is, however, preferable to use the DCFA, which allows the time required to complete the works and re-lease the property to be taken into account. Example 6.1 will serve to clarify the above.

The profit and loss account proposed presents different definitions of income: which one should be used in the valuation process? While the Net Operating Income (NOI) is the main reference in international theory and practice, potentially all the definitions of income presented can be used, provided that they are consistent with the definition that was used to determine the rates through the Comparables.

With regard to Table 6.2, the initial definitions of Potential Gross Income and Actual Gross Income do not take into account any kind of operating expenses and therefore represent a less accurate measurement of the real income-generating capacity, given that two properties which, *ceteris paribus*, generate the same amount of revenues, but have a different operating cost structure, cannot have the same value, as the net profit for the Owner is different. In theory, these definitions are therefore considerably criticised, although in practice they are the most frequently used definitions in less transparent markets or when there are few available Comparables. In fact, while it is relatively simple to estimate the profit and loss account structure of the subject property, potentially having access to all the information, it is difficult to carry out the same operation for the Comparables, for which often the only available information is related to the rents and the sale prices. Even though it is possible to determine the expenses structure by applying benchmark parameters extracted from the market, this exercise only increases the subjectivity and uncertainty of the valuation.

Definitions of income are not even commonly accepted in the more evolved and transparent markets. US valuers do not adopt a single definition and in *The Dictionary of Real Estate Appraisal* there is a definition of NOI which is not precise with respect to the treatment of investments and extraordinary maintenance: 'Net Operating Income (NOI): the actual or anticipated net income that remains after all operating expenses are deducted from effective gross income, but before mortgage debt service and book depreciation; may be calculated before or after deducting replacement reserves.'[22]

In reality, this uncertainty about the treatment of investments arises from the purpose of calculating the NOI:

■ When applying the Direct Capitalisation Approach, an average definition of income is sought, so a provision (in search for stabilised income) for (CapEx) investments and extraordinary maintenance as a cost item must be considered.
■ When applying the Discounted Cash Flow Approach, a precise definition of income is sought, as this will then be used to estimate the cash flows, so expenditure on investments and extraordinary maintenance must be considered at the exact time they are actually paid (in search for actual cash flows).

In practice, this distinction is often ignored, without any differences arising in the final result: from a financial point of view, whether a disbursement is classified as a cost or as an investment is irrelevant.

EXAMPLE 6.1: DEFINITIONS OF INCOME AND YIELD

In searching for Comparables and applying their parameters to the subject property, it is fundamentally important to choose a standard definition of income, as it will determine the Property Return Rates drawn or, alternatively, the value of the asset, as shown in the example.

The profit and loss account and the price recently paid on the market are shown for a property, which in the example is a leased office. The various definitions of income provide different definitions of rates for the same property.

TABLE 6.3 Definitions of income and yield

		Price	€ 35,000,000
Revenues		Yield	(Formula)
+ *Rents*	€ 2,700,000	7.71%	*Rents / Value*
+ *Other revenues*	€ 150,000		
Potential Gross Income	**€ 2,850,000**	8.14%	*Potential Gross*
− *Effective vacancy*	€ 350,000		*Income / Value*
− *Credit loss*	€ 30,000		
Effective Gross Income	**€ 2,470,000**	7.06%	*Effective Gross*
Property taxes € 120,000			*Income / Value*
Property insurance € 20,000			
Stamp duty € 11,750			
Reserve for Extraordinary maintenance € 150,000			
Tenant improvements € 23,500			
Property & Facility Management € 67,500			
Leasing fees € 18,000			
− **Total operating expenses**	**€ 410,750**		
Stabilised Net Operating Income	**€ 2,059,250**	5.88%	*NOI / Value*

Finally, one last note needs to be added regarding Trade-Related Properties, the value of which is strictly dependent on their business-related potential. In addition to estimating the income and the respective cap rate, the minimum sustainable turnover and, consequently, the maximum sustainable rent (if the property is leased) or the sustainable operating profit[23] (if the property is used directly by the Owner[24]) must also be determined.

Use, Advantages, and Limitations of the Direct Capitalisation Approach

As mentioned earlier, to ensure the correct use of the Direct Capitalisation Approach, the income must be stabilised, i.e. it must represent the actual long-term income-generating capacity of the property. For this to be verified, therefore, there has to be an actual rent that is at the same level of the ERV for the property and a 'normal' occupation rate for that type of property. Furthermore, the conditions of the Building must be such that no significant renovation works are necessary within a reasonable period of time.

In this ideal situation, the Direct Capitalisation Approach is most suitable because it allows the cap rate to be drawn from the Investment Market, as further explained in Chapter 7, thus ensuring that the valuation is based on an objective parameter. Conversely, using the DCFA would not present any advantage because it would merely project the current income into the future, based on potentially arbitrary assumptions about growth rates and future ERVs, subsequently discounting it by using a discount rate which, by its nature, cannot be directly extracted from the market, but can only be estimated. Finally, an assumption would have to be made about the Terminal Value, which, in any case, would be based on forecasts of the estimated future income, and a going-out cap rate, that again is based on subjective assumptions.

As can be easily seen in the formula, the main limitation of the Direct Capitalisation Approach is the high sensitivity of the result to the slightest inaccuracy in its two parameters.

In anything other than an ideal case, in fact, if the income were not stabilised, corrections would have to be made to the income amount or to the cap rate in order to use it. These adjustments, however, introduce a high degree of arbitrariness and become difficult to quantify, but also to explain and justify in a valuation report. As for the income, it could be replaced by the ERV, making a correction directly to the estimated value. Otherwise, an adjustment to the cap rate would become even more arbitrary, because there would be no reference parameters from the market to rely on in order to quantify the variation of the specific case.

However, even an adjustment made to take into account any refurbishing work, albeit easily quantifiable and potentially applicable directly to reducing the estimated value, presents a problem in ensuring that the cap rate is correctly quantified, given that a property which needs redevelopment presents a higher risk.

Application of the Direct Capitalisation Approach

When you have estimated the income[25] and the cap rate (for the quantification of which see Chapter 7), the application of the Direct Capitalisation Approach is relatively simple.

As shown in Example 6.1, the use of different definitions of income does, however, lead to significantly different cap rates, which is why, when extracting the cap rate, it is fundamental to use the same definition for the whole sample of Comparables. It is also fundamental to maintain consistency between the definition used for the income and the yield thus obtained, avoiding any comparison between rates resulting from different definitions of income. When valuing a property, it is therefore essential to know how the cap rate has been obtained; using rates supplied by third parties requires knowledge of the income definitions used to obtain them since several definitions can be used.

The best definition is the Net Operating Income because it deducts expenses directly attributable to the specific property. In this way, it allows for the valuation properties with different cost structures.[26]

The use of the other definitions considered potentially correct is less rigorous, but may be acceptable if it is not possible to obtain accurate expenses information.

After having chosen the best definition of income, one must determine the exact period of time over which it will be calculated by using three different solutions:

- Historical or current values
- Potential values
- Market Values.

The first solution uses the same level of income as the previous period, the current period or an average of the most recent periods; this is based on the assumption that the property is already fully operational and this level of income can be maintained in the future. The problem with this solution is that it relates to the past rather than to the potential future revenues of the property.

Potential values consider the income from the property when fully operational. This solution should be used in particular when there is no information on its recent history (i.e. previously vacant) and/or the existing conditions do not reflect its potential revenues in the medium to long term (i.e. under-rent or over-rent).

If none of the above solutions is practicable, because the property is new or has been vacant for a long time, average Market Values may be used, assuming a potential income value obtained from comparable assets (i.e. ERV).

In practice, the income in the current or subsequent year is used (current and potential value), although distortions may occur if the income-generating capacity is not the same as the actual rent. Consider the case of a property with a rent that is higher than the value that could currently be obtained if the property were vacant and available on the market; this income is a temporary situation that will not be maintained beyond the period of validity of the lease agreement and, therefore, using it for the valuation process would not lead to a correct valuation of the property. The following example will better clarify this concept.

EXAMPLE 6.2: EXAMPLE OF THE APPLICATION OF THE DIRECT CAPITALISATION APPROACH

The subject property is an entire office building with $18,700\,\mathrm{m}^2$ of Net Lettable Area, located in a business district on the outskirts of a large city. Recently redeveloped, the property has been fully leased to a single tenant not long ago under a lease agreement which, after an initial period of 6 months' free rent, is now fully operational on a rent of € 4.675 million a year (equal to € $250/\mathrm{m}^2/\mathrm{year}$). The operating expenses (including property tax, insurance premium, property & facility management fees, extraordinary

(Continued)

maintenance costs, etc.) are estimated to be € 675,000 a year, resulting in an NOI of € 4 million a year.

The market analysis revealed an estimated cap rate (net yield) of 6.5% (see Chapter 7, Section 'How to Estimate Property Return Rates' for further information on how the rates are determined) and an ERV of € 255/m^2/year.

It is, therefore, a Flexible Commercial Property, with a typical cost structure, with a stabilised income (as it is fully leased and the existing rent is substantially in line with the ERV) and in a condition that will not require major renovation work for a reasonable period of time (as the property has been recently redeveloped). Consequently, based on the contents of the previous paragraph, the Direct Capitalisation Approach is the most suited to estimating its Market Value, which one can, therefore, calculate directly as the ratio between the NOI and cap rate (net yield drawn from the market).

$$\text{Market Value} = \text{NOI}/\text{cap rate} = € 4 \text{ million}/6.5\% \approx € 61.5 \text{ million}$$

Now consider the following cases as variations of the original example.

1. Partially leased property: assume that the property is leased under the same conditions, but only 70% of Net Lettable Area is actually leased. In this case, in practice, there is a tendency to use the Direct Capitalisation Approach, subtracting the loss of rental revenue from the estimated Market Value of the property for the period required to lease the currently unleased portion and/or to adjust the cap rate upwards to account for the greater rental risk. In reality, these solutions are subject to a high degree of uncertainty and subjectivity, especially as regards cap rate adjustments due to the vacancy risk, so it is better to use the DCFA.

2. Property fully leased with rent that is not at the same level of the ERV: assume that the property is fully leased, but for a higher rent (over-rented) or lower rent (under-rented) than the ERV. Again in both these cases, in common practice there is a tendency to use the Direct Capitalisation Approach, adding to the Estimated Market Value of the property (or subtracting from it) the difference between the existing rent and the ERV for the remaining years of the lease agreement. Once again, it is better to use the DCFA, which allows the valuer to make more precise assumptions on the possibility of re-leasing the property on expiry of the existing lease agreements.

3. Property requiring redevelopment: assume that the property is fully leased and the rent is at the same level of the ERV, but the building requires renovation. Again, one could use the Direct Capitalisation Approach, subtracting from the estimated Market Value of the property the cost of the CapEx to be incurred and adjusting the cap rate upwards to account for the higher technical risk of the property. In this case, as well, it is better to use the DCFA, which allows the exact timescale of the CapEx to be taken into account, mainly if they are incurred over more than one period of time.

In all the cases where there are two or more of the above scenarios, obviously the DCFA is the most suitable method for determining the Market Value of a property, as better described in the next section.

DISCOUNTED CASH FLOW APPROACH

The Discounted Cash Flow Approach (DCFA) is also based on the relationship between future expected income generated by a property and its value but, unlike the Direct Capitalisation Approach, it explicitly considers the evolution of rents, operating costs and any investments over time.

Speaking metaphorically, where the Direct Capitalisation Approach is like a photograph (which portrays a static income situation), the DCFA is like a movie, where to understand the meaning (estimate the value) a series of photographs (the movie frames, i.e. the various cash flows) are taken and must be viewed in sequence. This metaphor clearly illustrates when the two criteria should be applied: just as a movie is a better way of describing a moving scene, so the DCFA is able to give a better estimate of the value of an asset with an unstable income; conversely, a photograph is good to describe a stationary object, just as the Direct Capitalisation Approach is suited to estimating the value of an asset with a stabilised income. A photograph is more 'economical' than a movie as it requires fewer resources; moreover, its quality is higher since it has also a higher definition than film frames (i.e. more pixels). By analogy, the Direct Capitalisation Approach requires fewer parameters to be estimated than the DCFA and the data used are more objective, as they can all be drawn from the market, particularly with regard to determining the rates. As described in detail in Chapter 7, the cap rate can be directly drawn from the market, while the discount rate requires estimation processes that are more arbitrary.

The DCFA, based on updating future cash flows, is primarily used to determine the value of securities, shares and bonds, but also to estimate the value of companies: the value of any kind of asset depends on the economic benefits it is able to generate and the risk associated with them, i.e. it depends on its discounted cash flows. There are two major issues associated with applying this valuation method:

- Determining the expected cash flows
- Estimating the discount rate.

The economic benefit included in the calculation algorithm is a cash flow, meaning the amount of money generated (or absorbed[27]) by the property during the period under consideration. Unlike the Direct Capitalisation Approach, which is based on the direct capitalisation of a single income, estimating the expected cash flows requires accurate forecasts of future income, costs and investments for the various periods into which a specific time horizon is subdivided.

To make things clear, the DCFA will be illustrated by describing each of the following steps:

1. Choosing the time horizon
2. Estimating every cash flows
3. Determining the Terminal Value
4. Discounting the cash flows and calculating the value of the Asset.

This section provides the basic and theoretical elements, referring the reader to Chapter 9, where a case is presented, for a more detailed discussion of the various application issues. A joint reading of both chapters is therefore recommended.

Choosing the Time Horizon

Properties produce economic benefits for an extended period of time. However, the valuer's forecasting capability is limited, which is why a limited time horizon within which to conduct the analysis has to be defined. In practice, a time horizon similar to the length of the existing lease agreement, or a fixed period of 10 to 15 years, is often used. This immediately raises a question: how reliable can a forecast over such a long time horizon actually be?

While the real estate income is relatively stable, mainly thanks to the existence of lease agreements that guarantee a relative constant rent, other parameters, such as the ERV in particular, are undoubtedly uncertain and more varying over time.

Going back to the previous metaphor of the movie and the photograph, the time horizon should be as short as possible, in order to limit discretion and difficult in estimating future income flows. In fact, it is usually assumed that rents and, consequently, cash flows, periodically increase by a certain amount, equal to the expected growth in the Estimated Rental Value and a percentage of inflation for the Passing Rent. Once income stability has been achieved, why project cash flows into the future only to have to discount them then? This choice introduces a dual source of distortion and arbitrariness into the valuation: the choice of growth rate for the cash flows (from present to future) and the choice of discount rate (from future to present). On this second element, which is discussed in full in the Section 'How to Estimate Property Return Rates, it is enough to point out that, unlike the cap rate, which can be drawn directly from the market, drawing the discount rate from the market is an indirect process, with considerable amount of discretion in the hands of the valuer. According to this logic, the ideal time horizon would be the minimum beyond which the cash flow is stabilised. In extreme cases, the Direct Capitalisation Approach can be used when the cash flow is immediately stabilised.

Finally, although it should not be necessary, note that there is no relationship between the choice of time horizon and the investment time horizon of the current Owner. The Market Value of the asset is independent from its Owner and, consequently, the intention to sell by a specific or non-specific date in the future has no impact on this.

In this respect, consider the case of a property with a lease agreement running for a further 8 years, with cash flows that will only stabilise after 3 years, due to renovation work, owned by a closed-ended real estate fund which, in view of its impending liquidation, has decided to sell it over the coming 2 years. In this case, a valuer could reasonably choose a 3-year horizon, when the cash flows stabilise, without considering the (subjective) choice to sell made by the existing Owner (2 years), nor the expiry of the existing lease agreement (8 years).

After having established the period of analysis, the frequency of calculation of each cash flow must be determined. Discounting is a mathematical calculation in which, provided there is consistency between the frequency of the cash flow and the respective discount rate, the result does not change. Greater frequency seemingly results in a more accurate calculation, but in reality, this condition is only relevant when the time horizon is short, the cash flows are very different from one another, and the discount rate is high.

In practice, a quarter and a half-year time frequencies are often used, particularly in order to simplify the calculations. When the time horizon is quite long, within the previously stated limits, the year frequency is also used. Finally, in other cases, a monthly frequency is applied (e.g. in the case of properties with particularly complex rent rolls). Note, however, that the apparent greater accuracy is reduced if one resorts to an extended analysis horizon.

Estimating the Cash Flows

In the DCFA, the definition of relevant economic benefit is the cash flow, i.e. the amount of money available in each period, which is equal to the difference between all the income and expenditure arising from the property, pertaining to the property Owner.

The income, with reference to the suggested model of profit and loss account for a property (see Table 6.2), comprises all the revenue resulting from any existing lease agreements (e.g. rent, any revenue from renting out advertising space, etc.), net of credit losses. From the date of expiry of the agreement (the so-called 'reversion to market'), the Market Rent at which the property could be re-leased (ERV) has to be estimated and used.

Expenditure must be divided between operating costs, which are current expenses borne by the Owner (e.g. administrative and management costs, insurance, real estate taxes) and investments, which are made at irregular intervals or when particular events occur (e.g. replacement of the tenant and ensuing work to adapt the spaces). Anyway, it is worth noting that this distinction is not so relevant, since both the categories are negative cash flows.

Unlike the Direct Capitalisation Approach, in which an amount is set aside as reserve in order to determine the stabilised income, no provision should be required when determining the cash flow. One should instead consider the exact expenditure for the period in which the actual payment is expected. For example, assuming the lift has to be replaced every 20 years, one should not set aside 5% for each year (as in the Direct Capitalisation Approach), but enter the full amount in the year in which the expenditure is expected to take place. Our use of the conditional tense shows that in practice often a provision is nonetheless made, using an average cost for the period usually estimated as a percentage, rather than determining the expenditure accurately. This route is taken because of the difficulty involved in making an accurate estimate, considering that this simplification often has little impact on the final result.

Unlike the Direct Capitalisation Approach, TIs forecasts are also made when there is a change of tenant. In particular, costs will often have to be incurred to adapt the space to the different requirements of the new tenant or merely to carry out a series of operations to renovate the building. The expenses must also include marketing expenses, such as leasing fees incurred to find a new tenant and transaction costs (in particular brokerage fees) associated with the Terminal Value.

In Table 6.4, a simplified model applicable to an Income-producing Property is presented; the same model, applying a Multiple Periods Residual Value Approach, includes different income and expenditure items, such as the sale of realisable real estate units and the respective construction costs; see Section 'Residual Value Methods' for a detailed discussion.

In order to value an asset, all its cash flows generated until the end of its life will be considered.[28] Except in a few limited cases (e.g. leaseholds, concessions or usufruct), which place a relatively short limit on the duration of economic benefits, the estimated Terminal Value of the asset at the end of the identified valuation period[29] should be used.

Estimating the Terminal Value

The Terminal Value has a fundamental impact on the accuracy of the valuation because it often constitutes most of the value of the asset, mainly when the discount rate is low and the time horizon short.

TABLE 6.4   Cash flow of an Income-producing Property

	Revenues	
a	+ *Rents*	
b	+ *Other revenues*	
C = a + b	**Potential Gross Income**	
d	− *Effective vacancy*	
e	− *Credit loss*	
F = C + d + e	***Effective Gross Income***	
	Operating expenses	
g		*Property taxes*
h		*Property insurance*
i		*Stamp duty*
j		*Extraordinary maintenance*
k		*Property & Facility Management*
l		*Leasing fees*
M = g + [...] + l	***Total operating expenses***	
N = F − M	***Net Operating Income***	
	Investments	
o		*CapEx*
p		*Tenant improvements*
q		*Leasing fees*
R = o + p + q	***Total investments***	
S = N − R	***Intermediate Cash Flows***	
t		+ *Terminal Value*
u		− *Brokerage fees*
V = t − u	***Final Cash Flow***	
W = S + V	**Total Cash Flow to be discounted**	

There are two main methods for calculating the Terminal Value, based on the type of property, which are described in the respective chapters:

■ The Direct Capitalisation Approach
■ The Direct Comparison Approach.

The Direct Capitalisation Approach,[30] to be used in particular for Commercial Properties, is applied considering the income expected at the end of the time horizon and the respective outgoing cap rate (known as the going-out cap rate, referring to a cap rate applied in a future period). There is, therefore, a clear difference of application between the Discounted Cash Flow Approach and the Direct Capitalisation Approach, with the latter being a necessary component of the former if the useful life of the asset exceeds the valuer's forecasting capability.

It is appropriate to reflect very carefully on the choice of values to consider, as regards both the value of future income as the numerator and the rate used for the capitalisation. As we have seen, in fact, the value is very sensitive to these parameters. It is advisable to use the income for the period subsequent to the forecast horizon (i.e. year $N + 1$), as this will be a stabilised value.

The Terminal Value is then calculated by applying the usual Direct Capitalisation Approach formula as follows:

$$V_T = \frac{R_{n+1}}{GOCR}$$

where:

- R = income
- GOCR = going-out cap rate
- T = time
- n = last period in the time horizon.

The Terminal Value can also be estimated using the Direct Comparison Approach when, due to the nature of the asset being valued and based on the information actually available to make the forecast, this is more suitable for estimation purposes. In particular, in the Multiple Periods Residual Value Approach applied to a plot of Land for residential purposes, the Terminal Value must be assumed to be the sale price (future Market Value) of the real estate units that can be built, based on a Direct Comparison Approach (see Section 'Residual Value Methods' and Chapter 12 for further details).

There is no specific rule to choose between the two methods, but it is preferable to refer to the method where better and more information is available.

The last cash flow to be used in the DCFA may consider both the intermediate cash flow and the Terminal Value or the latter only. This depends if the sale is assumed after or before the current operating income collection.

Discounting the Cash Flows and Calculating the Asset Value

In order to compare the cash flows generated in different periods, they must be converted into equivalent flows measured at the same point in time, i.e. the valuation date. The discounting process allows to convert future cash flows into an equivalent current cash flow at time zero (as shown in Figure 6.1).

The DCFA is based on the Present Value[31] formula (PV), which is defined as the sum of all the cash flows, each one discounted at an appropriate discount rate.

In other words, it is the financial process that allows you to estimate at time zero (i.e. today) the value of capital available at a future date (future cash flow). The discount rate is the total return expected in relation to the risk associated with the capital payable at a future date that you intend to discount, i.e. to make equivalent to today (time zero).

Applying a discount allows you to identify the equivalent of two capital amounts with different maturity dates. This discount, or, more accurately, interest payable, is such that, capitalising the sum obtained (Present Value) at the same interest rate (discount rate) gives the same capital amount (Future Value).

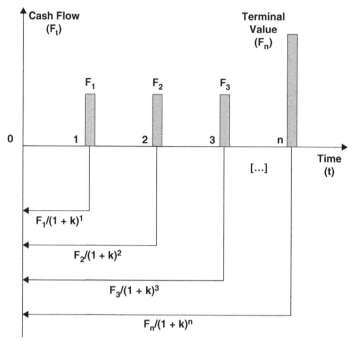

FIGURE 6.1   Graphic representation of the discounting process

The Present Value formula can be represented as follows:

$$PV = \frac{F_1}{(1+k)^1} + \frac{F_2}{(1+k)^2} + \frac{F_3}{(1+k)^3} + \cdots + \frac{F_n}{(1+k)^n} = \sum_{t=1}^{n} \frac{F_n}{(1+k)^t}$$

where:

- PV = Present Value
- F_t = cash flow at time t
- k = discount rate
- n = last period in the time horizon.

EXAMPLE 6.3: EXAMPLE OF APPLICATION OF THE PRESENT VALUE FORMULA

To illustrate the Present Value formula, we propose the following simple example of a valuation relating to an asset that generates the indicated cash flows and has a discount rate of 10%.

$$PV = \frac{€\,300}{(1+0.1)^1} + \frac{€\,300}{(1+0.1)^2} + \frac{€\,300}{(1+0.1)^3} + \frac{€\,300}{(1+0.1)^4} + \frac{€\,5.000}{(1+0.1)^5}$$

$$€\,272.73 + €\,247.93 + €\,225.39 + €\,204.90 + €\,3.104.61 = €\,4{,}055.57$$

The Present Value at time zero is the sum of all the discounted flows of € 4,055.57 and is the estimated value of the asset.

TABLE 6.5 Example of cash flow discounting

Period	1	2	3	4	5	Sum
Cash flows	€ 300.00	€ 300.00	€ 300.00	€ 300.00	€ 5,000.00	€ 6,200.00
Discounted Cash Flows	€ 272.73	€ 247.93	€ 225.39	€ 204.90	€ 3,104.61	€ 4,055.57
Discount rate	10%					

Graphically, the Present Value can be represented as a decreasing function of the discount rate: the Present Value falls as the rate used to discount the cash flows rises (as shown in Figure 6.2, which is based on Example 6.3). In economic terms, the explanation is found in the lower value attributed to future flows discounted at higher rates that express higher risk.

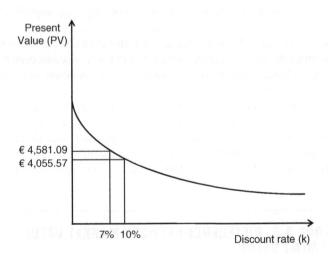

FIGURE 6.2 Graphic representation of the function of the Present Value

Use, Advantages, and Limitations of the Discounted Cash Flow Approach

The DCFA presents a number of advantages fundamentally associated with the fact that, compared with the Direct Capitalisation Approach, it allows the future economic dynamics of the asset to be determined more effectively. In particular, the DCFA is appropriate for valuing assets that do not yet have a stabilised income or, in the extreme case of a plot of Land or Development Project, which are not currently producing any income but only generate expenditure at the initial stage (see Section 'Residual Value Methods').

Furthermore, the need to estimate cash flows over a time horizon of several years requires the amount and distribution of the revenue over time, operating expenses and any other disbursement borne by the Owner to be stated, giving a clear explanation of the underlying assumptions. It also requires consideration of the rate of growth of the various elements that determine the cash flow and, consequently, an analysis of the market in which the property is located.[32] For example, it is appropriate to not only estimate the foreseeable rent increases, taking into account market conditions, legal and contractual constraints, but also to evaluate the quality of maintenance of the Building.

The model is also suited to analysing the sensitivity of the value of the property to any variation in the various valuation parameters. The value can easily be recalculated if the rental growth rate is 2% and no longer 3%, or if the extraordinary maintenance begins five years later rather than the following year, and so on, although simulations are more suited to assess the economic feasibility of an investment project than for the purpose of estimating the Market Value.

The main limitation of the DCFA is the difficulty, and often the subjectivity, involved in determining the discount rate. Valuers often dedicate many pages to giving a physical description of the property and to the assumptions used to determine the cash flows, while failing to explain or support the methods used to determine the discount rate.

Despite these undeniable advantages, one must not forget an implicit paradox in this model, which is that to calculate the value of an asset today, we first need to estimate, among the other parameters, its future Terminal Value at the end of the forecast horizon. When you do not know how much the asset you are valuing is worth today, it seems even more random to determine its Terminal Value; this just reinforces why so much attention is directed at exploring the difficulty of estimating it.

Finally, the detailed structure of the DCFA, with so many amounts of money set out over multiple periods of time, can give the illusion that the value obtained is necessarily reliable, which is not the case[33]: the soundness of the valuation will always depend on the quality of the parameters used, which are derived from a careful analysis of the property market (both the Space and the Investments Markets), i.e. of transactions which have actually taken place.

A CLOSER LOOK 6.3: DIFFERENCE BETWEEN MARKET VALUE AND INVESTMENT VALUE

The main difference between estimating the Market Value and the Investment Value is that in the former the valuer takes an objective stance, determining the value which the market is prepared to attribute to the asset, while in the latter the valuer looks at the asset from the perspective of a specific player. When applying the Discounted Cash Flow Approach, this translates in the first case into using the incomes, cash flows, and a cost of capital considered appropriate for a potential buyer and, for this reason, the cash flows will not be net of tax but necessarily gross, given that, based on this, the tax payable on the income from the property will vary according to different Owner categories.[34] Equally, the discount rate, i.e. the cost of capital, cannot refer to a specific entity; it must be the cost of capital required by the market participants for the specific property based on its operating risk and the typical financial structure of that kind of transaction.

Furthermore, regarding assumptions on expected income and costs in the future, while Market Value estimations are based on expectations regarding the most likely use of the asset according to type and location, where Investment Value is concerned, different players could have a different operational view of the actual use of the property, resulting in different expectations regarding the cash flows.

In calculating the cash flows, when determining the Investment Value, it is also worth remembering that, as the entity analysing the investment is known, one can use both operational cash flows, net of the tax burden, as well as levered cash flows, already net also of the actual financial structure effect the player intends to use for this specific investment.

To conclude, it is clear that in estimating the Market Value one has to use operating cash flows before tax, discounted using a market Weighted Average Cost of Capital (WACC) that, consistent with the cash flows, does not consider any tax benefit from the use of the debt. However, when estimating the Investment Value, the cash flows may be operational cash flows already net of adjusted operating tax, discounted at the Investor's WACC or, alternatively, one could use the shareholder's cash flows (Free Cash Flows to Equity, FCFE), i.e. not only already net of tax, but also of the estimated debt servicing on the actual financing; in this latter case, however, the cash flows should be discounted at a rate that represents the cost of equity.

Also with regard to the Investment Value, one can see that the discount rate is not the same for all Investors and, consequently, a property will not have the same value for everyone. So what is the market price of a property that constitutes its objective value?

The price of the property will be the result of a comparison between the supply and demand at a given time. The concept of marginal demand is often considered, i.e. the demand of the Investor who will actually buy the property. In the dynamics of the market, there are many elements to consider that lead an Investor to become the marginal Investor. Apart from tax and borrowing policy, a key role will be played by elements such as risk forecasts and expectations regarding increases in the income (i.e. future cash flow growth) and value of an investment, available liquidity, other types of investments' returns, the Investor's current asset allocation, and any legal or regulatory restrictions, as well as potential 'behavioural' elements.[35] Consequently, the marginal Investor will vary over time.

RESIDUAL VALUE METHODS

Introduction

Land and, generally speaking, properties at the end of their life cycle[36] which cannot be used to generate any income, have a value based on the Buildings that could be constructed on them. For this purpose, a valuation procedure based on transformation is used. This can be applied using the Income Capitalisation Methods; in literature and in practice, this procedure can be traced to a series of models also known as 'Residual techniques' or 'Residual methods'.[37] For this reason, we decided not to categorise this procedure as an independent valuation method but as the application of the Income Capitalization Approach to a specific case of a property that does not currently generate a cash flow.

The Residual Value Methods consist of identifying the 'best' use of a plot of Land subject to the legal and economic feasibility constraints (Highest and Best Use, HBU). In the first case, reference is made to local planning rules, local authority regulations and construction permits. This condition, albeit necessary, is not sufficient, as the economic feasibility condition also has to be fulfilled. Being legally allowed to build the property is not enough; there must also be an actual demand to use it. The HBU is not necessarily what will generate the highest selling price, but what allows the higher profit (meaning the difference between costs and revenues). In fact, in order to apply the process effectively, as better illustrated in the following sections, the construction costs must be considered in addition to estimating the future value of the realisable property.

The Residual Value Methods could also be applied in a more complex way by using the real options theory.[38] Although potentially also applicable to estimating the Market Value, this rather complex method is usually used to analyse investments and in feasibility studies for Development Projects. Although a large amount of literature exists on the subject in real estate,[39] its practical application is limited due to the scarcity and unreliability of some of the data required.

For simplicity, two different models to applying the Residual Value Method have been set up, which are based mainly on the Income Capitalisation Methods and differ in the number of periods considered:

- Single Period Residual Value Approach
- Multiple Periods Residual Value Approach.

The application of both procedures requires the use of different criteria based on the nature of the asset: in the next section, a sample profit and loss account is presented for a Development Project, suitable for the Single Period Residual Value Approach, from which the cash flows, to be applied with the Multiple Periods Residual Value Approach, can be obtained.

Single Period Residual Value Approach

This is known as a single period process because the sale value of the property that can be built and its construction costs are gathered in a single period, without directly considering the time required for the actual construction and sale of the property.[40] The process, therefore, is based on the difference between the price obtainable from the sale of the property that can be built and the total of all the costs of building it, including the cost of the whole capital.

The price obtainable from the sale is estimated, as the future Market Value, using different methods depending on the type of asset, as per the Terminal Value estimation.[41] If the property that can be built is for residential purposes, an estimate will be made of the future Market Value resorting to the Direct Comparison Approach. Otherwise, in the case of a Commercial Property, the Direct Capitalisation Approach is easier to apply. In both cases, the values must refer to the future date of the potential sale, e.g. the end of the construction phase.

For illustration purposes, the cost of building the property can be divided into two categories: construction and financial costs. The first category includes all the costs related to creating the Building; for example, the construction costs (known as hard costs), the planning fees, the development costs, the project management fees, etc. (known as soft costs). The second category considers the financial costs, usually subdivided between the cost of the financial charges on debt and the developer's margin,[42] or rather the Investor's expected return on capital or cost of equity.

The financial charges are generally quantified by considering, in a somewhat approximate way, an interest rate applied by the banks to an average amount of debt capital, all based on the duration of the work. For example, if the development phase is going to take a total of 2.5 years to build, and the average exposure to banks is estimated to be € 10 million for 2 years at a rate of 4.5% – given that the loan will be used based on the Work Progress Reports – then the financial charges can be quantified approximately at € 900,000, which is 4.5% for 2 years on an average capital of € 10 million. On the contrary, the developer's margin or, more correctly, the remuneration of the equity component, is often quantified as a percentage of the building costs,[43] including hard and soft costs. For example, if the equity remuneration is 18%, and the building costs amount to € 20 million in total, the developer's margin can be quantified as € 3.6 million.

Finally, the value is estimated as the difference between the two amounts, as in the simple example in Table 6.6.

Multiple Periods Residual Value Approach

The cash flow model for a Development Project given in Table 6.7 may be used in the Multiple Periods Residual Value Approach. To simplify the illustration, it is assumed that the income consists exclusively of proceeds from sales[44] (which may be received at the signing of preliminary contracts of sale, in instalments based on the Development progress, or at the notary's deed), therefore assuming that once the real estate units are completed they are sold without being previously leased, while the outgoings consist primarily of the construction costs, i.e. all the costs incurred to construct the Building, even though there may also be Operating Costs to be borne (e.g. tax on the properties). Finally, the transaction costs also have to be considered, which consist primarily of the brokerage fees.

TABLE 6.6   Example of Single Period Residual Value Approach

+	Market Value of the property once built	€ 28,000,000
–	Construction cost	–€ 20,000,000
–	Financial costs	–€ 900,000
–	Developer's margin (% Full construction cost)	–€ 3,600,000
=	**Land Market Value**	**€ 3,500,000**

TABLE 6.7   Cash flow of a Development Project

		Sales
	a	*+ Downpayments and balance payments*
	A = a	***Positive Cash Flows***
B = c + [...] + k		**– Development Costs**
	c	*Demolition*
	d	*Land drainage*
	e	*Hard costs*
	f	*Urban development costs*
	g	*Soft costs*
	h	*Connections to public utilities*
	i	*Trials*
	j	*Contingency*
	k	*Other costs (insurance, marketing, general expenses)*
	L = m + n	**– Operating Expenses**
	m	*Property taxes*
	n	*Brokerage fees*
	O = B + L	***Negative Cash Flows***
	P = A – O	***Net Cash Flows***

In order to value Land based on a Development Project, one must, of course, analyse all the cash flows it will potentially generate until the sale of the assets built is completed, considering that usually the cash flows recorded in this initial phase are almost exclusively negative.

The Multiple Periods Residual Value Approach considers the return on invested capital based on the financial value over time. Unlike the previous Single Period Residual Value Approach, which is limited to the simple difference between the total revenue and costs, in this case, an estimate is made of the cash flows and their distribution over time, applying the DCFA. This seemingly more complex method has the advantage of being able to quantify the margin, i.e. the expected rate of return on the Investors' capital, more correctly and objectively.

Similarly to the Single Period Residual Value Approach, one needs to estimate the sale prices of the asset that can be built, by the same methods, and also the building costs, but only the ones previously defined as construction costs.

The financial costs, in fact, which include both the debt and the equity, are included in the discount rate; that is, the expected return of all the sources of capital. This value, as described in detail in Chapter 7, depends on the financial structure, i.e. the amount and cost of debt, and the return that Investors require on the equity, based on the risk associated with the Development Project. Compared to the developer's margin, therefore, one can more accurately assess the required expected rate of return; furthermore, while the developer's margin is fixed, and must therefore also include the duration of the operation, using a DCFA, the distribution over time does not strictly affect the discount rate.

A simple example of a Land valuation with the Multiple Periods Residual Value Approach is given in Table 6.8.

TABLE 6.8 A simplified example of a Multiple Periods Residual Value Approach

Timing	0	1	2	3	4	5	6	7
Positive Cash Flows								
Sales					€ 200,000	€ 600,000	€ 600,000	€ 600,000
%					*10%*	*30%*	*30%*	*30%*
Total Positive Cash Flows	**€ 0**	**€ 0**	**€ 0**	**€ 0**	**€ 200,000**	**€ 600,000**	**€ 600,000**	**€ 600,000**
Negative Cash Flows								
Urban development costs	€ 84,000	€ 36,000						
%	*70%*	*30%*						
Hard costs		€ 200,000	€ 200,000	€ 200,000	€ 200,000			
%		*25%*	*25%*	*25%*	*25%*			
Soft costs	€ 40,000	€ 15,000	€ 15,000	€ 15,000	€ 15,000			
%	*40%*	*15%*	*15%*	*15%*	*15%*			
Total Negative Cash Flows	**€ 124,000**	**€ 251,000**	**€ 215,000**	**€ 215,000**	**€ 215,000**	**€ 0**	**€ 0**	**€ 0**
Net Cash Flows	**−€ 124,000**	**−€ 251,000**	**−€ 215,000**	**−€ 215,000**	**−€ 15,000**	**€ 600,000**	**€ 600,000**	**€ 600,000**
Discount rate	*8.86%*							
Discounted Cash Flows	−€ 124,000	−€ 230,571	−€ 181,427	−€ 166,661	−€ 10,681	€ 392,473	€ 360,530	€ 331,187
Land Market Value	**€ 370,849**							

NOTES

1. The classification was initially proposed by Barber (1992).
2. When computer calculations were not available, direct capitalisation formulas with limited periods represented good shortcuts. Nowadays, with the ease of using spreadsheets, the difficulties in estimating factors of correction overwhelm the benefit of using shortcuts.
3. In the UK market, numerous variations of the formula and a variety of methods are used (e.g. 'core & top slice' and 'passing rent & reversionary') which we have chosen to 'ignore' as they are rarely used in other markets. Furthermore, if the Income is not stabilised or the duration of the lease is quite short, we recommend reporting directly to the Discounted Cash Flow Approach rather than applying variants of the Direct Capitalisation Approach formula for which it is in practice difficult to find objective parameters.
4. Gordon (1956). For further details also see Damodaran (2012) or any corporate finance book.
5. This section illustrates the profit and loss account of an Income-producing Property, to which the Income Model can normally be applied. The Section 'Residual Value Methods' will illustrate the peculiarities of the profit and loss account of a Development Project.
6. In most of countries, tax liabilities differ between individuals, partnerships, corporations, and REITs.
7. The subjective conditions of the Investor conducting the analysis also play a part in valuing the economic convenience of an investment. For this reason, the same investment could be feasible for one player but not for another with a different financing capacity (cost of the debt and equity) or a different tax liability.
8. On the subject of the best financial structure in the property sector, see Morri and Cristanziani (2009) and Morri and Artegiani (2015).
9. Differently from Investment Value or economic feasibility analysis, there is a sole Market Value for a specific asset.
10. The terms 'cost' and 'expense' are often used as synonyms in business practice, and in this book they have been used interchangeably. However, cost usually implies a one-time event, like a purchase, and for accounting and fiscal purposes is related more to assets that can be depreciated (which therefore will be shown on the balance sheet and will reduce revenues with depreciation amounts), while expense usually implies an ongoing payment and it is related more to business income being shown directly on the profit and loss account.
11. As suggested by Brueggeman and Fisher (2010).
12. The term 'rent roll' can literally refer either to a list of properties belonging to an individual or company, stating the rents owed by and received from each tenant, or to the gross income generated by a rented property.
13. For simplicity, reference is made here exclusively to lease agreements, but there are other typical forms of agreement, such as business branch leases.
14. In some legislations lease agreements include break options.
15. According to Geltner et al. (2013), it is possible to distinguish between:
    Flat rent: 'provides for a fixed, constant rent level throughout the term of the lease'.
    Graduated rent: 'provides for a changing rent which includes specified step-ups (or steps) in the rent. [. . .] both the timing and the amount of the rent changes are specified upfront in the lease contract'.
    Revaluated rent: 'specifies in the lease contract the times when the rental payments may change, but it does not specify in advance the exact [. . .] amounts of rent changes. Instead the lease specifies that the property [. . .] will be appraised by a professional real estate appraiser, and the rent will be adjusted accordingly. Sometimes, such revaluations call for upward-only adjustments in rent, while other leases allow the adjustment to be in either direction. In the latter case, this becomes a mechanism to keep the rent current with the changes in the local rental market. [. . .] Revaluation leases are particularly appropriate for very long-term leases'.
    Indexed rent: calls 'for the rent to be adjusted according to some publicly observable and regularly reported index, such as the consumer price index (CPI) or the producer price index (PPI). A

typical indexed might require rents to be adjusted annually at some percentage of the CPI. [...] Full (i.e., 100%) CPI adjusted leases are not uncommon, but often the adjustment is less than full [...] because it may be perceived that building operating expenses typically do not grow as fast as inflation, or that the market rents that the building could charge would not grow as fast as inflation'.

Percentage rent: involves 'changes in rent over time. [...] the motivation and nature of the change is rather different from the foregoing examples, and the application of percentage rent is limited to retail property space. [...] the rent is a specified percentage of the sales revenue or net income earned by the tenant in the rented space. Often the rent will include both a fixed component referred to as the base rent (which may or may not have any of the previously described change provisions) plus a percentage component. Sometimes the percentage component only applies to revenue or profits above a specified threshold amount'.

16. And also all the expenses paid by tenants.
17. See the case discussed in Chapter 9 for a detailed description of the methods for calculating these.
18. If they are borne by the Owner, the rent will be relatively higher.
19. Ordinary overheads are usually borne by tenants and, therefore, should not be included in the profit and loss account of the property for valuation purposes.
20. As suggested by Brueggeman and Fisher (2010).
21. Again, as suggested by Brueggeman and Fisher (2010).
22. Appraisal Institute (2002).
23. This being the level of profit, before amortisation and financial charges, which an ordinary market operator could earn on the basis of a sustainable turnover net of all costs and expenditure required to generate such revenue, and of an adequate annual appropriation for periodic investments, such as unscheduled maintenance or the renewal of equipment.
24. Also see 'VPGA 4 – Valuation of individual trade related properties', RICS (2017), for an in-depth look at this subject.
25. As illustrated in the Subsection 'Profit and Loss Account of an Income-producing Property'.
26. The choice of the NOI is also supported by the Appraisal Institute (2001) because it provides an indication of the income to be used in determining the cap rate according to the structure presented earlier.
27. For example, if significant maintenance work is due to be carried out over a period of time.
28. And beyond as well, if you consider any expenses incurred for renovations or other costs incurred after the period in which the Property generates revenue! In this perspective, Properties have an infinite life because of the Land component.
29. A period which could be significantly shorter than the residual economic life of the asset.
30. The Discounted Cash Flow Approach is therefore only an extension of the Direct Capitalisation Approach, to which it refers not only in the economic principles, but also in the calculation algorithm. The advantage of the former is that it mitigates the difficulties of applying the latter which, by using only one income and one rate, is particularly sensitive to any errors in estimating these parameters.
31. The Present Value, albeit very similar, must not be confused with the Net Present Value (NPV), used as an economic feasibility valuation criterion for investments. From a mathematical point of view, the only difference between the two formulas is that the latter also considers a negative flow at time zero, i.e. 'net' of the intended investment, while the former does not consider any initial cash disbursement. In summary, from a valuation point of view, the Present Value formula is used to estimate the value of an asset, while the Net Present Value formula is a criterion used to assess the economic viability of investments. Sometimes, in practice, some operators incorrectly use the term NPV instead of PV.
32. Baum et al. (2017) synthesise clearly the advantages of the method: 'The strongest criticisms of the normal approach [Income Capitalization Approach] are that it fails to specify explicitly the income flows and patterns assumed by the valuer, and that growth implicit all risk yields are used to capitalize flows of income. The DCF approach requires the valuer to specify precisely what rental income and expenses are expected when, and for how long. The valuer therefore is forced to concentrate on the national and local economic issues likely to affect the value of a specific property as an investment'.

33. Financial models also suffer from 'Garbage In, Garbage Out', an expression often used in the field of IT and communication technology to illustrate the fact that computers process even obviously meaningless incoming data (Garbage In) uncritically, and, in turn, produce meaningless results (Garbage Out).

34. Remember in this respect that different rates of income tax apply to individuals, partnerships, corporations, listed property investment companies, and property funds.

35. There are many studies on behavioural finance and its effects on the property sector, e.g. see Beracha and Skiba (2014).

36. For simplicity, in the rest of the chapter we will always refer to Land.

37. Other well-known definitions include the Transformation Method, the 'Land Residual Method' (Brueggeman and Fisher, 2010), the *'Méthode Dite du Bilan Promoteur'* – Developer's Balance Sheet Method or *'Méthode compte à rebours opérateur'* – Land Recovery Method (IFEI, 1993), Developer's Margin Method, Residual Method, etc. See also Coleman et al. (2013) for further details of the literature and models used to value the feasibility of a Development Project.

38. The theory and application of real options were developed by Myers (1977) using the financial options and formula devised by Black and Scholes (1973). The term 'real options' is understood to be the opportunity to delay one or more decisions to a time in the future when new information will be available. On this subject see Brealey et al. (2016).

39. Among the other contributions on this subject, see Williams (1991), Lucius (2001), D'Amato (2005), Guthrie (2009) and Bravi (2013).

40. In practice, it is known also as the Cost-Revenue Analysis.

41. See Subsection 'Estimating the Terminal Value'.

42. Based on this, the process takes one of the various names currently used.

43. Or, sometimes, of the total expected revenues.

44. These are often referred to in practice as 'Sales Revenues', although revenue is actually an income item (profit and loss account) rather than a financial one (Cash Flow).

CHAPTER 7

Property Return Rates

For the purpose of applying the Income Capitalisation Methods, different rates of return must be used depending on the model adopted. In the Direct Capitalisation Approach, where the reference amount is the income, the formula requires the use of a cap rate, which ideally projects the current income into the future, determining the value of the asset. Differently, in the Discounted Cash Flow Approach (DCFA), where the reference amount is the cash flow, the formula requires the use of a discount rate, which ideally relates future income flows to the present. In order to provide a clear illustration, the two rates will be discussed separately, although they have several points in common.

Both rates are in fact an expression of the amount of return expected by Investors, as more clearly described in the following sections. In particular, given that it is an expected return, they will depend on the implicit risk in the asset or, more accurately, the risk factors associated with its expected income/cash flows.

The methodology for determining Property Return Rates remains, however, one of the most critical elements of the Income Capitalisation Methods and often a source of errors or estimates that are insufficiently supported by empirical evidence. As will be seen more clearly in the Section 'How to Estimate Property Rates', the opportunity to derive the rates directly from the market is limited to the cap rate, while different techniques will have to be used to determine a discount rate.

MEASURING THE RETURN ON A PROPERTY INVESTMENT

Without any claim to be exhaustive on this subject, this section provides a simple description of the most common methods for calculating the return on investments.[1]

When an investment is made, particularly in an asset that generates a regular stream of income and has a residual value, the total return is derived from two return components, as simplified in Figure 7.1:

- Yield or current return (for simplicity just referred to as 'yield'), which is the ratio between the income and the value/price of the asset
- Capital gain return (or 'growth return'), which is the ratio between the increase in value during the period (equal to the difference between the value of the asset at the end of the period – sale or reimbursement value – and the value of the asset at the beginning of the period – purchase price or cost of the asset) and the value of the asset at the beginning of the period.

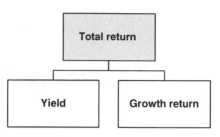

FIGURE 7.1   Return composition

Where an investment is made in an Income-producing Property, the calculation method is simple, as shown in Examples 7.1 and 7.2.

EXAMPLE 7.1: CALCULATION OF THE RETURN ON AN INCOME-PRODUCING PROPERTY IN A SINGLE PERIOD

Purchase price	€ 100
Income for the period	€ 6
Sale price	€ 110

$$\text{Current return} = \frac{€\,6}{€\,100} = 6.00\% \text{ (yield)}$$

$$\text{Capital gain return} = \frac{€\,110 - €\,100}{€\,100} = 10.00\% \text{ (growth return)}$$

$$\text{Total return} = \frac{(€\,110 - €\,100) + €\,6}{€\,100} = 16.00\% \text{ (total return)}$$

The example, which is extremely simple and easy to use, relates to a single period. If these calculations are applied over multiple periods, a method must be found to distribute the Capital Gain Return component.

EXAMPLE 7.2: CALCULATION OF THE RETURN ON AN INCOME-PRODUCING PROPERTY OVER MULTIPLE PERIODS

Purchase price	€ 100
Income in period 1	€ 8
Income in period 2	€ 10

Income in period 3	€ 12
Income in period 4	€ 14
Income in period 5	€ 16
Total periods	5
Total income in periods	€ 60
Sale price	€ 115

$$\text{Current return} = \frac{€\,60}{€\,100} = 60.00\% \text{ (yield)}$$

$$\text{Capital gain return} = \frac{(€\,115 - €\,100)}{€\,100} = 15.00\% \text{ (growth return)}$$

$$\text{Total return} = \frac{(€\,115 - €\,100) + €\,60}{€\,100} = 75.00\% \text{ (total return)}$$

$$\text{Periodic total return} = \frac{75\%}{5} = 15.00\%$$

The periodic total return has been calculated as a simple average. Usually, when returns over multiple periods are being determined, a compounded average return is used.[2]

Indeed, the return (15.00%) calculated as simple division by time periods is not correct because it does not consider differences in the time distribution of intermediate cash flows. In the example, these are the periodic revenues. In standard practice, the Internal Rate of Return (IRR) is used when there are different intermediate cash flows, corresponding to a compounded return. From a mathematical point of view, the IRR is the discount rate that makes the sum of discounted cash flows equal to zero. This represents the total return of an investment:

$$\sum_{t=0}^{n} \frac{F_t}{(1 + IRR)^t} = 0.$$

This formula assumes, for simplicity, that the investment results in a single initial negative flow of F_0, but nothing changes if there are multiple negative flows. Interpreting the IRR is easy if it is clearly understood that it is the discount rate that makes the sum of the values of the discounted positive and negative values identical.

If the economic feasibility analysis of an investment project is taken as an example, ignoring any evaluative consideration, the IRR is the maximum cost of capital an investment can sustain before it becomes uneconomical (i.e. until its Net Present Value, including the initial investment, remains positive). See Figure 7.2 and Example 7.3.

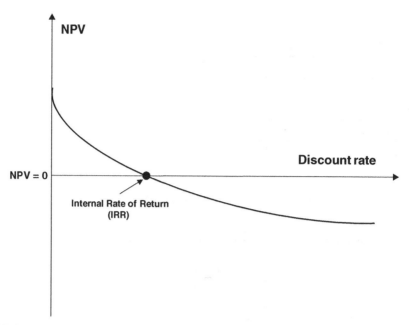

FIGURE 7.2 Graphic representation of the function of the Net Present Value (NPV)

EXAMPLE 7.3: CALCULATING THE IRR OF AN INCOME-PRODUCING PROPERTY OVER MULTIPLE PERIODS

TABLE 7.1 Calculating the IRR of an Income-producing Property over multiple periods

Period	0	1	2	3	4	5
Acquisition price	−€ 100					
Income	€ 0	€ 8	€ 10	€ 12	€ 14	€ 16
Sale price						€ 115
Cash Flow	**−€ 100**	**€ 8**	**€ 10**	**€ 12**	**€ 14**	**€ 131**
IRR	*13.77%*					

Period	0	1	2	3	4	5
Cash Flow	−€ 100	€ 8	€ 10	€ 12	€ 14	€ 131
Discount rate	*13.77%*					
Discounted Cash Flow	−€ 100.00	€ 7.03	€ 7.73	€ 8.15	€ 8.36	€ 68.74
Sum of Discounted Cash Flow	−€ 100.00	−€ 92.97	−€ 85.24	−€ 77.09	−€ 68.74	€ 0.00
NPV	**€ 0.00**					

Given that any rational Investor will make an investment provided that the return it may produce will be at least equal to the cost of the resources used (cost of capital), the IRR can be assumed to represent the gross return one can expect from an investment. From an economic point of view, the IRR is, therefore, the expected return (discount rate) that makes the Net Present Value equal to zero and therefore represents the implied return on an investment. In summary, the return depends on two elements: the size of the outgoing and incoming cash flows and their distribution over time.

For illustrative purposes, the above can be simplified by saying that the cap rate corresponds to the expected current return (yield), while the discount rate corresponds to the expected total return (IRR). Furthermore, going back to the simple relationship stated in Figure 7.1, it is clear that the relationship between the two rates of returns is linked to the expected variation in the value of the asset. The latter, however, with the same income yield, depends exclusively on the variation in the future income (future cash flows). Consequently, the relationship between the cap rate and discount rate is closely linked to the expected growth in future flows.[3]

It is useful to note that, depending on the various kinds of real estate transactions, different income components will prevail. In an extreme case, in a Development Project, assuming the properties developed are sold without being leased, there will only be the capital gain return component, which is the difference between the sale price and the purchase and transformation costs. In an Income-producing Property, however, again assuming an extreme case in which there are no variations in market rates (cap rate) or variations in income (no rental growth), there will only be an income yield component (current return).

While these two examples are provided to facilitate understanding of the issue, they are not unrealistic. Considering the risk of the operation and the resulting high cost of capital, a developer will need to avoid, or at least minimise, the period for which the property is leased before being sold. And conversely, in the case of an Income-producing Property, the assumption that there will be no change in income is realistic because, if there is no economic expansion leading to a higher demand for Space, one can assume that an ordinary operator will be able to maintain the quality of the property constant over time.

Finally, it is worth noting that the expected rate of returns for Development Projects and Income-producing Properties differ considerably, as can be expected, based on the different levels of risk assumed by the Investor. Therefore, any consideration of the Property Return Rates, for both types, has to include an analysis of the risk[4] connected with the property.

RATES AND CAPITAL MARKET

Before concluding the introduction and looking at individual Property Return Rates in detail, it is important to point out that, since both cap rates and discount rates are an expression of expected returns, the following function applies to both:

Property Return Rate = risk-free rate + property risk premiums

The risk-free rate is the return required by investors to reliably defer their consumption over time (which ensures that the actual return is equal to the expected return). The risk-free expression indicates the absence of two risks.

1. Default risk: represents the possibility that the debtor will be unable to return the capital received. This is why usually a bond with maximum rating is used, usually a government

bond issued by a State with a solid economy. However, if the country risk is going to be included from the outset, without having to estimate it subsequently in the risk premium component, a government bond of the State in which the property is located can be considered. The absence of any risk that the government bonds will not be reimbursed stems from the opportunity for the State issuing the debt always to meet its commitments, even in the case of difficulty, by increasing taxes. This is obviously only a nominal return as there is always uncertainty regarding changes in price levels.

2. Uncertainty regarding reinvestment rates:[5] a risk-free security will have no cash flows (zero-coupon bond) until the end of the reference time horizon. Otherwise these would have to be reinvested at rates that are not known today. Furthermore, although sometimes only short-term government bonds, such as Treasury bills (T-bills) in the US, are considered to be risk-free, in reality, one needs to be consistent with the time horizon over which the risk-free rate is being estimated: over a time horizon of 5 or 10 years, a 6-month T-bill will be subject to a reinvestment risk because the future return on the security is currently unknown.

To summarise, therefore, a risk-free rate can be assumed to be the return on a zero-coupon government bond with a duration that is consistent with the relevant time horizon. A five or ten-year maturity is commonly used in practice.[6]

There are various alternatives for estimating the risk-free component, always considering the consistency between the life of the security and the time horizon of the valuation:

1. Use the return on a government bond with no 'default risk' by definition. However, this requires subsequent consideration of the risk premium component, which is also a country risk factor. Secondly, these financial instruments might provide for annual coupons, so they cannot be considered entirely 'risk-free' because of the coupon reinvestment risk, although in practical terms this has a limited impact on the valuation.
2. Use the return on a government bond of the country where the property is located.
3. Use an average weighted return on a basket of government bonds, a choice often adopted in practice by valuers.
4. Use the interest rate swap, as we saw in relation to quantifying the cost of debt. Once again, however, one has to consider a country risk factor in the risk premium component.

As regards the duration, a further point needs to be made: in a Property Valuation, the cash flows are estimated over multiple periods (typically lasting six months) over several years, so in order to be consistent with the above, one would have to use different risk-free rates for each period. In reality, in standard practice, a security with a duration equal to the time horizon of the valuation is generally used. This is an acceptable simplification, considering that no significant differences are found in terms of the result when the yield curve is normal.[7] The property investment premium (risk premium) is the additional return required to invest in risky activities as opposed to risk-free activities. Once again, there are two fundamental aspects to consider when determining the risk premium: which risk factors need to be remunerated and how should they be estimated (*ex-post* or *ex-ante*)?

With regard to the first aspect (which risk factors), it is important to consider that talking about a single risk premium in a property investment seems restrictive because of the considerable differences in risk between individual properties. In other words, the higher return will need to remunerate not only the non-diversifiable risk (or market risk) but also the specific risks of each property.

With regard to the second aspect (how to estimate the risk factors), one has to consider instead how, assuming one has adequate historical time series available, the risk premium can be measured as the difference between the average historical return on the activity and the risk-free rate (this is referred to as the 'historical risk premium'). This is quite commonly done when valuing listed securities, since there are data time series; many data providers supply estimates of the average difference between the total return, e.g. a stock market index for a particular market, and its risk-free rate. However, this is less common in the real estate sector, where, at most, one can measure the difference between the yield and the return on its risk-free rate, as stated in market reports commonly published by real estate consultants. Furthermore, an *ex-post* approach of this kind has two main limitations: what happened in the past may not be representative of what should have happened or what will happen in the future and the fact that all the risk factors are combined into a single value, without the option of determining to what extent each of them has contributed to the total.[8]

If historical series are going to be used to calculate this parameter, an adequate time horizon has to be identified that will account for the cyclical nature of the market. In fact, a sufficiently long time span must be used to overcome the short-term effects due to the cyclical nature of the property market. Furthermore, a long time span incorporates exceptional events better, allowing their impact on the risk premium[9] to be reduced.

The alternative method consists in estimating the risk premium *ex-ante*. This may refer to past returns, particularly as regards non-diversifiable risk factors, while it must necessarily be based on experience and adjustments to the base rate as regards specific risk factors.

It is useful to remember that, generally speaking, risk premiums depend on the return expected by investors and therefore on market sentiment.[10] In particular, it is believed[11] that, while economic fundamentals play a crucial role in determining rates, in part they depend specifically on market sentiment.[12]

CAP RATE

Definition and Description of the Cap Rate

In financial literature, a cap rate is a figure which ties the value of an asset, whether it is a transferable security, a specific income-generating asset, a business or a property, to the flow of income generated in a particular period.

In the property market, the commonly accepted definition of cap rate is provided by the Appraisal Institute (2002): 'Overall capitalisation rate: an income rate for a total real property interest that reflects the relationship between a single year's net operating income expectancy and the total property price or value; used to convert operating income into an indication of overall property value.'

With reference to property return rates, the term 'overall cap rate' (or simply and commonly 'cap rate') and the term 'all risks yield' (or more simply and commonly 'yield') are used interchangeably. The difference between cap rate and yield is very subtle and has more to do with terminology[13] than substance; they both refer to the same concept, although yield typically defines the annual percentage of return on an investment. Therefore, although the two terms are often used synonymously, the yield is an (actual or expected) rate of current return and it is the output of a formula, while the cap rate is a capitalisation rate to be used as input in the valuation formula, i.e. the element used to convert income into value. Metaphorically, one could say that they represent the two sides of a coin: yield is the output obtained by calculating the current return, while the cap rate is the input data used in the Direct Capitalisation Approach valuation algorithm.

Going-In and Going-Out Cap Rate

The Direct Capitalisation Approach can be used to estimate the value of an asset in the present, as well as in the past or in the future. The first two cases are undoubtedly more intuitive, but the third case is no less common, as will be shown more clearly below.

Applying the Direct Capitalisation Approach to a specific date in the present or in the past is one of the choices available when estimating an asset. Information on the cap rate is available from the market at these dates, based on the transactions actually completed, by extracting the yield based on income and price of Comparables. However, applying the Direct Capitalisation Approach to a future date is not often in itself a final method for estimating the value of an asset, but it is used in the DCFA to determine the Terminal Value.[14]

Consequently, depending on the moment to which the estimate relates along the time horizon, two definitions of cap rate[15] are commonly used:

1. Going-in cap rate (GICR or, also, 'initial cap rate' or 'initial yield'): the relationship, at the valuation date, between the initial income and the value/price of the asset.
2. Going-out cap rate (GOCR or, also, 'terminal cap rate' or 'exit yield'): the rate used in order to convert the final income into the expected value of the asset at the end of the time horizon of the valuation (Terminal Value). In contrast to the former, this rate cannot be extracted from the market – given that there is no current knowledge about future transactions – it can only be estimated. It represents the estimate of the expected ratio between the final income and the expected value/price of the asset at a future date.

In order not to confuse the reader, we should clarify straight away that the GICR, where it does not need to be distinguished from the GOCR, is referred to just as the cap rate and is the one that is usually referred to. Clearly, therefore, the GICR and the GOCR are not two components of the cap rate, but the same rate considered in two different periods of time: at the beginning (valuation date) and at the end (last period in the future), respectively. Evidently, therefore, while there is only one GICR for a specific date, usually the valuation date, in the case of a DCFA valuation, different GOCRs must be used along the time horizon depending on the date to which one is referring.

The GICR can be estimated in different ways, as explained in Section 'How to Estimate Property Return Rates', while the GOCR has to be estimated by referring to the future market conditions. This may be estimated either 'guessing' the rate in the future, on a stand-alone basis, or starting from the GICR and adding/subtracting a spread based on the different risk in the time.

In valuation practice, the (often positive) difference between the two rates is quantified as a certain number of basis points (bps).[16] Only a few and not recent studies[17] demonstrate or refute the validity of this relationship, which is widely acknowledged among valuers, but it is possible to identify a few decisive factors behind this increase.

The first reason is the uncertainty that exists about the future, which is reflected in a higher risk inherent in the GOCR (and therefore a higher rate). The second reason why valuers prefer to use a GOCR higher than the GICR is the obsolescence of the Building[18]: when the GOCR is determined, in the absence of any refurbishment work (CapEx), account has to be taken of a reduction in the economically useful life compared to what it was at the beginning. Consequently, the Building loses part of its capacity to generate income and requires costly structural and functional maintenance (renovation of the Building). The wasting asset theory,[19] according to which all assets lose their productive capacity over time, is always applicable to properties. It is consistent with the concept of inevitable physical deterioration of the Building whereby ageing produces a deterioration which, in practical or economic terms, cannot be avoided.[20] For example, the cap rate of a property with a residual life of the Building estimated at 25 years will be lower than that of another property with all the other features being the same, but with a residual Building life estimated at 5 years.

Quantifying a GOCR to be used in estimating the Terminal Value within the DCFA remains one of the weaknesses of its application. A response that would be valid in all cases cannot be provided, but it is advisable nonetheless to take a few elements into consideration.

- The length of the valuation time horizon: a difference between the GICR and GOCR, at least at the forecasting stage, only makes sense if the time horizon is relatively long. For example, if the time horizon were just a few half-year periods, it would make little sense to consider a significant difference between the two rates and it would perhaps be more correct, if the other elements previously listed do not exist, to use the same cap rate.
- The existing conditions of the Building which, particularly in view of the previous point, can be a particularly significant factor. If the Building has only recently been completed, over a time horizon of a few years, it may not be necessary to attribute a differential. However, if the time horizon is longer and/or the Building is not recent, it is essential to consider the consistency between the maintenance costs and CapEx forecasts and the cap rate spread.
- The expected or foreseeable investments needed to maintain the Building or potential redevelopment work that may significantly alter the quality of the Space and, consequently, the risk (and therefore value) of the property: the potential to carry out even significant redevelopment work on the Building (for example a Building that has reached the end of its life cycle) can have a considerable impact that lowers the GOCR. An alternative route proposed[21] involves estimating the GOCR considering the existing GICR for properties with a residual life equal to that of the asset being valued on the future reference date; albeit theoretically interesting, in practice this is hard to quantify, but may nonetheless contribute to the valuer's opinion on the rate to be used.
- Any expected changes in market rates: these will depend in particular on a general variation of expectations regarding market conditions, in relation to both the risk-free rate but also to the additional risk premiums of property investment in general or specifically for the property. Therefore, all the above considerations are valid assuming that there are no economic changes which have a significant impact on the specific property, variations in expected interest rates, economic growth and other exogenous factors which, however, have an impact on the future value of the asset.

To conclude, while the considerations that lead to the GOCR being higher than the GICR may prevail where the aim is to estimate the Market Value, for investment purposes it is highly likely that an Investor will seek investment opportunities in which the expected GOCR can be lower than the GICR, generating a Capital Gain Return as well. It is worth noting in this respect that, mainly when economic growth is weak, some Investors in any case prudently base their estimates on GOCRs that are higher or at most equal to GICRs, seeking to cover any future losses with the higher income yield.

EXAMPLE 7.4: IMPACT ON VALUE OF A VARIATION IN THE GOCR AND INCOME

TABLE 7.2 Example of how the value changes because of a variation in the GOCR and income

	Initial Period		Final Period	
Constant cap rate and income				
Cap rate	7.00%	GICR	7.00%	GOCR
Income	€ 70		€ 70	
Asset value	€ 1,000		€ 1,000	
Cap rate reduction and constant income				
Cap rate	7.00%	GICR	*6.00%*	GOCR
Income	€ 70		€ 70	
Asset value	€ 1,000		€ 1,167	
Cap rate increase and constant income				
Cap rate	7.00%	GICR	*8.00%*	GOCR
Income	€ 70		€ 70	
Asset value	€ 1,000		€ 875	
Constant cap rate and income increase				
Cap rate	7.00%	GICR	7.00%	GOCR
Income	€ 70		*€ 80*	
Asset value	€ 1,000		€ 1,143	
Constant cap rate and income reduction				
Cap rate	7.00%	GICR	7.00%	GOCR
Income	€ 70		*€ 60*	
Asset value	€ 1,000		€ 857	
Cap rate reduction and income increase				
Cap rate	7.00%	GICR	*6.00%*	GOCR
Income	€ 70		*€ 80*	
Asset value	€ 1,000		€ 1,333	

TABLE 7.2 (*Continued*)

	Initial Period		Final Period	
Cap rate increase and income reduction				
Cap rate	7.00%	GICR	*8.00%*	GOCR
Income	€ 70		**€ 60**	
Asset value	€ 1,000		€ 750	

In general, a reduction in the future cap rates (and, consequently, a greater Market Value of properties) stems from an unexpected increase of demand for Space and/or a reduction in risk-free rates, whereas an increase in rates (and a corresponding reduction in property values) stems from an unexpected increase in the supply of Space and/or risk-free rates.[22]

Finally, the cap rate is strongly linked to its historical value and, in particular, there is a strong link between its variation and the performance of the Space Market, especially with regard to the vacancy rate.[23]

DISCOUNT RATE

Definition and Description of the Discount Rate

As previously illustrated, the discount rate is used in the formula of the Present Value to make cash flows available on future dates comparable to one other. In other words, it represents the interest rate to be used to transfer to the present day a financial capital (or more generally a cash flow) obtainable on a future date, so that the discounted capital, i.e. obtainable today, is financially equivalent to the capital obtainable on the future date.

The level of this rate is equal to the total return achievable from alternative investments that broadly have the same risk profile, which is the rate of return required by the market participants for an investment with cash flows having the same level of risk. In other words, it is an opportunity cost associated with the total return offered by alternative investments that are comparable in terms of risk profile, which represents an adequate return based on the risk to which the Investor is exposed. Put simply, the discount rate[24] is the total return expected from an investment, i.e. the expected IRR.[25]

Finally, it is worth noting that theoretically there is no difference between the use of real and nominal flows, provided that there is consistency with the respective discount rate. Usually in valuation practice, one prefers to use nominal cash flows because they are often linked to inflation (e.g. index-linked rents or operating expenses) and Investors usually work with nominal return figures rather than with real returns expectations net of inflation. Inflation is, in any case, an important factor as it impacts on both rates and cash flows; in the case of cash flows, however, the effect on revenues might differ from the effect on costs.

Consistency Between Discount Rate and Cash Flow

Given that the discount rate is an expected total return, it makes sense to define how the return is calculated, i.e. to which cash flow it should be applied. The following points must be considered:

1. Financing and tax status
2. Rental situation
3. The yield curve.

Firstly, if the Investment Value is being estimated taking a subjective approach, the cash flow used – typically a Free Cash Flow from Operations[26] – is estimated by also considering the tax impact, since the subject to which the valuation relates is known as well as its tax status. Furthermore, where the actual financial structure of the project is already determined, using a project finance approach, it will also be possible to consider the actual financial charges and the debt disbursement and repayment dynamic using a Free Cash Flow to Equity.[27]

In the specific case of determining a Market Value, the cash flow chosen will be an amount that includes tax and financial charges,[28] the tax situation and financing strategy of the most likely buyer of the asset under valuation being unknown; consequently, the discount rate, i.e. the total rate of return required, must also be calculated at the same level. In other words, the discount rate must be the total return expected (IRR) in terms of operating cash flow, including financial charges and taxes. This rate will be higher than a similar rate of return calculated net of tax, while it may be lower than a rate of return for the Investor calculated after having considered the effect of the debt.[29]

To conclude, one could simplify by saying that the discount rate is the total return, including tax and ignoring the leverage effect, which the market expects from the cash flows of the specific asset, based therefore on the level of risk perceived in them.

Secondly, a specific consideration must be made regarding the lease agreements. While in the case of two properties, one leased and the other vacant, it is clear that *ceteris paribus*, a higher discount rate would have to be used in the second case, there may be situations in which it is less evident. Although it is advisable to avoid using extremely long time horizons, when necessary, one may be faced with the simultaneous presence of periods with flows derived from actual lease agreements and other periods in which, on expiry of the agreement, it is assumed that the property will be leased again under market conditions and, therefore, with merely potential cash flows. In this case, the risk profile in the two periods is different, given that in the first case one has a higher degree of certainty because of the existence of an agreement, while in the second case the cash flows are only estimated based on the future ERV and depending on the Space Market.

Pushing this concept to its extreme, one could argue that, not only can there be two different time periods – one with an existing agreement and one with a potential agreement – but more often the same property might include some units which are leased and others which are vacant.

The real estate literature[30] suggests using a different discount rate. In the first case, it would be an 'intralease discount rate' (lease in place), while in the second it would be an 'interlease discount rate', in order to account for the different levels of risk more accurately. In Property Valuation practice, however, this risk differential is not often made explicit and is implicitly included directly in the quantification of the discount rate, which therefore represents a weighted average: the term used for this single rate is a 'blended discount rate'. The grounds for making this choice are that a blended IRR is used, i.e. an 'average return', as a starting point for estimating the discount rate. The distinction, without expecting any practical application, is primarily made for illustrative purposes, to make it easier for the reader to understand the constant relationship that exists between return and risk.

Similarly, in a Development Project, a distinction would have to be made between the construction phase, in which the properties are built, and the sale phase, in which the units are sold (either individually or all together). Clearly, the risk profile of the two phases is different, so different discount rates would have to be used (just as within the individual phases the risk profile changes based on the time that elapses). In this case too, however, a single blended discount rate is commonly used in practice. A distinction does have to be made in this respect, however, taking the two most common cases as an example.

- In the case of Development Projects for Residential Properties, with the units being sold individually, the choice of a single discount rate seems correct, particularly considering that often the initial sales phase takes place while construction work is still in progress, which means that the Development Project is an entirely uniform operation.
- In the case of Development Projects for Commercial Properties, which are intended to be sold altogether once they have begun to generate an income (for example, a shopping centre or a hotel), the choice of a single rate seems correct provided that the Operation is completed within the period of time required to make the property fully operational (e.g. a period of three to five years for a hotel business to be established). However, if a decision is made in the valuation to consider both the development phase and the subsequent income-generating phase, the choice of two different discount rates seems more appropriate (e.g. assuming a leasing period of several years after the completion of the development phase); it should, however, be borne in mind that, in this case, prolonging the valuation time horizon, as already shown in Chapter 6, Subsection 'Choosing the Time Horizon', may not be the best choice as the ideal time horizon should be the minimum beyond which the cash flow stabilises.

Thirdly, similarly to the previous point, rarely valuers consider the yield curve.[31] Usually this curve is positively inclined, where longer maturities correspond to higher returns. The market yield curve is calculated for government bonds and interbank rates, which are a basis frequently used to estimate the cost of equity and debt.

As previously stated in the Section 'Rates and Capital Market', different discount rates should be used to discount cash flows with different maturity dates, each of them considering the different return required based on the different maturity. In practice, however, as in the previous example, a single (blended) discount rate is commonly used for all the maturities of the cash flows of the asset.

Again, in this case, the rate is derived from the average return expected according to the maturity date. To extract the rate, therefore, for consistency, reference must be made to the rate of returns required for investments with the same time horizon used for the valuation.

Finally, care must be taken to avoid counting the risk twice by reflecting it both in the cash flows and in the discount rate. For example, if in estimating the cash flows is already assumed that all the contractual break-options and the resulting vacancy periods are used by the tenants, the discount rate, *ceteris paribus*, must be lower because the respective leasing risk is already reflected in the cash flows themselves.

The Components of the Discount Rate

It is worth summarising that the discount rate is the total return expected from an investment. Up until now we have not considered whether the potential buyer of the property will use equity alone or also some debt capital, but we have referred to a generic notion of capital. Its return has to be ensured by the expected cash flows, which are therefore destined to remunerate and reimburse all the capital providers, i.e. they are intended to provide an overall remuneration for both banks (debtholders in general) and equity holders (the share of equity of the Investor). Real estate investments are often characterised by a complex financial structure which frequently includes both components, each one also possibly having different forms.[32]

Consequently, a discount rate, which is representative of the expected total return (or even called 'cost of capital') on all the financial resources used, must be employed for the purpose of discounting the FCFO. This discount rate can be identified as the weighted average cost of capital (WACC).[33]

In its simplest form,[34] i.e. when there are only two major sources of finance, debt and equity, the WACC[35] is determined by the following formula:

$$WACC = k_d * D\% + k_e * E\%$$

where:

- k_d = cost of debt
- $D\%$ = relative percentage of debt
- k_e = cost of equity
- $E\%$ = relative percentage of equity

The financial structure, i.e. the ratio between equity and debt, is estimated at market values and on the basis of a long-term target. See Figure 7.3.

Similarly, when estimating the Market Value of an asset, figures for the expected return on equity and debt and the financial structure are used. However, unlike in Investment Value estimation, rather than using subjective rates, i.e. the financial structure and cost of capital for a specific player, the rates currently requested by the market for a specific asset are used. For consistency, no tax benefit derived from the debt is considered as the cash flows are gross of taxation. In other words, the discount rate can be broken down into three components (financial structure, cost of debt, and cost of equity), each of which can be estimated independently.[36]

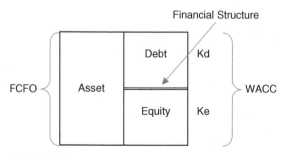

FIGURE 7.3 Cash flow and cost of capital

The WACC formula can also be used to estimate the cap rate (using the so-called band of investment technique, see Section 'How to Estimate Property Return Rates' based on the separated estimate of its debt and equity components: in this case an equity cap rate (i.e. the immediate rate of return expected on the equity, considering a certain level of debt) is weighted against the cost of debt. Example 7.5 shows a breakdown of the discount rate with some examples of changes to its components.

EXAMPLE 7.5: DISCOUNT RATE WITH SOME EXAMPLES OF CHANGES TO ITS COMPONENTS

TABLE 7.3   Discount rate with some examples of changes to its components

	Base Case	k_E increase	k_D increase	D (%) reduction	D (%) increase	k_E increase & D (%) reduction	k_E reduction & D (%) increase
k_E	15.0%	18.0%	15.0%	15.0%	15.0%	18.0%	12.0%
k_D	5.0%	5.0%	6.0%	5.0%	5.0%	5.0%	5.0%
E (%)	70%	70%	70%	80%	60%	80%	60%
D (%)	30%	30%	30%	20%	40%	20%	40%
WACC	12.00%	14.10%	12.30%	13.00%	11.00%	15.40%	9.20%

The WACC technique, albeit interesting in terms of method, in practice is rarely applied to determining the cap rate because it is hard to extract equity cap rates directly from the market. Instead, it is more widely used to determine the discount rate as it is easier to estimate, often by qualitative analysis, the rate of return required on the equity for an investment in a particular kind of property or in a specific asset.

Similarly, the band of investment technique could be used by assigning rates separately to the Building and the Land components characterised by different risk/return profiles.[37] While theoretically valid, this method is hard to apply in practice because it is difficult to extract from the market specific rates attributable to the individual components.

The Financial Structure   The market returns on debt and equity must be weighted using the financial structure available on the market for the subject property. The financial structure, i.e. the percentages of debt and equity, is assumed as the typical capital financing available on the market at a given time for the subject property in the period of analysis of the cash flows.

The availability of credit for real estate investments varies over time and space (depending on the broader capital market), as well as depending on the type of property and the characteristics of the specific asset.

With regard to variability over time, it is worth pointing out that the granting of credit to the real estate sector depends both on the general availability of credit in the banking system and on its actual exposure to this sector. Immediately following the global financial crisis of 2008, banks in almost every country reduced the amount of credit granted in general (in the so-called 'credit crunch period'); subsequently, once the market situation was normalised, credit for the real estate sector was restricted for several years owing to the excessive concentration of risk on the sector.

With regard to different types of properties, there is a considerable difference in the extent to which debt financing is available for Income-producing Properties as opposed to Development Projects. In the first case, without going into detail,[38] debt financing is more readily available for Income-producing Properties as its cash flows are more stable over time and more predictable; in other words, they present a lower level of operational risk, which allows banks to finance them, thus 'investing' with a low level of risk, in accordance with the characteristics of the lender (banks). Conversely, the cash flows of Development Projects are riskier because they depend on many unpredictable factors, such as unforeseen circumstances during construction or variability in the market, which can affect timings and sale prices, as well as the actual ability of the developer to complete the project. Consequently, as the level of operational risk is higher, a greater share of the capital is represented by equity which, by its nature, can cope better with the higher uncertainty.[39] It is unsurprising, therefore, particularly after the global financial crisis of 2008, that, in general, the banking system has reduced the debt component granted to Development Projects. In some cases, where the risk of the project is quite high (e.g. a new real estate concept in a secondary market), the financial structure might consist of equity alone.

Finally, it is worth pointing out that, as the quantity of debt obtainable depends fundamentally on the risk associated with the financed asset, the financial structure will depend on all the characteristics of the specific property, including existing lease agreements and, consequently, the creditworthiness of the tenants.

Debt   The cost of debt (K_d) expresses the current cost required by the financial market, mainly banks, to finance a property similar to the one being valued.

The rate has to be representative of the cost of the loan which could be obtained on the valuation date. The loan amount to be considered is only the amount that banks would grant by offering as collateral the subject property, without external guarantees that may reduce the cost and increase the debt amount granted.

The cost of debt can be subdivided into two components: the base rate and the margin required by the banks.

As regards the base rate, as stated earlier in the Section 'Rates and Capital Market', the debt financing must be a fixed rate loan as the valuation must not take into account any exogenous risk of a change in interest rates. For this reason, the base rate deemed most appropriate is the Interest Rate Swap, such as Eurirs[40] (or just 'IRS') in the Euro area or USD Swap curve in the USA, which is the parameter for indexing fixed-rate mortgages.[41]

Secondly, its maturity must be consistent with the time horizon used to discount the cash flows: for this purpose, the IRS quotations are typically calculated at 1 to 30-year intervals, which are thus entirely compatible with the valuation time horizons for property operations. Finally, while historical data (*ex-post* returns) are available, one can also obtain future forecasts (*ex-ante* returns) based on futures rates.[42]

As regards estimating the margin requested by banks, a specific market research is required to gather information from the banks on the spread they would be prepared to apply if they were to finance the purchase of the subject property.

The cost of debt, as already illustrated with respect to the financial structure, varies over time and depending on the asset being analysed. For this reason, a valuer has to check for consistency when estimating the value of several assets that may not present the same characteristics in terms of eligibility for financing.

Equity The cost of equity (K_e) expresses the total return currently required by the market participants to invest in a property similar, in terms of overall risk, to the one being valued.

The expected return will always have to be higher than the cost of debt as its repayment is postponed and, consequently, its risk is higher. Any use of resources is made with the aim of achieving a return within a specific time horizon. However, the return actually achieved may not be the same as the expected return.

For the purpose of estimating the Market Value, in accordance with the adopted definition of the cash flow, the return referred to is gross of tax.

Furthermore, the cost of equity is based on the overall risk of the investment, i.e. it considers the operational risk (property) and the financial risk (the financial structure, i.e. the debt/equity ratio). For this reason, in order to estimate the equity, one has first to determine the financial structure to be applied. Without wanting to go into too much detail here, the same investment poses a higher risk to the shareholder when its cash flows are subordinate to an amount of debt as compared to having no prior rights; considerations regarding the risk of debt use must be based on each individual euro invested, not on the total investment amount (which might lead to the mistaken conclusion that the risk of an investment made partly with debt is lower because the total invested equity amount is smaller).

Estimating the cost of equity is complex, particularly in the case of real estate assets, which are not traded on a regulated market where all the information are easily available; furthermore, unlike securities, two properties cannot be precisely the same.

The cost of equity also requires two components to be estimated, as already described in the Section 'Rates and Capital Market': a risk-free rate and a risk premium. For the latter please refer also to the Subsection 'Build-Up Approach'.

HOW TO ESTIMATE PROPERTY RETURN RATES

One of the main problems encountered when applying the Income Capitalisation Methods is quantifying the rates to use. These rates represent the return the market requires to invest in the asset being valued. Consequently, this being an economic comparison (as seen in Chapter 4), they should be drawn from the market. While there is a considerable conceptual difference between cap rate and discount rate, both of them essentially refer to the same concept: an expected rate of return, which is therefore based on the asset risk, albeit calculated in two different ways. Theoretically, it is possible to draw both the expected cap rate and discount rate from the market, in both cases seeking the actual returns (current return in the former and total return in the latter) for Comparables. In practice, it is not possible to observe total returns for Comparables, since the Capital Growth component is only implicit.

In the financial market, a discount rate can be drawn from the historical data series for listed securities using risk pricing models[43] which, however, are based on strong assumptions,[44] which are just about acceptable in financial markets[45] and are even harder to verify in the real estate market, given its specific characteristics.

The real estate market characteristics make it hard to determine or estimate the total return (IRR) of a property as there are no historical series with all the characteristics of the investment[46]: the only return that is easy to determine is the current return (yield), which is obtained by dividing the income price and the market of comparable transactions. Therefore, only the cap rate, which expresses the current return component only, can be determined. Otherwise, to determine the discount rate, the reference would have to be made to the total return expected by the market participants for the specific property, considering assumptions regarding the expected future Terminal Value and the investment period. Therefore, other methods must be used to estimate the discount rate.

In real estate, both theory and practice identify different methods for determining property rates, some of them usable for both cap and discount rates, and others being more specific; the choice of method depends on the data available.

1. Yield extraction from the market based on a sample of Comparables recently traded, whose income and price must be known.
2. Determining the discount rate from the cap rate.
3. Using a Build-Up Approach that involves the identification of specific risk factors, the sum of which is used to determine the rate.
4. Analysis of opinions on the return expressed by market players.
5. Using a band of investment technique that consists of deriving the rate from the basic components, based on the DCFA (equity and debt) or a property criterion (Building and Land)[47].
6. Ellwood,[48] Akerson,[49] and other 'financial archaeology' formulas for estimating the rate developed for the most part in eras when the calculation itself was a limitation.[50]

The various techniques will be analysed and described in the following sections. Some are applicable to both rates and others are specific, as summarised in Table 7.4. The description will exclude the band of investment technique, which is rarely used in European valuation practice and is similar to the WACC formula, as well as the Ellwood and Akerson formulas, as they are obsolete and are now of little practical use.[51]

Market Extraction

The Market Extraction method involves extracting the cap rates, corresponding to the current returns on the property (yield), directly from the market. This is a similar way to the Direct Comparison Approach, with qualitative analyses of the assets to be compared, making the appropriate increases or decreases based on differences in the characteristics of the Comparables.

One of the most challenging stages of valuing a property with the Income Capitalisation Methods is determining the correct rates. The advantage of direct extraction from the market is that a rate that includes all the property's risk components can be obtained.

TABLE 7.4   Main techniques for determining Property Return Rates

	Cap rate	Discount rate
Extraction from the market	This involves extracting yields directly from the market, in a similar way to the Direct Comparison Approach, with qualitative analyses of the assets to be compared, making the appropriate increases or decreases based on differences in the characteristics of the Comparables. It is the most widely used technique from practitioners.	*Not directly applicable*
Determining the discount rate from the cap rate	–	It is based on the relationship between the total return (IRR) and the income yield. Care must be taken to use the same level of income and cash flow.
Build-Up Approach	Even if it is more typically used in order to estimate a discount rate, it can also be used in order to determine a cap rate.	It expresses the discount rate as a function of the specific risk components (WACC). It is the most widely used technique among practitioners.
Analysis of opinions on the return expressed by operators	This is based, similarly to the extraction from the market, on the opinion of operators which provide hints on rates for different locations and asset typologies.	It can be useful in order to provide benchmarks for single components of the Build-Up Approach (e.g. cost of equity).

A cap rate extracted from the market is based on the income for a single year divided by the sale price of the property, without the various risk components being highlighted individually.

$$\text{Cap Rate} = \text{Yield} = \frac{\text{Income}}{\text{Price}}$$

The main obstacle encountered in using market extraction is the small number of comparable transactions that take place within a reasonable period of time and in the same geographical area. Nevertheless, when there are enough data with respect to the sale of similar properties and at market prices, deriving yields directly from transactions of Comparables is the best approach[52].

Therefore, in order to obtain a meaningful rate, there must be:[53]

- A sufficient number of comparable transactions
- The possibility of determining the historical series of income and expenditures for each comparable transaction, or the availability of sufficient data to estimate the income, expenditures and occupation rate at the time of the transaction.

The property under analysis (for which a rate is being sought) and the Comparables for which the information is available, must have the same features (uniformity condition) in terms of[54]:

- Highest and Best Use
- Location
- Physical condition of the Building (which influences both the current income, due to planned maintenance, and the future value, due to extraordinary maintenance)
- Residual life
- Current situation and future expectation of income: duration and type of lease agreements, quality of tenants, current and anticipated occupation rate
- Potential financial structure (possibility of using the same financial structure).

While the above characteristics are the most commonly used, there is no universally accepted method for extracting market rates and even the data published by analysts and consultancy companies are often diverse, which places a limit on their actual use.[55] A simple example will serve to clarify this (see Example 7.6).

EXAMPLE 7.6: EXAMPLE OF THE MARKET EXTRACTION OF A CAP RATE

In order to obtain a correct cap rate, recent transactions which have occurred in the same area involving assets with similar characteristics to the subject property need to be analysed:

- Area: CBD – Central Business District
- Type: offices
- Property: whole Building
- Conditions: Class A
- Tenant: prime tenant
- Rental: new contract at Market Values.

Four properties with the same risk characteristics have been sold in the last quarter, for which the market prices and income, expressed as the gross rent, are known.

TABLE 7.5   Market extraction of a cap rate through market yield estimation

Comparable transaction	*Alpha*	*Beta*	*Gamma*	*Delta*
Income	€ 2,740,000	€ 2,350,000	€ 3,105,000	€ 2,930,000
Price	€ 38,000,000	€ 32,000,000	€ 45,000,000	€ 42,000,000
Yield	7.21%	7.34%	6.90%	6.98%
Average Yield	**7.11%**			

> Using the data extracted from the market, one can estimate an average yield of 7.1% applicable as the cap rate to the subject property. Note that, although an arithmetical average has been calculated in the example, in practice the analysis and, specifically, the calculation, are only needed to form an opinion of the market yield to choose a cap rate to be applied to the valuation. For example, if the subject property is more similar to property Gamma than to the others in the sample, the valuer could decide that estimating a cap rate of 7% would be more appropriate than the average value.

Note furthermore that the market extraction of the cap rate must be done directly, without making the mistake of determining the rates by estimating them as a ratio between the average rents and the Market Values of comparable assets or values drawn from secondary sources.

If the rate thus extracted is based on an inaccurate definition of income, such as the rent (Potential Gross Income), which fails to consider any differences in the cost structure, the estimate could be less accurate. The use of the Potential Gross Income is acceptable if it can be assumed that the comparable assets present similar cost structures.[56]

The following are some of the most common errors that could be made when extracting a property market rate:

- Choosing inappropriate comparable transactions: properties of the same kind must be considered.
- Using comparable transactions that took place too long in the past: market conditions may have changed,[57] given that factors such as interest rates, expectations of the property value, the supply and demand and occupation rates in the market have a significant effect on the rates.
- Differences between buyers: the motivations and profile of the typical buyer (Investor) must be similar, as the return required and the cost of capital for different kinds of Investors differ and are reflected in the rates. Any strategic motivations can also potentially lead to a price higher than the Market Value being offered, which thus influences the extraction of the comparison rate.

If there are differences in the characteristics of an asset (or in the other specifications of the type of property being analysed), corrections will have to be made to the rate identified in order to account for the differences between the properties, which are reflected in the risk and therefore in the expected return. To this end, also see the determination of the risk premium in the Build-Up Approach model.

Determining the Discount Rate from the Cap Rate

As described in the Section 'Measuring the Return on a Property Investment', the discount rate also represents the total return expected from the investment. Since the cap rate represents a current return, the discount rate is different as it also implicitly considers the growth return depending on the expected variation in the Terminal Value of the asset. Consequently, in order to extract the discount rate from the market, the expected IRR would have to be calculated for each transaction that has taken place on the market, i.e. the total return rate expected by the buyer, therefore based also on future expected cash flows (especially the Terminal Value). In the real world, this measurement cannot be taken because only the expected current return (corresponding to the implicit cap rate in the transaction price) can be determined by analysing the yields extracted from the market, while the part of the return derived from the expected Capital Gain return is only potential and depends on the buyer's expectations.

However, the relationship between the two rates of return is useful for estimating the discount rate based on the extraction of a cap rate calculated for similar assets (which is, therefore, an expression of the income yield), by estimating an addendum which considers expectations regarding future flows, i.e. the Capital Gain expected.[58] In other words, it is the reverse procedure to the previously analysed method based on the Gordon model:[59]

$$Value = \frac{Income}{k - g}$$

where k represents the discount rate, a figure that can be calculated by adding the cap rate i to a coefficient g which represents the future income growth rate expected, which means that $k = i + g$. A simple numerical example that compares the two criteria illustrates this mathematical relationship.

EXAMPLE 7.7: RELATIONSHIP BETWEEN CAP RATE AND DISCOUNT RATE

The value obtained by discounting, at a rate of $k = 8\%$ ($i + g = 6\% + 2\%$), the cash flows (amounting initially to € 100) projected into infinity (in the example for 'only' 200 years), with an annual cash flow growth rate of 2%, returns (almost) the same value that would be obtained with the Direct Capitalisation Approach, by capitalising the initial income at a 6% cap rate.

TABLE 7.6 Example of the relationship between cap rate and discount rate

Period		1	2	3	4	5	6	7	8	198	199	200
Income / Cash Flow		€ 100.00	€ 102.00	€ 104.04	€ 106.12	€ 108.24	€ 110.41	€ 112.62	€ 114.87	€ 4,946	€ 5,045	€ 5,146
Cap Rate	6% i											
Growth rate	2% g											
Discount Rate	8% $k = i + g$											
Discount Cash Flow		€ 92.59	€ 87.45	€ 82.59	€ 78.00	€ 73.67	€ 69.58	€ 65.71	€ 62.06	€ 0.0012	€ 0.0011	€ 0.0011
Market Value with the DCFA		€ 1,666.6486	*(Present Value, sum of Discounted Cash Flows)*									
Market Value with the Direct Capitalization Approach		€ 1,666.6667	*(Income/Cap Rate)*									
Difference		*−€ 0.0181*										

If this estimation technique is used, however, care must be taken to use the same level of income and cash flow; in other words, as often happens, the discount rate sought is net of the operating costs (i.e. NOI level). For consistency even the cap rate must be calculated at the same profit and loss account level. It would be wrong, in fact, to use a cap rate calculated on the rent (Gross Income) as a basis for determining the discount rate applied to a cash flow net of operating costs.[60]

In practice, the expected inflation is often used as an approximation to the growth rate of future income. This simplification, which may be acceptable in the long term, assuming that there is a correlation between inflation, economic growth and growth in the demand for space, may, however, originate errors in the short-term, when on the contrary a contraction (e.g. because of a temporary economic crisis) may occur with a consequent reduction in the ERV.

It is also important to understand that the current yield is a summary rate, not necessarily an accepted current return rate.[61] It merely reflects the value because Investors are interested in the total rate of return (IRR), not only in part of it (yield or current return). The following simple example[62] clarifies this concept.

EXAMPLE 7.8: INITIAL YIELD AND TOTAL RETURN

Two properties A and B present the same risk, and therefore the same total return should be required by Investors, which corresponds to a discount rate (or IRR) of 9% a year. There is no growth in the cash flows of property A, while those of property B are expected to grow by 2% a year. While the two properties present the same risk and the same initial income, no Investor would pay the same price for both.

Property B value is higher than Property A and its yield lower (7% compared to 9%), implicitly considering the positive growth rate (2%).

TABLE 7.7   Initial yield and total return comparison

Discount rate	9.00%									
Growth rate Cash Flow Asset A	0.00%									
Growth rate Cash Flow Asset B	2.00%									

Period	1	2	3	4	5	6	7	8	9	10
Cash Flow Asset A	€ 100	€ 100	€ 100	€ 100	€ 100	€ 100	€ 100	€ 100	€ 100	€ 1,211
Cash Flow Asset B	€ 100	€ 102	€ 104	€ 106	€ 108	€ 110	€ 113	€ 115	€ 117	€ 1,861
Discounted Cash Flow Asset A	€ 92	€ 84	€ 77	€ 71	€ 65	€ 60	€ 55	€ 50	€ 46	€ 512
Discounted Cash Flow Asset B	€ 92	€ 86	€ 80	€ 75	€ 70	€ 66	€ 62	€ 58	€ 54	€ 786

Value Asset A	€ 1,111									
Value Asset B	€ 1,429									
Initial Yield Asset A	9.00%									
Initial Yield Asset B	7.00%									

Build-Up Approach

The Build-Up Approach is generally used in estimating the discount rate, but it can also be used to determine the cap rate because this rate also expresses an expected return based on the level of risk resulting from the sum of several elements. Indeed, more generally, it consists in the identification of the main elements according to which the risk of an investment can be defined, in the research of a tool in order to quantify them and, at the end, in a synthesis of those quantities, applying the necessary weighting factors, in order to obtain a single number representative of the intensity of the risk considered.

The Build-Up Approach allows a rate to be defined based on the specific risk components; for this reason, it can also be used to modify the rates obtained with the market extraction method, with the appropriate upward or downward corrections needed to account for the differences in risk compared to the Comparables used. It is advisable, however, not to abuse the correction because, if excessive, it demonstrates the actual non-comparability of the assets used for the extraction (exactly as shown in Chapter 5, Section 'Direct Comparison Approach').

The main merit of the Build-Up Approach is to force valuers to focus their attention on the various risk components and their varying degrees of importance. Furthermore, it forces valuers to explain their choices when determining the rate, thus identifying the logical route followed in building it. However, the main drawback of its application is specifically the need to choose and, above all, to quantify the risk factors and their weighting.

The general formula for summing up the returns required based on each risk factor can be refined and applied to seek a rate, identifying two main components: a risk-free rate and specific risk component of the asset influenced by numerous factors.

$$\text{Property Return Rate} = \text{risk-free rate} + \text{property risk premium}$$

In order to obtain the rate, all the specific risk components (specific risk premium) affecting a particular asset must be identified, adding them to the risk-free rate[63] required by the market to defer consumption over time.

In corporate valuation, the specific risk premium is determined by many factors: risk of equity investment, dimensional risk, sector risk, financial risk, the degree of diversification, growth prospects, etc. Each factor explains part of the specific risk and can be quantified by a number of basis points of specific additional return required by market participants to bear this specific risk. When determining a rate to use in doing Property Valuations, the risk premium can be built by determining the contribution of each significant factor.

The main problem is how to identify, or somewhat quantify and weight, the factors the valuer has to consider in calculating the specific risk premium. In practice, the choices made by valuers are fairly diverse and the estimates are based on ranges that are expected to vary over time. In practical terms, the factors are usually quantified in basis points, which can be exclusively positive, where the valuer decides to start with the return based on the 'ideal' lowest risk property, i.e. with the lowest level of risk per individual element, to which incremental risk factors are added (see Example 7.9). When the valuer decides to start with the return on an 'average' property, representing the average risk level, both positive and negative adjustments are applied. While there is nothing scientific about identifying and estimating individual risk factors, consistency checks can be performed, e.g. checking that, considering the level of risk, the estimated rate is consistent when compared to the return on alternative forms of investment (bonds, shares, etc.) or to the actual or estimated return on other properties.

EXAMPLE 7.9: EXAMPLE OF DISCOUNT RATE ESTIMATION WITH BUILD-UP APPROACH

The subject of the valuation is an Income-producing Property and the valuation horizon is set at 10 years. Once the intermediate cash flows and the Terminal Value have been estimated, the discount rate must be estimated in order to convert the future cash flows into a Present Value (the sum of which is the Market Value of the subject property). For this purpose, the three components of the discount rate are determined as follows:

- The financial structure (D% and E%) determines the weighting of the various forms of capital used (debt and equity) and depends on the operating risk of the asset and on financial markets. A suitable financial structure for this property is considered to be as follows:

$$\text{Debt (D\%)} = 70\%$$

$$\text{Equity (E\%)} = 30\%$$

- The cost of debt (K_d) expresses the current cost required by the banks to finance a property similar to the one being valued, considering the specific operating risk and the financial structure. This can be subdivided into two components:
  a) The basic reference rate (as seen in the Subsection 'Debt', which could be estimated as the 6-month average of the 10-year interest rate swap (or any other base rate)
  b) The margin required by the lenders (spread), which could be estimated by surveying a number of banks.
    As of the valuation date, this can be quantified as follows:

  K_d = base rate + spread = six-month average of the 10-year interest rate swap

  + average spread on the market = 1.00% + 3.00% = 4.00%

- The cost of equity (K_e): expresses the total return currently required by the equity investor to invest in a similar property to the one being valued, considering its operating risk, cost of debt, and financial structure. For the purpose of estimating the cost of the equity with the Build-Up Approach, the following return components required for the various risk factors listed below have been added together. Again, there is a risk-free component and a remuneration component of the specific risk premium:
  a) Risk-free rate: the 10-year government bond rate (average of returns over the last 6 months) has been chosen as it is consistent with the valuation time horizon.

(Continued)

b) Risk premium: the following factors have been identified and quantified on the basis of an ideal property with the minimum level of risk, based on the judgement of the valuer.

i. Property sector risk estimated at 400 bps

ii. Location risk estimated at 150 bps

iii. Intended use and type of property risk estimated at 100 bps

iv. Physical and technical risk estimated at 50 bps

v. Rental and contractual risk estimated at 50 bps.

$$K_e = \text{base rate} + \text{risk premium}$$

$$= \text{10-year government bond rate} + \sum \text{specific risk factors}$$

$$= 1.80\% + (4.00\% + 1.50\% + 1.00\% + 0.50\% + 0.50\%) = 9.30\%$$

After having determined the financial structure, the cost of debt (K_d) and cost of equity (K_e), the discount rate (WACC) is determined.

$$WACC\ (K) = K_d * D\% + K_e * E\% = 4.00\% * 70\% + 9.30\% * 30\% = 5.59\%$$

Analysing the Opinions of Market Players on the Return Expected

A different way of extracting market rates, without referring directly to comparable transactions, is to analyse the opinions of market players on the return expected.

In the more transparent and sophisticated markets, some consultancy companies periodically publish reports[64] based on the opinion of market players, which give indications about the rates for different property types and locations. The limitation of this method is immediately evident, as they are average values based on opinions connected with the past. However, where available, they can be a useful starting point to build the rate for the subject property based on the Build-Up Approach.

In markets where no systematic surveys are done, the valuer could try to achieve the same result by carrying out a direct survey among Investors operating in the specific market. In this case, while the problem is solved at the root, by seeking the rate of return required by the market, attention must be paid to how the survey is carried out and to ensuring that the data is justifiable if the sources need to be formalised in a valuation report. Moreover, it is important to be clear about the expected rate of return definition. If a cost of equity is required, it is also important to refer to the associated capital structure.

NOTES

1. Detailed discussions on the methods for calculating return on investment can be found in any finance manual. This section only details the simplest methods to contribute to understanding and estimating the rates to use in the Income Capitalisation Approach Methods algorithms. For further details, see Damodaran (2012).

2. The principles for calculating this can be found in textbooks on financial mathematics.
3. We shall return to this subject when describing how to derive the discount rate from the cap rate in the Subsection 'Determining the Discount Rate from the Cap Rate'.
4. Risk elements are described in Chapter 2.
5. 'No uncertainty about reinvestment rates', quoted from Damodaran (2012).
6. In practice, since there are only few zero-coupon bonds listed, coupon bonds returns are also commonly used.
7. The yield curve is simply the graph that represents the rate of return paid by bonds with different maturity dates. A yield curve is said to be 'normal' when it has an upward trend; in fact, the shorter the bond duration, the smaller the return, because of the lower associated risk.
8. RICS (2010).
9. Consider for example the shock and the economic crisis that resulted from the bankruptcy of Lehman Brothers in 2008.
10. Some of the latest research in the fields of economics and finance concerns behavioural finance and behavioural economics, which apply scientific research in the field of cognitive psychology to understand economic decisions, based on the rationality, or rather the non-rationality, of economic agents.
11. Clayton et al. (2009).
12. In particular, House (2004) shows how in many property markets, between 2002 and 2007, much of the growth in value resulted from an investment surge mainly driven by market sentiment.
13. In practice, the term 'yield' is mostly used in the British market and the term 'cap rate' is used in the US market.
14. See Chapter 6, Subsection 'Estimating the Terminal Value' for further details.
15. There is no single definition of yield and cap rate and among operators, as well as academics, different definitions are used. An interesting result in this respect was achieved by Boydell (1998), in which theory and market practices are analysed by interviewing managers and valuers to reconcile their actions with theory; one of the areas in which no single conclusion is reached is specifically the definition of 'reversionary yield' which, in practice, is often considered to be the terminal cap rate or GOCR.
16. A basis point is one hundredth of a percentage point (one basis point corresponds to 0.01%).
17. Others include Gunnelin et al. (2003) and Wang et al. (1990).
18. Wincott (1991).
19. Wurtzbach and Miles (1987).
20. Appraisal Institute (2001).
21. Brueggeman and Fisher (2010).
22. Brueggeman and Fisher (2010).
23. McDonald (2015).
24. 'Equivalent yield' in British terminology.
25. See Section 'Measuring the Return on a Property Investment'.
26. Free Cash Flow from Operations (FCFO), also known as unlevered cash flow, refers to the cash flow generated by operations.
27. Free Cash Flow to Equity (FCFE), also known as levered cash flow, refers to the cash flow generated for the shareholders.
28. See Chapter 6, Subsections 'Profit and Loss Account of an Income-producing Property' and 'Estimating the Cash Flows' for the reasons behind this choice.
29. There is, however, no possibility of identifying a relationship between the discount rate net of financial charges and debt service and the gross rate, as the two previous elements have an opposite effect, the prevalence of which depends on the quantity and cost of the debt and the tax rate.
30. Including Geltner et al. (2006), page 204.
31. The market yield curve represents the rate of return achievable by a specific financial security on different maturity dates.

32. While it is not the topic of this book, it is worth pointing out that there are different forms of equity (ordinary and privileged shares and units of various kinds in property funds having different economic rights, etc.) and debt (senior and junior bank loans, ordinary and convertible bonds, mezzanine loans, etc.). In this respect, see Morri and Mazza (2015) for a deeper analysis.

33. On this subject, see Damodaran (2012).

34. The WACC used in capital budgeting, where the economic feasibility of an investment in the perspective of a specific player is estimated, also considers the tax shield. The cost of debt is, therefore, reduced due to the tax deductibility of the financial charges.

35. If the investment is made using equity alone, the discount rate will be equal to the cost of capital (equity), i.e. the minimum return expected by the equity Investor. Given that in reality most investments are made using debt capital as well, a weighting formula is used.

36. Even if each of them can be estimated separately, there are strict relationships among the three components. Both the cost of equity and the cost of debt depend on the leverage ratio and the operational risk, and moreover the cost of equity depends also on the cost of debt.

37. Fisher and Martin (1994).

38. On this subject, see Morri and Mazza (2015).

39. Without wanting to go into specifics, as financial structures are a very complex subject widely discussed in financial literature, we simply want to point out that, unlike debt, equity has no repayment deadline and, consequently, while requiring a greater return, it copes better with changes in the remuneration timetable.

40. The acronym for Euro Interest Rate Swap, which is the reference rate calculated by the European Banking Federation as a weighted average at which Europe's leading lending institutions enter into Interest Rate Swap contracts to hedge against interest rate risks.

41. Alternatively, some valuers use the Interbank Offered Rate as the Euribor in the Euro area or the Libor in UK, which is the interest rate used as a parameter for indexing variable rate mortgages. In this case, the spread also has to consider the cost of hedging against interest rate risks.

42. In practice, either the IRS rate on the valuation date or an average of values over the previous 6–12 months is used in order to account for market fluctuations.

43. The most famous and most frequently used ones are: *Capital Asset Pricing Model* (CAPM) and *Arbitrage Pricing Theory* (APT).

44. As an example, here are the main assumptions of the CAPM, one of the most widely used models for pricing risk (Damodaran, 2012):
    - no transaction costs
    - all assets are traded on the market
    - investments are infinitely divisible
    - symmetry of information
    - possibility of unlimited borrowing at a risk-free rate.

45. A critical analysis of the CAPM and its limits is presented in Fernandez (2015) and in Fernandez (2017).

46. In a study of the US market, Breidenbach et al., (2006) use *Betas*, elements used in the CAPM to calculate the return on investments in Property (using the NCREIE direct property index) and listed vehicles (REITs) in order to estimate the discount rate. They conclude that in the first case, owing to the typical smoothing of indexes based on valuations, among other factors, the data are not suitable and they suggest using a representative index of listed vehicles. However, one can immediately see the limitation stemming from the different liquidity of the listed vehicles compared to properties, as well as the difficulty involved in applying the method due to the absence, in almost all markets, of vehicles that are specialised by type or geographical area.

47. Fisher and Martin (1994).

48. Ellwood (1959).

49. Akerson (1984).

50. Goddard and Marcum (2012).

51. Kelly et al. (1995).
52. Appraisal Institute (2001).
53. Strickland (1999).
54. Accetta (1998).
55. Reenstierna (2008).
56. Rent is often used in less transparent markets where Net Operating Income information is not available.
57. The time span concept is not an absolute value, as it can depend on particular events that change market conditions. For example, transactions cannot be considered comparable if they took place a few days before and after the collapse of Lehman Brothers, when risk premiums on all asset classes increased considerably, with direct consequences on the falling prices.
58. Also see Geltner et al. (2006), page 254.
59. Gordon (1956).
60. The issue is well described in Wincott et al. (1996) with a series of simple examples showing how the relationship between the two rates is only valid if the same profit and loss account level is used.
61. McDonald (2015) summarises the relationship as follows: 'Capitalisation Rate is related to the risk-adjusted Discount Rate chosen by the investor minus one very important factor – the expected percentage change in value. In particular: Capitalisation Rate = Discount Rate minus Expected Percentage Change in Value' and also 'The risk-adjusted Discount Rate is a target rate set by the investor based in part on perceived risk'.
62. Taken from Geltner et al. (2006).
63. See Section 'Rates and Capital Market'.
64. Such as those published by PwC (Real Estate Investor Survey) and Korpacz Realty Advisors.

CHAPTER 8

Structure of the Valuation Report

This chapter provides a description of the main elements of what is known as a 'valuation report', i.e. the document relating to the appraisal of a property which 'clearly and accurately set[s] out the conclusions of the valuation in a manner that is neither ambiguous nor misleading, and which does not create a false impression'.[1]

The following is a non-exhaustive list of what are considered to be the main elements of a valuation report, indicating those that are fundamental requirements (also called 'minimum terms of engagement'[2]) and those that constitute good practice and therefore contribute to maintaining a high standard of professional competence. In practice, the content of a valuation report depends significantly on the quality and quantity of the information available, so it is essential to specify the sources of the information used, as well as to report the assumptions on which the valuation is based.

The structure and the level of detail depend also on the purpose of the valuation. If the report is for internal purposes, some parts may be omitted (e.g. part of the Preamble) and other parts (e.g. the Description of the property when known to all the readers) may be minimal.

In this chapter, therefore, we shall describe the ideal case of a full valuation, without the limits set in the terms of engagement which, due to necessity (lack of information) or the client's requirements (e.g. to keep down the costs of the valuation by avoiding zoning analysis), could result in a less detailed analysis. Reference is also made to a so-called 'full' valuation, i.e. with an external and internal inspection visit. In this respect it is useful to distinguish between:

- 'Desktop' valuations: no inspection is carried out, but the valuer performs an indirect verification, where possible, of the documentation provided by the client using online maps, for example, to determine the location, or property portals and databases to analyse the market.
- 'Drive-by' valuations: after having examined the documentation provided by the client, the valuer carries out only an external inspection of the property gathering data and information on site.
- 'Full' valuations: the valuer also carries out an internal inspection of the property, as well as carrying out any further technical and administrative research if required (e.g. local town planning search involving the relevant local authorities).

Ideally, to provide the reader with a simple structure, the valuation report should consist of the seven main parts, better described in the following paragraphs:

1. Executive Summary
2. Preamble
3. Description of the property

4. Market Analysis
5. Valuation
6. Conclusions
7. Appendices.

EXECUTIVE SUMMARY

The Executive Summary provides a summary, on one or two pages, of the main information contained in the valuation report, allowing the reader to promptly understand the main assumptions, figures and conclusions of the valuation without having to read the whole document in detail. Clearly, the Executive Summary is only significant if it is accompanied by the respective full valuation report to which it relates.

PREAMBLE

The Preamble is a fundamental part of the Valuation report because it contains all the elements which contribute to defining the valuation requirement (as stated in Chapter 1, Section 'Determining the Valuation Requirement') as follows:

- Identification of the subject property
- Purpose of the valuation
- Basis of value
- Valuation date.

    The Preamble can also contain the following information:

- The terms of engagement set by the client and a statement of the potential conflicts of interest in respect of the client.
- The type of valuation (desktop, drive-by or full), the date of any inspection visit and the details of this visit.
- Any particular assumptions (so called 'special assumptions') on which the valuation is based that differ from the facts on the valuation date (e.g. the valuation of a Building as if it were completed, even if still under construction).
- The limits of the valuation, such as any non-verification of the information provided, lack of access to any parts of the property during the inspection, lack of environmental checks, etc.
- The documentation used, indicating the latest revision date and the respective source, stating whether it was supplied by the client or obtained during the inspection visit or from any research from the relevant technical offices.
- The work team, stating the name of the person responsible for the valuation, of the person in charge of the inspection and the other individuals involved and in what capacity.

DESCRIPTION OF THE PROPERTY

This part of the valuation report is dedicated to describing the property. It is worth remembering that the valuation report is not intended to be, nor to replace, a technical, administrative and environmental due diligence of the property. However, many of the elements of the two documents are the same and, indeed, having up-to-date due diligence is fundamental to carrying out the valuation properly. The aim is, in fact, to identify and describe all the elements that may have an impact, positive or negative, on the value of the subject property, obviously taking into consideration the type of asset that is being valued. For example, consider the proximity of an airport, which in most cases represents a negative factor for Residential Properties due to the noise of departing and arriving aircrafts, while being a positive factor for logistics-related properties benefitting from proximity to infrastructure, as the travel times and distances for the goods are reduced.

The description of the property must be complete and exhaustive in every respect, but it must not contain misleading or unnecessary information (for example, an analysis of the catchment area for a single residential unit, or an analysis of the presence of services – shops or public offices – for a logistic property, are of little use).

The elements that allow one to define a property from a technical, administrative and economic point of view can be listed as follows.

- Location, i.e. all the elements that unequivocally describe the location of the property and how it can influence the property's ability to generate a benefit, i.e. to be more attractive to a User.[3] The following elements define the location of a property:
  - Address.
  - Macro- and micro-location, using more or less detailed maps[4] and taking care to point out the distance from infrastructure and services of specific relevance to the property in question.
  - Identification of the perimeter of the plot of Land on which the property stands and any appurtenances.
  - Details regarding the accessibility of the property and its visibility, where relevant (such as in the case of retail properties).
  - Details of roads and infrastructure (particularly important for some kinds of properties, such as shopping centres or properties used for logistics purposes).
  - Presence and distance of the main forms of transport (local public transport, trains, airports, ports, etc.).
  - Description of the urban surroundings (e.g. any presence of other developments, the purpose of the Buildable Areas and the type and primary purpose of other properties in the surrounding area, the presence of public services – public offices, hospitals, post offices, etc. – and private ones – banks, pharmacies, shops, shopping centres, supermarkets, etc.).
  - Availability of public and private car parks.
  - Other specific factors that can vary depending on the type of property (e.g. analysis of the catchment area or pedestrian flows for retail properties, demographic trends and per capita GDP for a Residential Development Project).
- Technical description, i.e. all the elements needed to gain a clear and comprehensive picture of the physical characteristics and a quality assessment of the property. The analysis will differ according to the typology of properties:
  - In the case of a Buildable Area, one has to:
    - Determine the scope to build and the urban destination of the area.
    - Verify the presence of any restrictions or easements (rights of way, power lines, the presence of archaeological finds, etc.) which have an impact on the availability of the property.

- Analyse the presence of infrastructure (in terms of urbanisation and services).
- Check the potential presence of environmental issues (i.e. the industrial purpose of the area, pre-existing issues, the presence of unauthorised refuse dumps). This verification is extremely important as, at the executive planning stage, the construction of buildings in areas considered to be at risk always requires a preliminary investigation of these aspects and, if potential problems are detected, reclamation work which, particularly for Residential developments, can have a major impact on development costs and, consequently, on the value of the area.
- For an Income-producing Property, the additional aspects to consider include:
  - Type of property (existing use and condition as far as can be ascertained).
  - Year of construction and latest renovation.
  - Number of floors, above and below ground.
  - Details of pedestrian and vehicular access.
  - Architectural features of the Building (i.e. façades, doors and windows, roof, etc.).
  - The structural features of the Building (from the foundation to the roof) and their maintenance status, reporting any defects, damage or deterioration, if detected during the inspection visit, as well as the need for urgent work, ordinary or extraordinary maintenance carried out in recent years and/or planned in the future.
  - Technical equipment (such as water and drainage, heating, air conditioning, fire-prevention, safety, and lift systems) and their maintenance status, reporting any defects, damage or deterioration, if detected during the inspection, as well as any need for work, maintenance carried out in recent years and/or planned in the future.
  - External structures (car parks, manoeuvring areas, green spaces, etc.).
  - External finishes.
  - Internal areas and their space layout. In this respect, it is worth pointing out the increasing importance of identifying the characteristics of the Building with respect to its intended use. While this may be obvious and closely related to the measurement unit used for valuation purposes (e.g. the number of screens and seats in multiplex cinemas, the number of rooms in hotels, or the number of beds in student housing), it is increasingly important for traditional buildings, such as offices, where the number of workstations rather than the surface area is increasingly influencing the value (typically, modern office buildings have a better layout and can, therefore, host a higher number of workstations). For the latter, moreover, it may be useful to use an international classification, such as the one set up by the Building Owners and Managers Association (BOMA) that distinguishes between class A, B, and C offices, standing for high, good, and minimum quality office spaces respectively, although there is not, as yet, an unambiguous definition of these.
  - Geographic cardinal exposure (particularly important in the Residential sector).
  - The energy performance of the Building, its environmental characteristics (presence of geothermal, solar power, underfloor heating, and cooling systems, etc.) and any environmental certification protocols[5] (e.g. BREEAM[6] or LEED[7]).
  - Maintenance facilities (e.g. the presence of fixed installations for cleaning façades or areas that are difficult to access, such as ventilated façades or shelters).
  - Presence of any easements (rights of way, power lines, etc.) which have an impact on the availability of the property (e.g. the presence of a telephone aerial and/or the electricity operator's control unit, availability of public or publicly used parking areas, or protected areas).

- The availability of licenses in the case of a retail property.
- Presence of toxic materials or buried tanks that may have leaked and polluted the soil, in addition to any past or present contamination.
- Presence of any urban or archaeological restrictions (in particular for historical properties) which might limit the options of refurbishment of the Building.
- In the case of a Building under construction, the verification, in addition to considering the elements already mentioned, where applicable, must include a detailed analysis of the tender documentation, including contracts with the construction companies, including, by way of example, the executive designs (architectural, installations, structures), the descriptive reports, the specifications, the metric calculations for the construction and system installation work, the works schedule, the work progress report or all the various obligations and undertakings of the developer towards the public administration relating to public works to be carried out directly, with deduction of charges or any other compensation.
- Dimensions, i.e. details of the surface areas and their distribution. In this respect, it is useful to point out that technical measurement is definitely one of the most delicate aspects and a source of significant controversy. In most cases they are associated with the existence of specific uses based on the different professional categories of the different geographical areas or specific types of properties. One can easily see how, *ceteris paribus*, a different measurement can have a significant impact for the purposes of valuation. It is therefore fundamentally important to ensure that the following elements are reported in detail:
  - The subdivision of spaces by floor and intended use (as well as external parking areas, green areas etc.), main rooms and accessories, horizontal and vertical connections, covered and uncovered areas.
  - The types of surfaces (Gross Floor Area, Land registry, Net Leasable Area, etc.) with a clear indication of the criteria for determining and measuring them (and the relative source).
  - An indication of whether the surfaces were verified during the inspection visit (for example, sample verification of some units or full measurement of the whole Building) or whether these have been provided by the client or by third parties.
  - The criterion and the weighting factors whether used in order to standardise the different surfaces.
- Rental status, i.e. details regarding the spaces currently leased and the respective existing lease agreements (so-called 'rent roll', also see A Closer Look 6.1):
  - Identification of the spaces currently leased or vacant, highlighting any discrepancies found during the site visit compared to the documents provided by the client.
  - Identification of the tenants and characteristics of the existing lease agreements (e.g. type of agreement, passing rent, effective date, duration, presence of early withdrawal clauses – the so-called 'break option' – rental indexing, existence of any 'free rent' periods or stepped periods, any TIs paid for by the Owner, guarantees, or other specific clauses).
  - Description of any other forms of agreement that link the User of the property to the Owner, such as hotel management service agreements or business branch leasing agreements in shopping centres.
  - Identification of any spaces which are occupied illegally, indicating how these will be dealt with for valuation purposes.

- Verification of the reliability of the tenants (by means of a creditworthiness analysis) or, in the case of Trade-Related Properties where the activity carried out within them significantly influences the tenant's ability to pay the rent, such as shopping centres or hotels, the impact of the latter on the tenant's turnover and an indication of any potential default.
- Verification of the presence of the tenant in other properties within the same area, which might lead to the possible release of space especially in periods of economic downturn or may represent an element of strategic importance.
- Land registry status, i.e. the property's registration details (whether available) as it allows the property to be unequivocally identified, in terms of ownership, location and type (registration category), although discrepancies are often found between the contents of the registration documents (Land registry search report, map extract and cadastral plan) and the results of the site visit (e.g. the presence of illegal buildings or a failure to update the Land registry).
- Building and zoning compliance, i.e. details of the Building's town planning status, generally taken from a urban planning certificate, and compliance with building regulations (e.g. building practice, building permit, testing and habitability licence, or any requests for amnesty).
- Any presence and details of leasing, environmental or other restrictions, as well as any real rights which may restrict the availability of the property for the owners.
- Evidence of any problems and/or other elements of interest regarding the property not stated in the above categories.

A CLOSER LOOK 8.1: SURFACE AREA MEASUREMENTS

One of the main problems related to Property Valuation arises from the lack of uniformity in the definition of surface areas and the methods for measuring them. While on the one hand the problem can be reasonably solved for the subject property by means of a precise survey of the dimensions, on the other hand, it persists in the use of comparable property data for which it is difficult to obtain highly detailed information. A research carried out by JLL[8] has shown that the use of different measurement standards can lead to differences in the measurement of an area in the same property in the order of 24%. To cope with this problem, the International Property Measurement Standards Coalition (IPMSC), a group of over 80 professionals and non-profit organisations around the world, is working to develop and implement International Property Measurement Standards (IPMS) to ensure that the dimensions are determined consistently in order to create a transparent market and consequently to gain the greater trust of Investors and savers and, finally, the greater stability of the market itself.

In this book, as it is not a technical book, unless otherwise stated only the terms 'Gross Surface Area' and 'Net Lettable Area'[9] (or 'Net Sellable Area' for Residential Properties) will be used and will have the following meaning:

- Gross Surface Area: the sum of all the surface areas (covered and uncovered) of a property, divided by purpose and floor, as well as by primary purpose and secondary purpose (e.g. lift shafts, corridors, or utility areas).

- Net Lettable Area: the surface area of a property that is currently leased or could be leased to one or more tenants; generally, this excludes the entrance hall, atrium, utility area, lift shafts, etc., unless the property is of monumental historical value or prime real estate.

In several countries, moreover, in order to obtain a single uniform piece of data for each use of the property (such as office space), it is common practice to apply weighting factors to the various areas of the Net Lettable Area (such as archives, technical rooms or parking spaces). This method has the advantage of simplifying the research of comparable data to a single parameter (rent or sales value per m^2) for each use within the same property, but it has the drawback that the weighting factors are discretional and they might differ between valuers, thus leading to a further level of distortion beyond the measurement issue.

The alternative method would be to identify different comparable data not only for each use of the property but also for each different space (i.e. not only for the office space, but also for the archives, the technical rooms or the parking spaces).

While this latter approach would be theoretically more correct, from a practical point of view it is often inapplicable. Taking as an example a retail unit on 3 floors (basement, ground and upper floor), it is easier to apply different weights to the different floors based on their use and position (e.g. 50% to the basement if used as a storage and 80% to the first floor, which has a lower appeal as a retail space) in order to calculate a weighted surface for the entire shop, rather than identifying comparable data for each floor (as there may be no market for storage space at basement level or for retail units located on upper floors).

Beyond the simplification introduced by this book, it is important to use uniform measurement and weighting standards for the surface areas of the subject property and Comparable Properties in order to minimise the margin of technical error inherent in the valuation report.

MARKET ANALYSIS

The market analysis described in Chapter 3, begins with a macroeconomic overview and then focuses on the real estate market, both in terms of type and geography. The macroeconomic analysis is important, as it allows for the understanding of the overall current and prospective economic fundamentals, especially when the Discounted Cash Flow Approach (DCFA) is applied and the choice of some economic variables is necessary (such as the inflation rate, the Market Rental growth rate and the risk-free rate). It also serves to gain a better understanding of the supply and demand for Comparables based on economic trends.

The real estate market analysis must provide all the information needed to support the data used in the valuation, including, for example, the appetite of investors for the specific asset class in the subject macro- and micro-location, sale prices and yields impacting capital values, rental levels, vacancy rates, take-up, existing supply, and expected pipeline of comparable space.

The findings of the market analysis, combined with the specific features of the property, can finally be summarised in a SWOT Analysis, which allows the strengths and weaknesses of the property to be highlighted, as well as the opportunities and threats compared with other properties on sale or for rent.

VALUATION

The value estimation is the core of the valuation process, involving the selection and application of the valuation method deemed most appropriate considering the value base definition, the type of property and the data available. In particular, while applying the valuation method is often little more than a simple numerical exercise (even the most complex valuations with the DCFA are reduced to a relatively small number of lines on a computer spreadsheet), the choice of the method itself, which must be appropriately justified, is fundamental because it depends on the structure of the valuation itself and the choice of the most suitable market parameters to be used.

When applying the method, therefore, one has to justify the choice of each parameter used with references, as accurate as possible, to the market analysis.

Finally, it is essential to carry out a verification of the result obtained, at least to be sure that no mistakes have been made in applying the chosen method or, more simply, in performing the calculations. The verification can easily be carried out by converting the result into a comparable unit. One example might be a nursing home, which has been correctly valued using the DCFA, for which determining the Market Value per bed may be a useful element of comparison with other nursing homes. Or, a single office unit, correctly assessed using the Direct Comparison Approach, for which the implicit return, calculated as the ratio between the existing rent and the estimated Market Value, allows it to be compared to the market yield of other units leased and recently sold. Or again, in the case of a Buildable Area, correctly assessed using the Residual Value Methods, for which the unit value of $€/m^2$ calculated on the buildable surface area allows it to be compared to other areas recently sold or for sale with similar uses and in the same location.

It is important to note, however, that in some cases there is only one correct method to value a property, so taking the average between two or more different methods could worsen the reliability of the estimate.[10] Furthermore, at least for verification purposes, the actual comparability of assets should be considered. For example, having determined the value of a hotel, then determining the value per room, although it represents a useful metric in itself, does not necessarily make it more easily comparable with other properties recently sold, the dimensions of which could differ significantly, with different economic efficiency.

CONCLUSIONS

Briefly, this part goes over what has been previously reported and then states the value of the property, followed by the date and place of signing, as well as by the signature and any stamps of the valuer. Often the Conclusion can also make a comparison with the previous valuation carried out,[11] highlighting the main reasons that led to a change in value in the period between the two appraisals. In this case, it is very important to specify if there were any changes in the reference perimeter of the valuation, as for example in the case of a Development Project in which some of the units included in the previous valuation have been sold.

APPENDICES

At the end of the valuation report are the Appendices, containing everything which, due to its size or lesser importance, has not already been stated in the body of the text, or any documents produced by third parties (annexes) and referred to in the main body of the valuation report. The appendices often include:

- The details and terms of engagement (possibly attaching the assignment contract itself)[12]
- Maps for the purpose of identifying the geographical location
- Photographs shot during the site visit
- Floor plans of the property
- Land registry documentation (Land registry search reports and maps)
- Town planning documentation
- Details of Comparable Properties used
- Development of the valuation, particularly where it has been carried out using the DCFA.

NOTES

1. RICS (2017); TEGoVA (2016).
2. The terms of engagement, according to RICS (2017) can be listed as follows:
   (a) Identification and status of the valuer
   (b) Identification of the client and any other intended users
   (c) Purpose of the valuation
   (d) Identification of the asset(s) or liability(ies) valued
   (e) Basis(es) of value adopted
   (f) Valuation date
   (g) Extent of investigation
   (h) Nature and source(s) of the information relied upon
   (i) Assumptions and special assumptions
   (j) Restrictions on use, distribution and publication of the report
   (k) Confirmation that the valuation has been undertaken in accordance with the IVS
   (l) Valuation approach and reasoning
   (m) Amount of the valuation or valuations
   (n) Date of the valuation report
   (o) Commentary on any material uncertainty in relation to the valuation where it is essential to ensure clarity on the part of the valuation user
   (p) A statement setting out any limitations on liability that have been agreed.
3. For an explanation of the importance of a property's location, see Chapter 2, Section 'Characteristics of Property Investments', Subsection 'Location', and Chapter 2, Section 'Common Risk Elements in Real Estate Market', Subsection 'Location'.
4. In this respect it is worth noting the high level of detail provided by sites such as Google Maps, Google Earth, Google Street View, and Bing Maps, which allow images of the relevant Property to be obtained, sometimes even three-dimensional.
5. For a more in-depth look at the subject of green buildings, see Morri and Soffietti (2013) and Fedrizzi et al. (2014).
6. The BREEAM – *Building Research Establishment Environmental Assessment Method* (www.breeam .com) is a British voluntary building sustainability assessment method for master planning projects,

infrastructure and buildings. Applied in over 70 countries, it is the most widely used building sustainability certification system in the world.

7. The LEED – *Leadership in Energy and Environmental Design* (www.usgbc.org/cert-guide) is a US voluntary building certification system and is applied in over 140 countries worldwide. Developed by the U.S. Green Building Council (USGBC), it states the requirements to create environmentally sustainable buildings, in terms of energy and consumption of all the environmental resources involved in the construction process.

8. Professional services firm that specialises in real estate and investment management, as reported by ipmsc.org.

9. Also called 'Net Leasable Area'.

10. Even if model averaging, in order to account for model uncertainty, is a well-established procedure in the forecasting literature, in some cases, when the difference is too wide, reliance on the model based on the most reliable data may be suggested. See also Chapter 4, Section 'Choice of Valuation Method'.

11. This is common practice among entities which, by law, are required to value their Properties periodically, like real estate investment funds or REITs.

12. In this case the assignment contract does not state the valuation fees. This is agreed in a separate document to prevent the information being disseminated, since often the Valuation Report is forwarded to third parties as banks or advisors of the owner.

CHAPTER 9

Office Property Appraisal

The following case study is related to the valuation of a partially leased office property located in Milan, Italy. Even if nameless, it is based on realistic data with the main goal of describing a full application of the Discounted Cash Flow Approach as presented in Chapter 6 and Chapter 7. It is focused on the determination of key elements such as the time horizon, the intermediate cash flows, the Terminal Value, and the discount rate. Although this case study presents all the major elements of a valuation report, various sections have been simplified and some minor parts are omitted.

DESCRIPTION OF THE PROPERTY[1]

The asset being valued is an office property located close to the centre of Milan, Italy, completed approximately ten years before the valuation date. The property is part of a larger plan to regenerate a former industrial area which included the development of other office properties, as well as hundreds of residential units and a shopping centre. Due to the availability of public and private services, several overground public transport routes and good availability of car parks in the surrounding area, the location is excellent for office use. The railway station is about 1.5 km away and the junction for the motorway and the external ring road are about 5 km away.

The Building has a supporting structure of reinforced concrete and continuous glass façades. It consists of a basement, which houses archives, storerooms and a car park, and five identical open-plan floors above ground. The stairwell and lifts, which are accessed via the reception on the ground floor, are situated at the centre of the Building. Utilities are distributed to the floors via cable ducts and the power supply system is structured in such a way as to allow each floor to manage its own separate system. The boilers, air conditioning and cooling systems are installed on the roof. The fire-fighting system consists of hoses, fire extinguishers and smoke detectors.

The dimensions of the individual rental units are shown in Table 9.1. Surface weightings have been applied to the Net Leasable Area, already divided by tenant, in order to determine the Weighted Lettable Area[2] for valuation purposes (see A Closer Look 8.1).

Each floor of the Building is an independent unit leased to different tenants, with lease agreements that differ in terms of timescale and rental amount. As of the valuation date, two floors (the second and fourth) are entirely vacant, as summarised in the rent roll shown in Table 9.2.

Three of the four existing lease agreements are in the second six-year contractual period[3] and it has therefore been assumed that they will remain in force until expiry. Particular attention

TABLE 9.1   Net Lettable Areas and calculation of the Weighted Lettable Area

Tenant / Destination of use	Offices (m²)	Storage rooms / Archives (m²)	Uncovered parking spaces (m²)	Covered parking spaces (m²)	Weighted Lettable Area (m²)
Weighting factor	*100%*	*50%*	*10%*	*25%*	
Tenant "A"	2,750	350	300	400	3,055
Tenant "B"	1,500	250	250	250	1,713
Tenant "C"	1,500	200	300	200	1,680
Tenant "D"	3,000	250	350	300	3,235
Vacancy	6,000	450	400	350	6,353
Total Net Lettable Area (m²)	14,750	1,500	1,600	1,500	**19,350**
Total Weighted Lettable Area (m²)	14,750	750	160	375	**16,035**

TABLE 9.2   Rent roll

Tenant	Floor	Weighted Lettable Area (m²)	Passing rent	Passing rent (€/m²/year)	Indexation	Overall length	Residual length
vacancy	B	*353*					
Tenant "A"	G / B	3,055	€ 572,836	€ 187.5	75% CPI	6 years + 6 years	3.5 years (2nd six-year period)
Tenant "B"	1 / B	1,713	€ 309,549	€ 180.8	75% CPI	6 years + 6 years	5.5 years (2nd six-year period)
Tenant "C"	1 / B	1,680	€ 341,503	€ 203.3	75% CPI	6 years + 6 years	1.5 years + 6 years
vacancy	2	*3,000*					
Tenant "D"	3 / B	3,235	€ 591,443	€ 182.8	75% CPI	6 years + 6 years	4 years (2nd six-year period)
vacancy	4	*3,000*					
Total		**16,035**	**€ 1,815,331**				

will however need to be paid to the agreement with tenant 'C', whose existing rent (passing rent) is higher than the rent paid by the other tenants. If the rent is significantly higher even than the ERV, it is highly likely that the tenant will decide to vacate the property at the expiry of the first period. In this case, unless there are particular reasons for this not to take place, such as strategic reasons or the high direct and indirect costs of a transfer, it will be appropriate to consider this likelihood by adjusting the rent to the Market Rent (ERV) level for this unit for the following years. Obviously, the same consideration must be made not only when there are legal contractual expiry dates, but also in the case of contractual break-options, as shown in A Closer Look 6.1.

CHOICE OF VALUATION METHOD

The subject property comes within the category of Flexible Commercial Properties, which are usually hard to compare regarding physical characteristics, while often presenting a sort of separation between Owners and Users. With these properties, it is relatively easy to gather information regarding income (passing rents in the lease agreements and ERV as future or potential rent in the Space Market) and market expected return (yields based on trading values in the Investment Market for properties with the same risk) rather than to search for the sale price of assets that are not easily comparable. The best options for valuation purposes are therefore represented by Income Capitalisation Methods.

As seen in Chapter 6, Section 'Approach and Application Criteria', where the choice is between applying the Direct Capitalisation Approach and the Discounted Cash Flow Approach, it is important to check three elements: whether the property is fully leased, whether the rents are in line with the ERV, and whether the Building needs any CapEx to be refurbished and upgraded.

As for the subject property, considering that around 40% of the space is vacant and that, therefore, the time and cost involved in re-leasing this space have to be considered, the Discounted Cash Flow Approach is deemed to be the best way of estimating its Market Value.[4]

MARKET ANALYSIS

An analysis of the trend of real estate market at national level, which is not shown here, is conducive to a more specific analysis of the local property market, with a specific focus on the office segment.

On the Investors' side, market evidence suggests that, while prime locations for class A properties leased to primary tenants continue to be favoured, because of lack of supply of assets with these characteristics, Investors seeking higher returns are also investing in secondary locations with excellent road and public transport connections and leased to good, creditworthy tenants. On the tenants' side, however, the space market remains relatively buoyant, with good demand for leasing spaces, provided that they are energy efficient buildings with low operating expenses, even if the demand is not so strong as in the previous years. Moreover, there is some expectation of an increase of time required to lease units.

In addition to analysing the indirect data sources, which contain aggregate information, a survey was conducted via a number of real estate brokers in order to determine the ERV and the market yield to estimate the cap rate for the subject property. In particular, a number of transactions relating to recent leases of real estate units with similar characteristics in the same area (Table 9.3) and transactions of comparable properties were analysed (Table 9.4).

The data gathered show that the ERV is approximately € 185/m² which is consistent with the range of values shown by secondary sources.

The average gross yield value is around 7%, based on gross rent definition. The net yield could not be determined because the cost structure of the comparable transactions was

TABLE 9.3　Determining the ERV by comparison

Comparable Properties	Weighted Lettable Area (m²)	Passing rent (€/year)	Passing rent (€/m²/year)
1	3,425	€ 602,800	€ 176
2	2,630	€ 504,960	€ 192
3	2,890	€ 514,420	€ 178
4	2,570	€ 485,730	€ 189
5	2,240	€ 409,920	€ 183
6	2,940	€ 570,360	€ 194

TABLE 9.4　Determining the cap rate by comparison

Comparable Properties	Weighted Lettable Area (m²)	Gross Rent (€/year)	Sale price	Gross Yield
1	13,480	€ 2,320,000	€ 32,910,000	7.05%
2	18,350	€ 3,560,000	€ 51,450,000	6.92%
3	17,620	€ 3,220,000	€ 46,130,000	6.98%
4	14,890	€ 2,740,000	€ 38,560,000	7.11%

unknown and so it was not possible to estimate their Net Operating Income (NOI). Based on the yield extracted from the market, a decision is made to use a base cap rate of 7%.[5]

VALUATION

Discounting the intermediate cash flows (mainly based on net rental income) and calculating the Terminal Value (final cash flow), which is the expected income from the theoretical sale of the property at the end of the valuation time horizon, are the fundamental elements of a Discounted Cash Flow Approach valuation. In the following sections the main assumptions made for both components are reported.

Choosing the Time Horizon

As shown in Chapter 6, Subsection 'Choosing the Time Horizon', the ideal time horizon is the minimum one beyond which the cash flows stabilise. In this case 6.5 years is considered the most appropriate time horizon; in fact, given that the passing rent of tenants 'B' and 'D' is in line with the ERV and the rent of tenant 'C' will presumably be renegotiated to reflect the Market Rent at the end of the first six-year period (break option), the minimum time required to obtain stabilised cash flows (assuming that vacant spaces are leased in the meantime) is equal to the residual duration of the longest existing contract (the one relating to tenant 'B'), which is 5.5 years, plus the time (estimated in one year[6]) required to refurbish and re-lease this unit once it has been vacated.

For simplicity, a six-month period frequency has been used as a unit of time in modelling the cash flows. A quarter frequency would have not significantly improved the precision of the appraisal.

Estimating the Cash Flows

Determining the Income   The main economic benefit generated by the property is the rental income.[7] In order to estimate this value, reference must be made to existing lease agreements for which the amount and residual duration are known, and predictions must be made for the vacant property units based on the ERV. The existing lease agreements must be carefully analysed to check whether there are any clauses which allow tenants to withdraw early (i.e. contractual or legal break-options). For the vacant units, the valuer has to estimate the time needed to find a tenant and the rental level (ERV) determined by the market analysis shown in the Section 'Market Analysis'.

The actual rents are indexed at 75% of the inflation index, as required by the respective lease agreements.[8] Consequently, the assumptions made about future inflation rate are important.

A CLOSER LOOK 9.1: CHOOSING THE GROWTH RATE FOR THE CASH FLOWS

One of the most important factors in estimating the value of a property is undoubtedly the growth rate of its cash flows. The decision often taken in practice is to have the income and costs to grow at the same inflation rate, which is usually estimated based on the projections made by a number of institutional sources,[9] by some of the main economic study centres, or by some financial institutions or international consultancy firms over a period of 2–3 years, subsequently using the target growth rates for the medium to long term, such as the Euro Area inflation targeting rate.

While this approach is based on the previous predictions which the valuer may or may not decide to agree, several other points need to be made.

- For rented units, indexing of the rents at the inflation rate is a provision of their lease agreements, and it is therefore correct to predict that rents will grow in line with the expected inflation.
- ERV, however, may perform differently to inflation, based on expectations in the Space Market (supply of new properties arriving on the market and level of demand from Users). During periods of economic crisis, linking ERV growth to the inflation rate may lead to an overvaluation of the asset: one example of this is the period that followed the 2008 global financial crisis, when in many countries, even with positive inflation rates, rents fell significantly in all real estate market segments. Some valuers, therefore, assume that ERV will not grow at all in the initial periods of the plan and will then align themselves with inflation in the medium to long term. Another possibility might be to link the ERV growth estimates to those of the Gross Domestic Product, which is a better reflection of the national economic growth rate and, consequently, the potential demand for Space by Users.
- Regardless of which method is chosen, the valuer must remain consistent in the assumptions used. The choice of an inflation rate can and must be updated every

(Continued)

time new estimates are issued by the economic or institutional source used as a reference. However, on the same valuation date, the same estimated parameter must be used for all the properties being valued, even if they are not included in the same portfolio under valuation. In contrast to inflation, which affects contractual rent and costs, properties may have different rental growth rate if they are located in areas with different Space Market dynamics, or in case of different typologies.

- Particular attention must also be paid to Development Projects, particularly those that involve the sale of separate residential units, the value of which is strongly linked to the income expected from the sale. One has to assess carefully whether it is reasonable to assume that prices will grow in line with inflation, even over short periods of time, or if it is better to use estimation of future selling prices. In other words, a valuer may either estimate the expected sale price at the time of valuation, as if the units where already available for the sale, and then project these values in the future at the date of the forecasted sale using some growth rate or, perhaps theoretically more correct, the valuer may directly estimate the expected future selling prices at the time of sales.

- Subject to any different and adequately justified assumptions (such as a turnkey contract at a pre-established cost), it is reasonable to assume that operating costs and CapEx will grow consistently with the assumptions made about inflation.

In some cases, in addition to rents, other potential sources of income may be considered, such as billboards or telecommunication masts. This income is often based on agreements that are different from the main leases, in terms of form and duration, which must be correctly transposed into the valuation. They have to be considered the same as rent, with the major difference that the amount does not depend on the Space Market and that the contract may have different terms from those of a typical lease agreement.

Vacancy and Credit Loss Revenues do not take into account any partially or completely vacant units. A rectification is therefore made based on assumptions about how long some units may continue not to generate income during the time horizon or, possibly, what portion of this income will not be received owing to a dispute or the insolvency of the tenant.

For currently leased units, no vacancy rate is assumed during the term of the lease agreement, assuming therefore that none of the tenants will vacate the property before their lease agreement expires (there being no break-options). For the two currently vacant units it is assumed that they can be leased within 12 months. The choice of this seemingly long time period is based on the market analysis and it is due to a weak demand for space lease.

Based on the analyses carried out, all the tenants currently present a solid credit position, so it is assumed that they will not default before the expiry date. Similarly, for new lease agreements, no credit loss has been explicitly quantified, but the corresponding risk has been taken into account in estimating the discount rate.

A CLOSER LOOK 9.2: VACANCY AND CREDIT LOSS

There are three ways to take vacancy and credit losses into consideration, thus avoiding the risk of double counting, i.e. overestimating, by considering them multiple times within the same valuation.

1. Determining them accurately, where there is sufficient information for this purpose. For example, if it is known that a unit is going to be vacated by a tenant who has notified its withdrawal from the agreement, or when it is known that a loss will be made following the negative outcome of an existing dispute, the loss of income or the respective cost can be accurately posted to reducing the income for the respective period.

2. Considering percentage reductions in the Gross Income, even if based on historical data recorded by the property or on market benchmarks. Care must be taken when making these choices; while considering an average vacancy percentage of 5% to valuing a shopping centre or a multi-tenant property can be a plausible choice, considering the physiological rotation of tenants, the same assumption is meaningless in the case of a single-tenant property, in which the only two potential scenarios are that the property is fully leased (zero vacancy rate) or completely vacant (100% vacancy rate). Even if it is not correct, in practice, some valuers tend to apply an average fixed vacancy rate regardless of the property (i.e. mono or multi-tenant) and the market cycle phase (i.e. increase or decrease in space demand).

3. Considering the potential reduction in income due to vacancy or credit losses directly in estimating the discount rate, within the rental risk component, by increasing it. Even if theoretically acceptable, this solution increases the subjectivity of the discount rate estimation.

Determining Operating Expenses

A CLOSER LOOK 9.3: OPERATING EXPENSES BORNE BY THE OWNER

Even if operating expenses should be expression of the market, being the charges that the property should face regardless of the actual owner, in practice their estimation is sometimes based on the actual amount. In fact, one of the main decisions the valuer has to make when determining operating expenses is whether to use the existing data, which are normally supplied by the property Owner or asset/property manager, or make estimates based on market parameters. Some valuers assume the current values,

(Continued)

but particular attention must be paid when the entities providing property services to the subject property belongs to the Owner or manager, since the fees charged may not represent market prices; in these situations, it is preferable to use average market parameters or benchmarks.

Among the most common operating expenses, the following must be considered:

- Property taxes for the subject property are usually known. When they are unknown, as the case of a building not completed yet, they have to be estimated based on the rules applied. In some countries they can be estimated on the basis of some technical parameters, derived from Land registry information and municipal regulations.

- Insurance costs are calculated based on the Reconstruction Cost of the Building and do not, therefore, depend on the Market Value or profitability of the asset. If the business interruption clause is included, also the fee is influenced by the rent.

- Stamp duty taxes on rents or other charges, in those countries where they are due, should be considered.

- Extraordinary maintenance costs are usually borne by the Owner (unless otherwise agreed contractually, such as in triple net lease agreements[10]). As the figure being sought is the cash flow and not an accounting quantity, it is important to define correctly the time period in which the actual disbursements will take place. However, as described in Chapter 6, Subsection 'Profit and Loss Account of an Income-producing Property', it is not always possible to determine the timing and amounts very precisely; often an amount based on a percentage is attributed to each individual period. This amount, estimated as a reserve, should be an actual cash flow, so a fixed estimation is spread out over time to simplify. Due to the limited impact on the Market Value, this simplification is commonly accepted in practice.

- Ordinary Building management expenses, unless otherwise specified, are borne by the tenant; for estimation purposes, only the expenses borne by the Owner within the time horizon, such as the administrative costs (property management), often estimated as a percentage of income (or more often of the gross or net rental amount), should be considered. Other costs may be partly or entirely borne by the Owner, including some facility management and utility costs, estimated in absolute values (possibly indexed to inflation over time) or as a percentage of income. The allocation of the Building management expenses between the Owner and the tenant may differ in various markets, both countries and property sectors; as a general valuation principle, all the expenses actually paid by the Owner should be considered for valuation purposes.

In the present case study, Italian law[11] stipulates that property taxes, insurance and extraordinary maintenance expenses are borne by the Owner, so they have been considered as operating expenses and the following assumptions have been made.

- Property taxes: the actual amount currently paid, and appropriately indexed to inflation, has been used.[12] Even if property taxes are not inflation linked, the assumption is based on the possibility of a nominal variation in the future to keep the same real value. In any case, the impact of this assumption is quite limited.
- Insurance costs: the actual amount currently paid, appropriately indexed to inflation, has been used as it is considered to reflect current insurance premiums on the market.
- Stamp duty tax on rent: this has been estimated at 0.50% of the actual rents according to the fiscal rules.
- Extraordinary maintenance costs: considering the maintenance conditions of the property, an annual amount corresponding to the 0.50% of the Reconstruction Cost of the Building has been estimated based on a cost of construction of € 1.100/m^2 indexed to inflation.
- Property and facility management expenses: these fees due by the Owner are estimated to be 2.00% of the actual rents. This amount does not represent the fees paid by the current Owner, but it is estimated as market benchmark.

Determining the Investments During the first six months of the time horizon, capital expenditures for € 300,000 are estimated for compulsory adaptation works required by Fire Prevention Certificate regulations.

Furthermore, investments for TIs are required to restore the Building every time the tenants change to carry out the customisation they need. For the subject property, these are quantified at € 50/m^2 (indexed to inflation).

Finally, a leasing fee is payable to real estate brokers every time a unit is leased. This is estimated to be 10% of the first-year headline rent as market benchmark.

Determining the Terminal Value

A Terminal Value has been determined by applying the Direct Capitalisation Approach to the income subsequent to the last period (time N+1); in particular, the Effective Gross Income (EGI) has been chosen, which makes it easier to extract a market cap rate from market gross yields.

In fact, even if the subject property cost structure is well known, the valuer has no information about the cost structure of Comparables. So, even if the EGI level is not the most precise income definition, in this case, due to the information constraints on Comparables, it represents the most effective solution. As alternative, a market benchmark amount of operating expenses (e.g. 75 bps) may be used to estimate a net cap rate to apply to the NOI, starting from a gross cap rate based on the EGI extracted from market Comparables.

The cap rate (going-out cap rate) has been estimated by adding a spread (+50 bps to the initial market rate (going-in cap rate), estimated as 7% as previously determined by the market analysis. Since in this case it is unlikely to assume a new use for the property on expiry of the lease agreement, it is deemed prudent to use a going-out cap rate that does not include a potential increase in value due to a change in the HBU. The positive spread considers a future loss of value of the property due to the obsolescence of the Building.

This theoretical value represents the gross Market Value expected at the end of the valuation time horizon. Transaction and brokerage costs (estimated to be 0.5% of the estimated sale price, as a result of the survey done among real estate brokers) need to be deducted from this amount.

Determining the Discount Rate

The discount rate is the hardest element to determine in the Discounted Cash Flow Approach as no Comparables exist in the property market. In general, the discount rate represents the Internal Rate of Return (IRR) expected by market participants to invest in the subject property. Consequently, assumptions regarding the total return currently expected by market investors for an asset as the subject property at the valuation date has to be estimated.

In this specific case, among the various methods for determining the discount rate, as shown in Chapter 7, Section 'How to Estimate Property Return Taxes', the valuer has chosen the Build-Up Approach, which allows the discount rate to be defined based on the specific risk components, determined as follows.

- *Financial structure*. For the subject property, the financial structure commonly used by market participants at the valuation date is the following:

$$\text{Debt (D\%)} = 60\%$$

$$\text{Equity (E\%)} = 40\%$$

The estimated financial structure represents the assumption made by the valuer on the amount of Debt that banks would grant to finance the acquisition of the subject property.

- *Cost of debt*. This can be subdivided into two components:
  - *Risk-free rate*, estimated to be equal to the six-month average of five-year EURIRS values, publicly available data.
  - *Bank spread*, estimated by conducting a survey of some banks.
    As of the valuation date, the cost of debt was quantified as follows:

$$K_d = \text{base rate} + \text{spread} = six\text{-month average of 5-year IRS rate}$$

$$+ \text{average spread surveyed on the market} = 0.33\% + 3.50\% = 3.83\%$$

The estimated K_d represents the assumption made by the valuer on the market cost of Debt that banks would apply to finance the acquisition of the subject property at the valuation date.

- *Cost of equity*. For the purpose of estimating the cost of the equity, the following return components required for the various risk factors listed below have been added together.[13] As for debt, there is again the risk-free component and a return component of the specific risk premiums:
  - *Risk-free rate*: the total return on the 5-year BTP[14] (based on the average returns for the previous six months) was used. The bond maturity is consistent with the valuation time horizon.
  - *Risk premium*: the following factors were identified and added, using as basis an ideal property with minimum level of risk.
    1. *Property sector risk*: represents the minimum level of risk required for real estate investments that do not involve other incremental risk factors specific to the property.

In other words, the hypothetical return to having an exposure to real estate investment in a property with the minimum risk (i.e. best location, tenant, and high quality
Building). As of the valuation date, this was estimated at 600 bps.
2. *Location risk*: this is the risk of the Use of Space demand in the specific market in
which the property is located, related to the local economy. For the subject Property,
this was estimated at 150 bps and was based on the market analysis.
3. *Intended use and typology risk*: this is the risk of a lack of Space Use demand for
a specific purpose, owing to the nature of the property as opposed to the potential
Users. For the subject property, this was estimated at 150 bps.
4. *Physical and technical features risk*: this is the risk associated, in a broader sense,
with the quality of the Space, and therefore of the Building. This is inversely linked
to the ease of finding a User. For the subject property, this was estimated at 100 bps.
5. *Rental/contractual risk*: this is the risk of vacancy or credit loss by tenants and is,
therefore, the risk associated with the actual lease agreements and tenants. For the
subject property, this was estimated at 200 bps.
   As of the valuation date, the cost of equity was quantified as follows:

$$K_e = \text{base rate} + \text{risk premium} = \text{5-year BTP rate} + \Sigma \text{ specific risk factors}$$

$$= 1.80\% + (6.00\% + 1.50\% + 1.50\% + 1.00\% + 2.00\%) = 13.80\%$$

The estimated K_e represents the assumption made by the valuer on the levered equity IRR
expected by market investors to invest in the subject property.

After having determined the financial structure, the cost of debt (K_d) and cost of equity
(K_e), the discount rate (WACC) can be determined as follows:

$$\text{WACC(K)} = Kd * D\% + Ke * E\% = 3.83\% * 60\% + 13.80\% * 40\% = 7.82\%$$

The estimated WACC will be used to discount all the intermediate cash flows as well as
the Terminal Value.

Finally, in discounting the cash flows, it was assumed that the rents and costs were received
and incurred respectively halfway through the six-month period, with the exception of the
cash flow derived from the sale of the Property, for which the beginning of the period was
considered.

Calculating the Market Value of the Property

Only for a better representation of the valuation process, the model provides for two different
cash flows: Intermediate cash flows, relating to the whole rental period (operational component), and a Terminal Value (divestment component). Discounting of the two cash flows
separately leads to a breakdown of the total value of the property.

The Discounted Cash Flow Approach model, which summarises the assumptions made
in the previous paragraphs, is shown in Table 9.5.

The Market Value of the subject property at the valuation date is € 39,020,000.

TABLE 9.5 Calculating the Market Value of the subject property

	semester	1	2	3	4	5	6	7	8	9	10	11	12	13	14
Rents															
Tenant "A"		€286,418	€286,418	€289,640	€289,640	€292,681	€292,681	€297,072	€297,072	€302,592	€302,592	€307,131	€307,131	€311,738	€311,738
Tenant "B"		€154,775	€154,775	€156,516	€156,516	€158,159	€158,159	€160,532	€160,532	€162,939	€162,939	€165,384	€165,384	€176,472	€176,472
Tenant "C"		€170,752	€170,752	€172,672	€158,831	€158,831	€160,856	€160,856	€163,269	€163,269	€165,718	€165,718	€168,204	€168,204	€170,727
Tenant "D"		€295,721	€295,721	€299,048	€299,048	€302,188	€302,188	€306,721	€306,721	€311,322	€323,609	€323,609	€328,463	€328,463	€333,390
Vacant space (1)		€0	€295,998	€295,998	€299,217	€299,217	€303,032	€303,032	€307,577	€307,577	€312,191	€312,191	€316,874	€316,874	€321,627
Vacant space (2)		€0	€0	€298,210	€298,210	€301,341	€301,341	€305,861	€305,861	€310,449	€310,449	€315,106	€315,106	€319,833	€319,833
Potential Gross Income		€907,665	€1,203,664	€1,512,085	€1,501,463	€1,512,419	€1,518,258	€1,534,073	€1,541,032	€1,558,149	€1,577,498	€1,589,138	€1,601,161	€1,621,583	€1,633,786
Effective vacancy		€0	€0	€0	€0	€0	€0	€0	€297,072	€311,322	€0	€0	€165,384	€0	€0
Effective Gross Income		€907,665	€1,203,664	€1,512,085	€1,501,463	€1,512,419	€1,518,258	€1,534,073	€1,243,960	€1,246,827	€1,577,498	€1,589,138	€1,435,777	€1,621,583	€1,633,786
Operating costs															
Property taxes	140,000 €/year	€70,000	€70,000	€71,050	€71,050	€72,045	€72,045	€73,486	€73,486	€74,955	€74,955	€76,454	€76,454	€77,984	
Property insurance	27,500 €/year	€13,750	€13,750	€13,956	€13,956	€14,152	€14,152	€14,435	€14,435	€14,723	€14,723	€15,018	€15,018	€15,318	
Stamp duty	0.50% % on rents	€4,538	€6,018	€7,560	€7,507	€7,562	€7,591	€7,670	€6,220	€6,234	€7,887	€7,946	€7,179	€8,108	
Extraordinary maintenance	0.50% % on reconstruction cost	€44,096	€44,426	€44,758	€45,070	€45,384	€45,836	€46,292	€46,753	€47,218	€47,688	€48,162	€48,641	€49,125	
Property & Facility Management	2.00% % on rents	€18,153	€24,073	€30,242	€30,029	€30,248	€30,365	€30,681	€24,879	€24,937	€31,550	€31,783	€28,716	€32,432	
Total Operating costs		€150,538	€158,267	€167,566	€167,613	€169,391	€169,989	€172,564	€165,772	€168,067	€176,804	€179,363	€176,008	€182,967	
Net Operating Income		€757,127	€1,045,396	€1,344,519	€1,333,850	€1,343,028	€1,348,269	€1,361,509	€1,078,188	€1,078,760	€1,400,695	€1,409,775	€1,259,769	€1,438,617	

	semester	1	2	3	4	5	6	7	8	9	10	11	12	13	14
Investments															
Capex	€ 300,000 *una tantum*	€ 300,000	€ 0	€ 0	€ 0	€ 0	€ 0	€ 0	€ 0	€ 0	€ 0	€ 0	€ 0	€ 0	€ 0
Tenant Improvements	50 *€/m²*	€ 158,813	€ 159,999	€ 0	€ 0	€ 0	€ 0	€ 0	€ 161,952	€ 173,200	€ 0	€ 0	€ 94,451	€ 0	€ 0
Leasing fees	10% *% headline rent*	€ 0	€ 59,200	€ 59,642	€ 0	€ 0	€ 0	€ 0	€ 0	€ 60,518	€ 64,722	€ 0	€ 0	€ 35,294	€ 0
Total Investments		€ 458,813	€ 219,199	€ 59,642	€ 0	€ 0	€ 0	€ 0	€ 161,952	€ 233,719	€ 64,722	€ 0	€ 94,451	€ 35,294	
Intermediate Cash Flows		€ 298,315	€ 826,198	€ 1,284,877	€ 1,333,850	€ 1,343,028	€ 1,348,269	€ 1,361,509	€ 916,236	€ 845,041	€ 1,335,973	€ 1,409,775	€ 1,165,318	€ 1,403,322	
Terminal Value															
Exit value (on GOCR)	7.25% *GOCR*	€ 0	€ 0	€ 0	€ 0	€ 0	€ 0	€ 0	€ 0	€ 0	€ 0	€ 0	€ 0	€ 0	€ 45,069,970
Brokerage fees	0.50% *% Terminal Value*	€ 0	€ 0	€ 0	€ 0	€ 0	€ 0	€ 0	€ 0	€ 0	€ 0	€ 0	€ 0	€ 0	€ 225,350
Final Cash Flow		€ 0	€ 0	€ 0	€ 0	€ 0	€ 0	€ 0	€ 0	€ 0	€ 0	€ 0	€ 0	€ 0	€ 44,844,620
Total Cash Flows to be discounted		€ 298,315	€ 826,198	€ 1,284,877	€ 1,333,850	€ 1,343,028	€ 1,348,269	€ 1,361,509	€ 916,236	€ 845,041	€ 1,335,973	€ 1,409,775	€ 1,165,318	€ 1,403,322	€ 44,844,620
Time factor		0.25	0.75	1.25	1.75	2.25	2.75	3.25	3.75	4.25	4.75	5.25	5.75	6.25	6.5
Discount factor	7.82%	0.9814	0.9451	0.9102	0.8766	0.8442	0.8130	0.7830	0.7541	0.7262	0.6994	0.6736	0.6487	0.6247	0.6131
Discounted Cash Flows		€ 292,754	€ 780,852	€ 1,169,506	€ 1,169,242	€ 1,133,806	€ 1,096,192	€ 1,066,073	€ 690,924	€ 613,701	€ 934,401	€ 949,602	€ 755,950	€ 876,722	€ 27,494,338
Sum of Discounted															
Intermediate Cash Flows	29.5% € 11,529,726														
Discounted Final Cash Flow	70.5% € 27,494,338														
Market Value	€ 39,024,063														
Market Value (rounded)	€ 39,020,000														

149

A CLOSER LOOK 9.4: APPLICATION OF THE DIRECT CAPITALISATION APPROACH

While the Discounted Cash Flow Approach was deemed to be the best model for valuing the subject property, given that it was partially vacant, the valuation carried out using the Direct Capitalisation Approach is also shown below. This requires only the estimation of two elements, the income and the cap rate. While the calculation algorithm is simple, however, it is hard to determine the quantities to use exactly as the financial result is very sensitive to these values.

There are two ways of determining the income: either using the potential Market Rent or the actual rent of the property, and there are different ways of calculating this. Choosing the NOI – considering the actual cost structure – is more accurate; however, as previously shown in the market analysis, in this case it is harder to find Comparables as the operating expenses of the properties traded in the market are unknown, so there is no access to the same data available for the subject property.

Considering the estimated ERV (€ 185/m^2/year), and that the average weighted passing rent (€ 187.5/m^2/year) is similar to the ERV, it is reasonable to estimate a Potential Gross Income of € 2,966,475 (i.e. € 185/m^2/year * 16,035 m^2).

The second phase is the cap rate estimation that must be based on the average market yield (estimated to be 7%, as previously described), but which, however, refers to properties that are completely leased at the time of sale. The subject Property, however, presents a high vacancy rate, although the good conditions of the Building and the market conditions suggest that this situation will be temporary (12 months).

If the Build-Up Approach is applied, the changes needed to consider the risk differentials will need to be made, and, in particular, a vacancy risk premium, quantified at 0.50%,[15] resulting in an estimated cap rate (GICR) of 7.50%.

Finally, one has to consider the CapEx to be incurred for the Fire Prevention Certificate requirements (amounting to € 300,000) and the TIs for adapting the currently vacant spaces (amounting to € 317,625).

$$\text{Estimated Market Value} = \frac{Potential\ Gross\ Income}{\text{GICR}} - \text{CapEx} - \text{TIs}$$

$$= \frac{€\ 2,966,475}{7.50\%} - €\ 300,000 - (€\ 50/m^2 * 6,353\ m^2)$$

$$= €\ 39,553,000 - €\ 300,000 - €\ 317,625 \approx €\ 38,940,000$$

Overall, therefore, an estimated (rounded) Market Value of € 38,940,000 is obtained using the Direct Capitalisation Approach.

In the example shown here, the estimated value using the two methods is virtually identical. The reason is primarily that, despite the Property presenting two vacant floors out of five, the residual portion is leased at an average rent which is in line with the ERV. In such a case, the Discounted Cash Flow Approach is in any case preferable than the Direct Capitalisation Approach. The DCFA, indeed, allows the various assumptions on which the valuation is based to be explained; the latter is instead more sensitive to the choice of the cap rate (a variation of just a few basis points would have significantly changed the value of the Property) and income, as all the elements of the valuation can only affect these two parameters. The GICR in this case can only be estimated, since it is difficult to extract it directly from the market due to the current vacancy rate of the property.

NOTES

1. In a real appraisal report the description of the Property may be very detailed, both for location and Building characteristics.
2. It can be defined as the surface area resulting from the application of weighting factors, estimated by the valuer, to the various areas of the Net Lettable Area (such as archives, technical rooms or parking spaces), in order to obtain a single uniform piece of data for each use of the property.
3. In Italy, lease agreements related to Commercial Properties have a minimum legal duration of six years, after which the lease agreement is renewed automatically at the same terms for additional six years unless the tenant does not communicate its intention to vacate the property. At the end of the first six-year term, the Owner has the right of giving notice to the tenant to quit the property only in a limited number of circumstances.
4. See A Closer Look 9.4.
5. Please note that the yield estimation is not a mere average value of Comparable Properties, but it is based on the opinion of the valuer.
6. This period, quite long, reflects the current market situation with a weak demand of space and a good supply of similar properties.
7. Please refer to Chapter 6, Subsection 'Estimating the Cash Flows' for a detailed definition.
8. Different conditions may apply based on different contractual agreements and legal frameworks. See also Chapter 6, Subsection 'Profit and Loss Account of an Income-Producing Property'.
9. The most frequently used, according to the geographical area, are World Bank, International Monetary Fund, European Central Bank, European Commission, Bank of England, Federal Reserve, etc.
10. See also Chapter 2, Subsection 'Rental and Contractual Situation'.
11. The situation may be different in other countries.
12. Since the property is in Italy, the local estimation rules apply. These do not depend on income-generating capacity, but are determined by the fiscal rental revenue estimated in the Land registry ('*rendita catastale*'). Since this is periodically updated, an average increase over time consistent with inflation is an acceptable assumption.
13. A decision was made to estimate the cost of the levered equity directly. An unlevered equity cost could also be considered, recalculating it based on the financial structure, thus increasing it to consider the Financial Risk factor.
14. Italian government bonds known as '*Buoni del Tesoro Poliennali*'.
15. This element is very hard to quantify because there are no market data: the value would correspond to the difference required by the market participants to invest in a Property with similar characteristics, but with higher vacancy rate.

CHAPTER 10

High Street Retail Unit Appraisal

T he subject property is a high street retail unit located in a primary European capital city.[1] Based on the market analysis, the current use as a restaurant does not represent its Highest and Best Use. For valuation purposes, being a Trade-Related Property, as stated in Chapter 2, Subsection 'Trade-Related Commercial Property', it is also essential to perform a careful analysis of the economic sustainability of the rent for the envisaged User. The case also illustrates some of the peculiarities of high street retail units, with a focus on why they are so appealing for institutional investors and high net worth individuals (HNWI).

DESCRIPTION OF THE PROPERTY

The property, currently rented to a restaurant business (whose lease agreement is expiring in 24 months), is located on Alexandria Street, adjacent to one of the most prestigious worldwide luxury retail locations (Edward Street) in the centre of one of the main European cities. The property is facing Alexandria Street from the front side; the opposite side is facing a minor street, while lateral sides adjoin other properties.

The property is a low-rise building composed of 3 floors (underground, ground and mezzanine) for a total Weighted Lettable Area of 1,413 square metres (as shown in Table 10.1).

Surface layout is rather efficient for retail business, with approximately 50% of the total Weighted Lettable Area placed in the ground floor, suitable storage space and numerous shop windows, on average approximately one each $100\,m^2$ of Weighted Lettable Area (Table 10.2 shows some typical retail surface efficiency indicators).

As competitive factors with respect to other nearby units, the property has a mezzanine floor characterised by high ceilings and wide windows.[2] As a drawback, despite its relevant size, it can only be leased to a single tenant because a series of physical constraints do not allow a rational and economically efficient surface if split in more than one unit.

This case study has been written by **Fabio Cristanziani**.

Fabio Cristanziani is an investment manager with more than 10 years of experience in the financial services industry. He currently works at Generali Real Estate, where he has covered various roles within the capital market and investment management practice.

TABLE 10.1 Summary of Net Lettable Area and calculation of Weighted Lettable Area

Floor	Destination of use	Net Lettable Area (m²)	Weighting factors	Weighted Lettable Area (m²)	Weighted Lettable Area (% of total)	# shop windows
Mezzanine	Retail	489	60%	293	21%	6
Ground	Retail	673	100%	673	48%	8
Basement	Retail	750	50%	375	26%	-
Basement	Storage	240	30%	72	5%	-
	Total	**2,152**	**66%**	**1,413**	**100%**	**14**

TABLE 10.2 Retail surface efficiency indicators

Retail surface efficiency indicators	on Net Lettable Area	on Weighted Lettable Area
Ground surfaces on total surfaces	31%	48%
Storage on total surfaces	11%	5%
Surface per shop window [sq.m]	154	101

Maintenance conditions are substandard, with an ancient and old-fashioned façade and not properly maintained windows fixtures. The internal layout is structured to satisfy its current use as a restaurant, but it might be transformed to fulfil the requirements of a modern retail unit.

Accessibility and visibility are granted by the eight shop windows at the ground floor. At the valuation date, however, the current layout does not properly leverage the full potential of the shop windows at ground level: in fact, while one is used as restaurant entrance, the remaining seven are used as standard walls without enhancing restaurant visibility and appeal (in fact, the window fixtures are rusty and painted black).

CHOICE OF VALUATION METHOD

Due to its location, balanced surface distribution across ground and other floors and architectural features (eight visible shop windows on the ground and six on the mezzanine floor), the restaurant business does not represent the Highest and Best Use for the property.

Being a Trade-Related Property, as seen in the Chapter 4, Section 'Choice of Valuation Method', the most appropriate valuation method is deemed to be the Discounted Cash Flow Approach. This valuation approach takes into account the current humble maintenance status which requires the refurbishment of the property by creating appealing/visible façades and by creating efficient internal floor plans. Moreover, a Direct Comparison Approach is not suitable since the current use of the property is suboptimal. The property is indeed under-rented and it would be possible, at the expiry of the current lease agreement, to lease it out to a retailer operating in the medium-end luxury segment which has not been able to find a spot within the more prestigious streets close by.

A CLOSER LOOK 10.1: PROPERTY CLASS PECULIARITIES IMPACTING ON THE VALUATION OF PRIME WORLDWIDE HIGH STREET RETAIL PROPERTIES

Across the full spectrum of real estate asset classes, High Street Retail (HSR), particularly when referring to prime worldwide location, is typically characterised by a series of distinctive and unique features enhancing the complexity of its valuation.

To understand the complexity of HSR properties, it is useful to take a deep dive into the key dynamics of the underlying leasing market. High-end HSR[3] properties are typically occupied by a limited number of worldwide retailers operating in the luxury good industry and leveraging their flagship store both as:

- A 'pure' point of sale, as for any retail property
- A branding and marketing tool.

While the rent deriving from the 'pure' point of sale approach can be estimated, like any other retail property, by applying an effort rate, the branding and marketing advantage of placing a flagship store in a strategic location can be priceless to some types of tenants, and in any case quite hard to quantify.

For luxury firms, brand recognition is paramount to sustain the underlying business. They allocate part of their sizeable marketing cost to rent in prime worldwide shopping streets (such as New York's 5th Avenue, London's Bond Street, Milan's Quadrilatero, or Hong Kong's Causeway Bay). Because of that, differently from other properties (such as offices or logistic platforms), where the leasing cost is treated as a standard operational cost and the underlying Flexible Commercial Property is perceived as a 'commodity', for HSR the characteristics of the flagship store strongly influence the core business and companies recognise their prime and strategic value.

An HSR unit needs to be carefully analysed against a series of specific dimensions which affect its value more heavily than for any other property type and specifically:

- *City*: In order to have a consolidated luxury district, a city must be able to attract high spending capacity individuals with a comprehensive lifestyle offer and, of course, adequate infrastructure. For these reasons high-end HSR are located in main global cities (such as New York, Hong Kong and Tokyo) or in primary cities recognised as a fashion destination (such as Paris and Milan).
- *Micro-location*: HSR properties need to be placed in a well-defined/delimited street. Only a few exceptions exist for wider but well-defined adjacent areas (such as Paris's Golden Triangle, Milan's Quadrilatero and the recently established Design District in Miami). It is worth mentioning that immediately outside the street/area defined as prime, property rents and related values drop significantly because of the lack of branding value.
- *Visibility*: A flagship needs to be noted and walked in. Cornering shape, appealing architectural features, charming lighting are just a few of the physical features enhancing the property value especially in case it is leveraged as a flagship.

(Continued)

- *Shop windows and internal layout*: Although HSR properties have part of their value coming from branding purposes, the store operates also as point of sale for which the presence of wide and highly visible shop windows act as a sales accelerator as well as a good layout of the internal surface improves storage efficiency and client shop experience.

Due to intrinsic asset class characteristics (limited supply fostering resiliency and strong occupancy eventually resulting in a conservative risk-return profile), HSR exposure is particularly suitable for investors with a low risk profile, such as long-term institutional investors (insurance companies, pension funds and sovereign funds) and private investors (especially HNWI), with the latter representing a significant share of the market.

In order to back their investment decisions, sophisticated long-term institutional investors are equipped with robust research departments able to identify long-term asset class attractiveness. Those research departments leverage their data-driven approach both on the analysis of the underlying real estate market and on the investigation of wider macro-social trends able to severely affect investment returns and liquidity. As a matter of fact, today most of the debate on the retail asset class is focused on e-commerce development and its integration with physical retail stores.

Differently from institutional investors, private investors, on top of risk-return consideration, own HSR for a number of additional reasons and specifically:

- Historical repositioning of the location: Since top HSR location have developed over time from "standard" urban neighbourhood, the private individuals owning units in those areas before their transformation have inadvertently taken advantage from the repositiong into a HSR destination.

- Limited asset management activities (vs. different destination of use): Private investors typically lacking of professional asset management skills choose to invest in HSR because HSR tenants do prefer to manage the properties they occupy as much as independently as possible requiring only limited interaction with the owner / professional asset manager.

Although considered a safe harbour, HSR exposure, as any other investment, brings in some short-term risks that typically revert in the long run. Major risk drivers can be summarised as follows:

- *Global economic trend*: For example, this happens when a potential worldwide consumption recession is able to impact tenant profitability and thus rental sustainability.

- *Country-specific risk*: For example, this happens when exchange rates create an impact in tenant profitability because shops' clients are mostly coming from a country experiencing a currency crisis.

- *Local dynamics*: For example, this can occur when a city is losing attractiveness due to the lack of infrastructure and side services (such as direct flights or luxury hotels).

- *Social and economic trends*: For example, this might happen in conjunction with a side effect of e-commerce to the wider traditional retail distribution system.

MARKET ANALYSIS

Based on what has been previously stated, the market analysis of an HSR property is a tailored exercise in which, more than for any other destination of use, the valuer needs to carefully understand the underlying leasing market dynamics and estimate its sustainability in the long run. The following sections will provide guidance to estimate the most critical inputs for the application of the DCFA; namely, the ERV, the cap rate, the vacancy rate and the refurbishment costs.

Estimating the ERV

A CLOSER LOOK 10.2: BENCHMARKING ANALYSIS AND ERV SUSTAINABILITY EXERCISE

Given that HSR properties are often characterised by significant absolute ERV per square metre, even a small reduction in percentage terms might lead to significant changes in the valuation. For this reason, a structured benchmarking analysis and ERV sustainability exercise needs to be run with the following phases.

- *Phase 1 – Micro-location analysis.* The valuer needs to examine current location setting and anticipate short-term and long-term potential developments. For example, it is paramount to identify which store is considered the 'most prime' ('tier I') within the district and from it to design a so called 'heat map' able to show how adjacent properties are perceived with respect to it ('tier II' and 'tier III'). This exercise implies an analysis of the types of stores by footfall, property visibility, surface physical characteristics and underlying industry of the occupier. It is also required to run an investigation on the potential development of accessibility by collecting information on public transportation infrastructure projects (for example the opening of a new underground station nearby) or modification to vehicular traffic. The analysis should also be directed towards understanding the total size of the district (both in terms of square metres and in terms of number of units) to spot potential demand/supply mismatching.

- *Phase 2a – Store-by-store physical data collection.* The 'qualitative heat map' built through the micro-location analysis should be equipped with a comprehensive and granular store-by-store analysis. The valuer should collect for all nearby stores a series of property KPIs, such as:

  - Floors size (i.e. ground, mezzanine and underground)
  - Intended use (i.e. sales vs. storage surfaces)
  - Number and size of shop windows.

Differently from other property typologies, surface efficiency plays an essential role in determining property appeal and marketability (and thus ERV level and vacancy risk) across the tenant market, as shops with rational surface distribution and balanced ratio between shop windows and size are the most attractive to tenants (see Table 10.3).

(Continued)

TABLE 10.3   Example of store physical data benchmark

Shop	Floor	Destination of use	Net Leasable Area (m²)	Weighting factors	Weighted Lettable Area (m²)	# shop windows
Shoe shop	Mezzanine	Retail	150	60%	90	2
	Ground	Retail	350	100%	350	2
	Basement	Storage	60	30%	18	-
		Total	560	82%	458	
Eyewear shop	Ground	Retail	70	100%	70	1
		Total	70	100%	70	
Jewellery shop	Ground	Retail	600	100%	600	5
	Basement	Storage	400	30%	120	-
		Total	1,000	72%	720	

A data collection exercise on surface size and distribution might be facilitated through site visits: if needed, a valuer can physically access stores, since they are open to the general public.

The analysis of the physical characteristics of the Buildings, combined with micro-location analysis, allows the valuer to rank them according to their appeal for tenants. In the example Figure 10.1, the jewellery shop is the most efficient unit as far as 'pure' retail use is concerned: it has five large shop windows and the depth (i.e. the distance between the street and the most internal point of the store) is fairly limited, allowing for an efficient shop windows to total area ratio. The presence of an

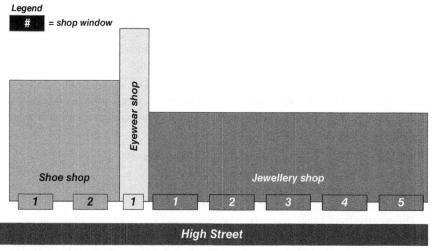

FIGURE 10.1   Example of store surface efficiency analysis

underground floor serving as vault for jewellery or traditional storage in the case of any other tenant, adds further appeal to the property. In contrast, the eyewear shop is the one with minor flexibility as far as 'pure' retail use is concerned: it has only one narrow shop window, depth surfaces and no storage space. The physical characteristics of the eyewear store (only one and narrow shop window, relevant store depth and lack of storage surface) represent constraints reducing its commercial property appeal for the final retail user and thus reducing the number of tenants willing to rent it. It is foreseeable that, as for any other market, lower competition on the demand side will translate in lower prices or longer time to lease (in the rental market this corresponds to lower ERV per square metre or longer vacancy periods). In the valuation process, the capitalisation of a lower ERV and/or longer vacancy periods will translate into lower property Market Values.

- *Phase 2b – Leasing benchmarking.* A proper analysis of comparable leasing terms is essential for rental sustainability estimation over time. The most important leasing KPIs to be collected are:
  - ERV per square metre
  - Total rental amount
  - Potential existence of break options
  - Lease closing date
  - Key money.[4]

     This exercise might be simplified by leveraging on the expertise of real estate brokers specialised in the luxury district under analysis.

     Rental level estimation and its sustainability are inferred by the careful analysis of the available data. A reliable database fed with granular data at property level is the starting point to have a solid foundation over which a valuation exercise should be developed. Of course, its construction requires relevant time and effort. Moreover, for HSR properties, given their strong influence in affecting the performance of tenant underlying core business, the valuer is required, more than in any other Property Valuation, to leverage its own judgement and expertise to interpret the data collected and to match real estate evidences with wider micro- and macro-economic dynamics and trends.

Alexandria Street has its own gravity centre at the crossroads with Edward Street (as already mentioned, one of the most prestigious worldwide luxury retail locations), in a point where the footfall is higher due to a street enlargement allowing for a smoother footfall flow and to an intersection with an adjacent street. The centrality of this point is confirmed by the nearby presence of a cornering trophy property representing the historical headquarters of a famous fashion brand which acts as destination for thousands of shoppers from all around the world. North of this point, the luxury street continues and hosts a series of top international tier I brands operating in the high-end luxury industry, whereas southbound, after very few highly reputable international brands, the commercial street continues hosting tier II shops, which are mostly national retailers operating at the medium-end segment.

In the last few years, the luxury shopping district originating from Edward Street has enlarged its capacity to surrounding streets. Nearby Alexandria Street, Frederic Street,

Veronica Street, and Mati Street have switched their vocation from pure residential to tier II and tier III retail areas. The enlargement trend is expected to keep growing, since a new underground station will be opened across the street.

Figure 10.2 offers a synthetic visualisation of benchmark leasing KPIs collected.[5] On average, data show a market timing effect in the previous 16 years, with 'older' contracts closed between years '–15' and '–13' characterised by higher ERV and key money paid for all store sizes. Later on, the leasing market has slowed down with the first transaction occurring in year '–9' and registering, despite the limited contract size, a low ERV and no key money (e.g. 'Accessories'). Recovery started in year '–6', with a series of transactions closed at increasing ERVs. Starting from year '–4' the leasing market was back on track registering closing terms in line with the previous cycle both in terms of ERV and of key money payment (e.g. 'Jewellery', 'Women's clothing' and 'Watches'). Intuitively, the slightly lower ERV per m^2 of 'Jewellery' vs. 'Women's clothing' and 'Watches' is due to the relatively significant total rental amount of 'Jewellery' (expressed by the size of the bubble): after a certain threshold, as soon as the total rent increases, the ERV per m^2 decreases (the market becomes less and less liquid, since only a very limited number of players can afford to spend such a large amount). As a rule of thumb, in developed countries, when the rental amount exceeds the € 2–3 million threshold, the number of potential tenants sharply decreases.

Estimating the Cap Rate

The cap rate estimation for the subject property takes into consideration a series of operating risk factors, among those ERV sustainability, vacancy, tenant market strength and investor's appetite (please refer to Chapter 7, Section 'Cap Rate' for detailed technicalities on how to approach cap rate estimation). Cap rate compression should take place only for properties where the quality of the space will be improved (e.g. through CapEx or TIs), therefore reducing letting risk and simultaneously increasing asset liquidity/cash flow generation capacity.

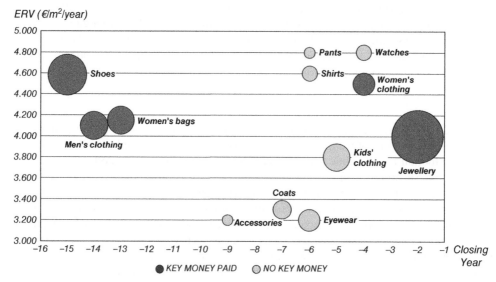

FIGURE 10.2 Leasing benchmarks – ERV by closing year, ERV by level (€/m^2), leasing contract size (bubble size) and key money payment (shading code)

From a valuer point of view, assumptions on potential expected trend of the capital market should be limited and in any case circumscribed to estimates widely accepted in the market.

Since the subject property has a value add potential because it is not currently expressing its HBU, the valuer should estimate a going-out cap rate coherent with the new lower risk profile and higher income potential after the completion of valorisation process and related CapEx. Matching the estimated stabilised cash flows with the estimated going-out cap rate will determine the Terminal Value for valuation purposes.

Estimating Vacancy and Leasing Time

For luxury HSR valuation (especially those located in prime worldwide luxury streets), a vacancy scenario should be treated as a 'tail' effect: under normal market conditions, their vacancy can be assumed close to none.[6]

Historically retail properties in Alexandria Street have registered on average less than two-month vacancy at lease expiration with only very few lease agreements not being renewed at natural expiration. As shown in Figure 10.2 the only proxy for vacancy effect suffered during low cycle has been the vanish of key money and ERV decrease, but no real vacancy.

In addition, as reported in Figure 10.2, the key money market practice that is peculiar to HSR properties shows that there exists some reward for tenants having the 'privilege' to rent in such locations; a concept that strongly conflicts with vacancy assumptions.

Estimating Refurbishment Costs

Refurbishment costs usually represent one of the easiest inputs to be estimated across all the pieces of information needed in a valuation process of an HSR property. Complexity in refurbishment costs estimation is limited since:

- Costs are parametric/proportional to the size of the Building (estimates by contractors are typically in line with effective costs).
- Specific/more complex fit-out costs are directly managed and borne by the tenant, thus reducing the risk for the Owner.
- Refurbishment costs represent a low percentage of the overall property value (which is rather due to location than to physical features).

Although fit-out works are usually managed and paid directly by the tenant, it is market practice for the Owner to grant a CapEx/fit-out contribution[7] to the tenant. It can be delivered either as a cash contribution or as a free rent equivalent (see also A Closer Look 6.1) and its amount depends on the market conditions, length of the lease agreement and type of refurbishment works to be realised. As a matter of fact, works able to enhance Building quality and remain within the property in the case of lease contract termination are typically sponsored by the Owner, while those not durable, or those that are movables, are not.

VALUATION

In order to define the inputs to apply to the Discounted Cash Flow Approach model, a detailed market analysis has been done to analyse the micro-location, to forecast potential developments for the area, to collect reliable market evidences, and to adjust the benchmarks to the unique characteristics of the property.

TABLE 10.4 Discounted Cash Flow model

	semester		1	2	3	4	5	6	7	8
Rents											
Current tenant (restaurant)	1,811	€/m²	1,280,000	€1,280,000	€1,299,200	€1,299,200	€1,318,688	€1,318,688		
New tenant	3,500	€/m²							€2,624,845	€2,624,845
Potential Gross Income			€1,280,000	€1,280,000	€1,299,200	€1,299,200	€1,318,688	€1,318,688	€2,624,845	€2,624,845
Effective vacancy			€0	€0	€0	€0	€1,318,688	€1,318,688	€0	€0
Effective Gross Income			€1,280,000	€1,280,000	€1,299,200	€1,299,200	€0	€0	€2,624,845	€2,624,845
Operating costs										
Property taxes	256,000	€/year	€128,000	€128,000	€130,560	€130,560	€133,171	€133,171	€135,835	€135,835
Property insurance	12,000	€/year	€6,000	€6,000	€6,120	€6,120	€6,242	€6,242	€6,367	€6,367
Stamp duty	1.00%	% on rents	€12,800	€12,800	€12,992	€12,992	€0	€0	€26,248	€26,248
Extraordinary maintenance	0.50%	% on reconstruction cost	€10,601	€10,706	€10,813	€10,920	€0	€0	€11,249	€11,361
Property & Facility Management	1.50%	% on rents	€19,200	€19,200	€19,488	€19,488	€0	€0	€39,373	€39,373
Total Operating costs			€176,601	€176,706	€179,973	€180,080	€139,414	€139,414	€219,072	€219,184
Net Operating Income			€1,103,400	€1,103,294	€1,119,227	€1,119,120	-€139,414	-€139,414	€2,405,773	€2,405,661
Investments										
Capex & Capital contribution	2,000	€/m²	€0	€0	€0	€0	€1,470,501	€1,485,134	€0	€0
Leasing fees	10.0%	% headline rent	€0	€0	€0	€0	€0	€0	€524,969	€0
Total Investments			€0	€0	€0	€0	€1,470,501	€1,485,134	€524,969	€0
Intermediate Cash Flow			€1,103,400	€1,103,294	€1,119,227	€1,119,120	-€1,609,915	-€1,624,547	€1,880,804	€2,405,661
Terminal Value										
Exit value (on net GOCR)	3.00%	net GOCR	€0	€0	€0	€0	€0	€0	€0	€160,377,377
Brokerage fees	0.50%	% Terminal Value	€0	€0	€0	€0	€0	€0	€0	€801,887
Final Cash Flow			€0	€0	€0	€0	€0	€0	€0	€159,575,490
Total Cash Flows to be discounted			€1,103,400	€1,103,294	€1,119,227	€1,119,120	-€1,609,915	-€1,624,547	€1,880,804	€161,981,151
Time factor			*0.25*	*0.75*	*1.25*	*1.75*	*2.25*	*2.75*	*3.25*	*3.5*
Discount factor	5.20%	*discount rate*	*0.9874*	*0.9627*	*0.9386*	*0.9151*	*0.8922*	*0.8699*	*0.8481*	*0.8374*
Discounted Cash Flows			€1,089,504	€1,062,134	€1,050,506	€1,024,116	-€1,436,374	-€1,413,153	€1,595,116	€133,632,194
Sum of Discounted Intermediate Cash Flows	2.2%	€2,971,850								
Discounted Final Cash Flow	97.8%	€133,632,194								
Market Value		€136,604,044								
Market Value (rounded)		€136,600,000								

The valuation model is based on the assumption that at the expiry of the current lease agreement (after 24 months from the valuation date), the current tenant will leave the property. Then, the Owner will undertake some substantial CapEx (€ 2,000/m^2 including the capital contribution to the new tenant) in order to refurbish it. At the end of the refurbishment period (12 months), the HSR unit will be leased to a new tenant with a rent aligned to the ERV (€ 3,500/m^2/year). As the Terminal Value, a net going-out cap rate estimated at 3.0%, aligned with market net yields, will be used.

The cost of capital can be estimated with a Build-Up Approach, or with any other approach as described in the Chapter 7, Section 'How to Estimate Property Return Rates', of course bearing in mind the risk profile of the property.

The estimated discount rate for the subject property is 5.20%. This takes into account the low market risk profile of HSR in that specific location and, for a minimum amount, an increase due to the value add nature of the property (repositioning) (see Table 10.4).

The Market Value of the subject property at the valuation date is € 136,600,000.

NOTES

1. Even if based on a real case, fictitious names have been used and numerical data have been sanitised.
2. In order to factor in the high quality of mezzanine surfaces, the surfaces in the mezzanine floor have been weighted at 60% (vs. 50% typically used to for retail surfaces placed in the mezzanine/first floor).
3. HSR properties is a wide definition since there are high streets in almost every city above a certain dimension and in high streets it is usually possible to find most of mass market brands. Most of the comments in this case instead specifically refer to those prime streets where predominantly luxury goods retailers are located.
4. The 'key money' is the amount of money paid from a new tenant in order to 'buy' the lease agreement from the current tenant of an HSR unit. In this way the new tenant will substitute the old one in all its contractual obligations.
5. Leasing benchmark refers to a series of retail units located around Alexandria, Edward, Frederic, Veronica and Mati streets. The benchmarks showing the highest values are the ones located in Edward Street (top retail location worldwide). The ERV per m^2 is typically directly proportional to the proximity to Edward Street.
6. The same statement may not apply to any HSR, since in less prestigious streets usually there are vacant spaces.
7. Owner contribution can usually be estimated to be an equivalent rental amount included in the three-month to nine-month range.

CHAPTER 11

Hotel Appraisal

The following case study[1] is related to the valuation of a four-star hotel[2] located in a primary UK city and currently managed by an international hotels and resorts chain. This case represents another example of valuation of a Trade-Related Property where, as better described in the Chapter 2, Subsection 'Trade-Related Commercial Property', it is first necessary to perform a careful analysis of the economic result for the User. Additional advice is provided, in particular with respect to the market analysis.

DESCRIPTION OF THE PROPERTY

A CLOSER LOOK 11.1: LOCATION AND PHYSICAL FACILITIES

As for any other Commercial Property, a hotel's site and its location within a specific neighbourhood can have a direct impact upon the hotel's performance relative to a competitive market. This explains the need for a detailed analysis of the location of the hotel in relation to its immediate surroundings and its market area. Similarly, the quality

(Continued)

This case study has been written by **Ezio Poinelli** and **Pavlos Papadimitriou**.

Ezio Poinelli is Senior Director Southern Europe (Italy and Spain based) of HVS, a global hotel consulting and valuation firm with offices in Europe, North America, Asia, South America and the Middle East. Ezio has more than 20 years experience in Hospitality, Real Estate, and Leisure Real Estate markets in Europe, Caribbean, Latin America, and South Africa. Before joining HVS, Ezio was Head of Southern Europe at Northcourse Advisory Services (Madrid), the hospitality and real estate consulting arm of Wyndham Worldwide, one of the largest hospitality companies in the world. He was also Head of Expansion & International Development at Compañia de Las Islas Occidentales (Canary Islands) and Director – Head of Real Estate and Hospitality at Ernst & Young Financial Business Advisors (Milan). He started his career with Investment & Tourism Consulting Associated with exposure to European and Latin America markets and REVA – Real Estate Value Advisors – a boutique firm focused on real estate and financial advisory.

Pavlos Papadimitriou is Director Southern Europe (Athens based) of HVS, specialising in hotel valuation and financial consultancy, and a member of the Royal Institution of Chartered Surveyors. A former hotelier himself, he joined HVS Athens in late 2007 after completing the MBA programme of Les Roches School of Hotel Management in Switzerland and a BSc in Marketing and Communication from the Athens University of Economics and Business. Since then, he has conducted numerous valuations, feasibility studies, and market research analyses for hotels in the Balkans, Cyprus, Georgia, Greece, Italy, Poland, Spain, and Turkey.

of a hotel's physical facilities has a direct influence on its marketability and attainable occupancy and average rate. The design and functionality of the structure can also affect operating efficiency and overall profitability. Again, it is therefore essential that a detailed analysis of the hotel's physical premises and facilities is carried out in an effort to determine how they contribute to its total value.

The subject hotel enjoys an excellent location, being located in the city centre of one of the primary UK cities outside London, near the business district and easily reached by several modes of transport. It also benefits from its proximity to all the major hospitality demand generators in the same area.

The subject property is a four-star hotel with 250 guest rooms, a café, a restaurant, a bar/lounge, 955 m² of meeting space, an indoor pool, an exercise room, a business centre, a gift shop, a guest laundry room and appropriate back-of-the-house facilities. The hotel is affiliated with an international hotels and resorts chain.

TABLE 11.1   Summary of the hotel facilities

Guest Room Configuration		Number of Units	Approximate Area (m²)
Single		85	25
Double		90	28
Executive		60	35
Suite		15	40
Total/Weighted Average		**250**	**29**
Food and Beverage Facilities	**Location/Floor**	**Seating Capacity**	**Approximate Area (m²)**
Café Restaurant	Ground	125	200
Speciality Restaurant	Top Floor	80	120
Bar/Lounge	Ground	50	70
Total		**255**	**390**
Meeting and Banqueting Facilities	**Location/Floor**	**Maximum Capacity (Persons)**	**Approximate Area (m²)**
Ballroom	Ground	400	500
Pre-Function Room	Ground	–	185
Board Room	Ground	20	40
Meeting Room 1	First	120	150
Meeting Room 2	First	60	80
Total		**600**	**955**
Car Parking	Approximately 75 underground spaces		
Leisure Facilities	Fitness centre with sauna, solarium and whirlpool spa; indoor swimming pool; gift shop		
Other Facilities	Business centre		

Opened 10 years ago, it has been well maintained since then. In general, the property's premises appear to be very well suited for hotel use. The building is straightforward in design and configuration, permitting efficiency of operation and convenient guest and staff flow. The exterior design of the building is both modern and inviting and the interior finishes are of a high quality. The guest rooms are excellent in terms of size and decoration and the hotel's ancillary facilities are appropriate for the operation of a four-star, commercial, city centre hotel in the UK.

Table 11.1 summarises the facilities available at the hotel.

CHOICE OF VALUATION METHOD

A CLOSER LOOK 11.2: PECULIARITIES OF HOTEL VALUATION

The valuation of hotels presents some peculiar characteristics which make the valuation process more complex compared to other properties, based on the analysis of some fundamental principles, widely accepted at international level:

- The physical facilities of the property are rigid and difficult to be modified in order to eventually change the intended use of the Building. Moreover, they are characterised by substantial prospective obsolescence in the different components of the Building (core structure, machinery, finishing, and furniture).
- The need for specialised know-how for the management of the property, which has led to the birth of hotel management companies with specific know-how, conveniently regulated through typical and atypical management contracts.
- Periodic fluctuations in the performance of the operating management of the properties, which is reflected in the projections of profit and loss statements and, consequently, in the cash flows which represent the base for the valuation.

Being a Trade-Related Property, as seen in the Chapter 4, Section 'Choice of Valuation Method', the most appropriate hotel valuation method is deemed to be the Discounted Cash Flow Approach (DCFA).[3] This approach is often selected as the preferred valuation method for Income-producing Properties because it most closely reflects the investment thinking of knowledgeable buyers, mainly professional investors. The evidence in the international markets, with numerous hotel buyers and sellers, indicates that the procedures used in estimating the value by the DCFA are preferred by most of the hotel investors. For this reason, the DCFA produces the most supportable value estimate and it is generally given the most important role in the hotel valuation process. Use of the Direct Capitalisation Approach is indeed limited to the valuation of hotels which present certain stability in the income generated and for which no major changes (in terms of CapEx, competitive set, etc.) are expected over the years.

The Direct Comparison Approach has some limited use in the estimate of the Market Value of a hotel. Differences in location, facilities, property rights transferred and many other variables make a precise comparison between the comparable sales and the subject hotel difficult. Subjective adjustments used to lessen these differences are highly speculative. Moreover, there is no accurate way of determining whether the sales prices actually paid represent Market Values, because it is difficult to determine the exact motivations of the buyers and sellers, or what special conditions may have influenced the sale. Although the Direct Comparison Approach is generally unsuitable for indicating a specific final estimate of value, it may serve to establish a range that can test the reasonableness of the values indicated by other approaches.

Finally, the Depreciated Cost Methods, as stated in Chapter 4, are even less appropriate. First of all, they do not reflect the economic factors that motivate knowledgeable hotel investors (that is, projected EBITDA – after FF&E[4] reserve – and return on investment) and therefore they are not suitable for the valuation of Income-producing Properties. Secondly, the difficulty in estimating and substantiating a number of highly subjective variables (such as effective age, accrued depreciation, and the remaining economic life of the improvements) limits the applicability of the Depreciated Cost Methods as effective valuation methods. Finally, hotels are rarely sold or purchased on the basis of depreciated cost. Therefore, these methods are considered as inapplicable in the valuation of the subject hotel.

MARKET ANALYSIS

Macroeconomic Climate

A CLOSER LOOK 11.3: ECONOMIC AND GEOGRAPHIC TRENDS

The macroeconomic climate in which a hotel operates is an important consideration in forecasting hotel demand and income potential. Economic and demographic trends that reflect the amount of visitation provide a basis from which the demand for hotel accommodation can be projected.

The purpose of the market area analysis is to review available economic and demographic data to determine whether the defined market area will undergo economic growth, stability or decline. In addition to a prediction of the direction of the economy, the rate of change must be quantified. These trends are then correlated based on their propensity to reflect variations in hotel demand with the objective of forecasting the amount of growth or decline in transient visitation by individual market segment.

The review of various national, regional and local economic data indicates that the subject city benefits from strong levels of commercial room night demand generated from local businesses, supported by modest numbers of leisure visitors. Specific local economic activity appears to be increasing beyond general national levels owing to a combination of factors, including the ongoing development of good quality offices and business parks.

Supply and Demand Analysis

A CLOSER LOOK 11.4: SUPPLY AND DEMAND

Under the economic principle of supply and demand, price varies, but not proportionately, directly with demand and inversely with supply. In the hotel industry, supply is measured by the number of guest rooms available and demand by the number of guest rooms occupied; the net effect of supply and demand towards equilibrium results in a prevailing price, or average rate. To evaluate an area's competitive environment, the following steps should be taken:

1. Identify the area's hotel facilities and determine which are directly and indirectly competitive with the hotel.

2. Determine whether additional hotel rooms (net of attrition) will enter the market in the foreseeable future.

3. Quantify the number of existing and proposed hotel rooms available in the market.

4. Review the rate structure, occupancy, market orientation, facilities and amenities of each competitor.

From an evaluation of the occupancy, rate structure, market orientation, chain affiliation, location, facilities, amenities, reputation and quality of the subject area's hotels, as well as the comments of management representatives, two properties have been identified as primary competitors of the hotel. Including the subject hotel, these primary competitors have a total of 781 rooms.

An additional 12 hotels are judged to be secondary competitors. Although the facilities, rate structures, or market orientations of these hotels prevent their inclusion among the supply of primary competitors, they do compete with the hotel to some extent. The room count of each secondary competitor has been weighted to reflect the degree to which it competes with the hotel. The aggregate weighted room count of the secondary competitors is 740.

A CLOSER LOOK 11.5: SEGMENTING THE MARKET FOR DEMAND ANALYSIS

For the purposes of the demand analysis, the overall market is divided into individual segments based on the nature of travel. The segmentation of a market (which can be done either through official reports or through interviews with hotel executives during

(Continued)

---

the market research on the field) is a useful procedure because individual classifications often exhibit unique characteristics in terms of growth potential, seasonality of demand, average length of stay, double occupancy, facility requirements, price sensitivity, and so forth. By quantifying the room night demand by market segment and analysing the characteristics of each segment, the demand for transient accommodation can be projected.

The purpose of segmenting hotel demand is to define each major type of demand, identify client characteristics and estimate future growth trends. Various types of economic and demographic data are then evaluated to determine their propensity to reflect future changes in hotel demand.

The following tables summarise the important operating characteristics of the competitors. This information has been compiled with personal interviews, inspections, hotel directories and databases. Table 11.2 sets out each property's estimated segmentation and aggregate weighted room count, while Table 11.3 shows market-wide occupancy, average rate and rooms revenue per available room (RevPAR[5]), whose calculation serves to gauge how well a hotel is maximising its rooms revenue.

As well as analysing the existing supply of competitive hotel facilities, it is important to consider any new hotel Development Projects that may have an impact on the hotel's operating performance. From the market analysis four developments, as shown in Table 11.4, have been considered as becoming competitive with the hotel.

Hotel demand in the surroundings of the subject city is generated primarily by the following five market segments (as shown in Table 11.5): Commercial, Meeting, Incentive, Conference and Exhibition (MICE), Individual Leisure, Group Leisure, Airline.

From a review of the market dynamics in the hotel's competitive environment, growth rates have been forecasted for each market segment. Using the calculated potential demand for the market, market-wide accommodated demand has been determined based on the inherent limitations of demand fluctuations and other factors in the market area.

A CLOSER LOOK 11.6: AVERAGE RATE AND OCCUPANCY

Average rate and occupancy are the foundations of a hotel's financial performance and Market Value. Most of a hotel's other revenue sources (such as food and beverages) are driven by the number of guests; many expenses also vary with occupancy.

To a certain degree, the occupancy achieved can be manipulated by management. For example, hotel operators may choose to lower rates in an effort to maximise occupancy. Forecasts should reflect an operating strategy that would be implemented by a typical, professional hotel management team to achieve an optimal mix of occupancy and average rate.

Table 11.6 details projection of hotel demand growth for the subject market, including the total number of occupied room nights and any residual unaccommodated demand in the market.

TABLE 11.2 Estimated segmentation and weighted annual room counts of primary and secondary competitors

| Primary Competitors | Number of Rooms | Estimated Segmentation | | | | | Total Comp Level | Base Year Weighted Annual Room Count |
		Commercial	MICE	Individual Leisure	Group Leisure	Airline		
Hotel	250	55%	15%	20%	5%	5%	100%	250
Primary Competitor #1	242	60%	10%	20%	5%	5%	100%	242
Primary Competitor #2	289	60%	10%	20%	5%	5%	100%	289
Subtotals/Averages	**781**	**58%**	**12%**	**20%**	**5%**	**5%**	**100%**	**781**

| Secondary Competitors | Number of Rooms | Estimated Segmentation | | | | | Total Comp Level | Base Year Weighted Annual Room Count |
		Commercial	MICE	Individual Leisure	Group Leisure	Airline		
Secondary Competitor #1	187	55%	15%	15%	7%	8%	75%	140
Secondary Competitor #2	40	55%	8%	30%	0%	7%	75%	30
Secondary Competitor #3	182	55%	15%	20%	5%	5%	75%	137
Secondary Competitor #4	201	50%	20%	10%	10%	10%	75%	151
Secondary Competitor #5 (*)	40	60%	5%	20%	10%	5%	50%	2
Secondary Competitor #6	128	55%	15%	20%	5%	5%	50%	64
Secondary Competitor #7	142	40%	25%	25%	5%	5%	50%	71
Secondary Competitor #8	200	55%	15%	20%	5%	5%	25%	50
Secondary Competitor #9	68	50%	10%	25%	10%	5%	25%	17
Secondary Competitor #10 (**)	167	55%	15%	15%	10%	5%	25%	27
Secondary Competitor #11	94	55%	0%	15%	25%	5%	25%	24
Secondary Competitor #12	112	45%	20%	20%	10%	5%	25%	28
Subtotals/Averages	**1,517**	**52%**	**16%**	**18%**	**7%**	**7%**	**50%**	**740**
Totals/Averages	**2,342**	**55%**	**14%**	**19%**	**6%**	**6%**	**65%**	**1,521**

*open for 31 days
**open for 240 days

TABLE 11.3 Market-wide performance of primary and secondary competitors

	Weighted Annual Room Count	Estimated Year (-2)			Estimated Year (-1)			Estimated Base Year		
		Average Rate	Occupancy	RevPAR	Average Rate	Occupancy	RevPAR	Average Rate	Occupancy	RevPAR
Hotel	250	£ 83	76%	£ 63	£ 84	75%	£ 63	£ 85	74%	£ 63
Primary Competitors (*)	781	£ 75	75%	£ 56	£ 78	76%	£ 60	£ 89	74%	£ 66
Secondary Competitors	740	£ 59	76%	£ 44	£ 60	75%	£ 45	£ 61	75%	£ 46
Totals/Averages	**1,521**	**£ 67**	**75%**	**£ 51**	**£ 70**	**76%**	**£ 53**	**£ 76**	**75%**	**£ 56**

*Including subject Hotel

TABLE 11.4 Proposed new supply

Proposed Property	Number of Rooms	Total Competitive Level
New hotel #1	128	100%
New hotel #2	220	25%
New hotel #3	123	25%
New hotel #4	110	25%
Total	**581**	

TABLE 11.5 Accommodated room night demand – competitive market and hotel

	Market wide		Hotel	
Market Segment	Accommodated Demand	Percentage of Total	Accommodated Demand	Percentage of Total
Commercial	229,455	55%	37,139	55%
MICE	57,552	14%	10,129	15%
Individual Leisure	77,990	19%	13,505	20%
Group Leisure	25,783	6%	3,376	5%
Airline	24,239	6%	3,376	5%
Total	**415,018**	**100%**	**67,525**	**100%**

Forecast of Average Rate and Occupancy

In Table 11.7, the penetration factor attained by the primary competitors and the aggregate secondary competitors are set out for each segment for the base year.

A CLOSER LOOK 11.7: PENETRATION FACTOR

The penetration factor is the ratio of a property's market share to its fair share. In this equation, market share is that portion of total market demand accommodated by a property, and fair share the hotel's portion of the total supply (calculated as the hotel's room count divided by the market's total supply).

If a property with a fair share of 5% is capturing 5% of the market in a given year, then its occupancy will equal the market-wide occupancy, and its penetration factor will equal 100% (5%/5% = 100%). If the same property achieves a market share in excess of its fair share, then its occupancy will be greater than the market wide occupancy, and its penetration factor will be greater than 100%. For example, if a property with a fair share of 5% has a market share of 7%, then its penetration rate is 140% (7%/5% = 140%). Conversely, if the property captures less than its fair share, then its occupancy will be below the market-wide average, and its penetration rate will be less than 100%. Penetration factors can be calculated for each market segment of a property, and for the property as a whole.

(Continued)

If one hotel's penetration performance increases, thereby increasing its achieved market share, this leaves less demand available in the market for the other hotels to capture and the penetration performance of one or more of those other hotels consequently declines (other things remaining equal). This type of market share adjustment takes place every time there is a change in supply or a change in the relative penetration performance of one or more hotels in the competitive market.

TABLE 11.6   Accommodated demand

	Base Year	Year 1	Year 2	Year 3	Year 4
Commercial					
Occupied Room Nights	229,455	242,591	252,276	259,688	266,051
Residual Demand	4,589	0	0	0	0
Accommodated Demand Growth	–	*5.7%*	*4.0%*	*2.9%*	*2.5%*
MICE					
Occupied Room Nights	57,552	60,801	63,188	65,047	66,643
Residual Demand	1,151	0	0	0	0
Accommodated Demand Growth	–	*5.6%*	*3.9%*	*2.9%*	*2.5%*
Individual Leisure					
Occupied Room Nights	77,990	81,563	85,553	87,652	89,803
Residual Demand	780	0	0	0	0
Accommodated Demand Growth	–	*4.6%*	*4.9%*	*2.5%*	*2.5%*
Group Leisure					
Occupied Room Nights	25,783	27,259	28,851	29,545	30,256
Residual Demand	258	0	0	0	0
Accommodated Demand Growth	–	*5.7%*	*5.8%*	*2.4%*	*2.4%*
Airline					
Occupied Room Nights	24,239	25,093	25,721	26,364	27,023
Residual Demand	242	0	0	0	0
Accommodated Demand Growth	–	*3.5%*	*2.5%*	*2.5%*	*2.5%*
Totals					
Occupied Room Nights	415,018	437,307	455,588	468,296	479,776
Residual Demand	7,020	0	0	0	0
Accommodated Demand Growth	–	*5.4%*	*4.2%*	*2.8%*	*2.5%*
Available Room Nights per Year	555,220	573,081	583,220	613,565	660,285
Available Room Night Growth	–	*3.2%*	*1.8%*	*5.2%*	*7.6%*
Market-wide Occupancy	**75%**	**76%**	**78%**	**76%**	**73%**

TABLE 11.7 Penetration factors in the base year

Property	Commercial	MICE	Individual Leisure	Group Leisure	Airline	Overall
Hotel	98%	107%	105%	80%	85%	99%
Primary Competitor #1	106%	70%	104%	79%	84%	98%
Primary Competitor #2	109%	72%	107%	81%	86%	100%
Secondary Competitors	95%	118%	94%	121%	116%	101%

As a result of its varying levels of penetration among the five market demand segments, the subject hotel achieved an overall penetration rate of 99% in the base year. The hotel's forecast market share and occupancy have been based on its expected competitive position within the market, as quantified by its penetration factor.

The projections of penetration, demand capture and occupancy performance for the subject hotel account for these types of adjustments to market share within the defined competitive market. Consequently, the actual penetration factors applicable to the hotel and its competitors for each market segment in each projection year may vary somewhat from the adjusted penetration factors shown in Table 11.8.

Penetration factors drive the estimates of demand capture and occupancy for the subject hotel, as can be seen in Table 11.9 which sets out the result of these market share adjusted (output) penetration factors by segment upon the subject hotel's future demand capture and occupancy performance, the annual market-wide occupancy and the resultant market mix, or total captured demand analysed by market segment. These projections are in calendar years from year 1 to year 4, by which time it is considered that the hotel will have reached a stabilised level of performance in terms of market penetration and occupancy.

Table 11.10 sets out the resultant market mix, or total captured demand analysed by market segment.

It has been chosen to use a stabilised occupancy level of 74%. The stabilised occupancy is intended to reflect the expected results of the property over its remaining economic life, given any and all changes in the life cycle of the hotel. This stabilised occupancy is intended to reflect the expected results of the hotel, excluding from consideration any abnormal relationship between supply and demand and non-recurring conditions that may result in unusually high or low occupancies. Although the subject hotel may operate at occupancy rates above this stabilised level, it has been considered equally possible for new competition and temporary economic downturns to force the occupancy rate below this selected point

TABLE 11.8 Market segmentation forecast

Market Segment	Base Year	Year 1	Year 2	Year 3	Year 4
Commercial	98.5%	107.4%	112.2%	111.7%	111.9%
MICE	107.1%	74.0%	73.8%	73.2%	72.9%
Individual Leisure	105.4%	101.0%	103.7%	105.2%	105.2%
Group Leisure	79.7%	88.0%	88.0%	88.1%	88.3%
Airline	84.8%	84.3%	84.4%	84.3%	84.4%
Overall Penetration	**99.0%**	**99.0%**	**102.2%**	**102.1%**	**102.2%**

TABLE 11.9 Forecast of occupancy of the hotel

	Market Segment	Base Year	Year 1	Year 2	Year 3	Year 4
	Commercial					
	Demand	229,455	242,591	252,276	259,688	266,051
	Market Share	*16.2%*	*17.1%*	*17.6%*	*16.6%*	*15.5%*
	Capture	37,139	41,472	44,276	43,140	41,138
	Penetration	*98%*	*107%*	*112%*	*112%*	*112%*
	MICE					
	Demand	57,552	60,801	63,188	65,047	66,643
	Market Share	*17.6%*	*11.8%*	*11.5%*	*10.9%*	*10.1%*
	Capture	10,129	7,159	7,297	7,077	6,718
	Penetration	*107%*	*74%*	*74%*	*73%*	*73%*
	Individual Leisure					
	Demand	77,990	81,563	85,553	87,652	89,803
	Market Share	*17.3%*	*16.1%*	*16.2%*	*15.7%*	*14.5%*
	Capture	13,505	13,123	13,875	13,719	13,057
	Penetration	*105%*	*101%*	*104%*	*105%*	*105%*
	Group Leisure					
	Demand	25,783	27,259	28,851	29,545	30,256
	Market Share	*13.1%*	*14.0%*	*13.8%*	*13.1%*	*12.2%*
	Capture	3,376	3,818	3,973	3,870	3,690
	Penetration	*80%*	*88%*	*88%*	*88%*	*88%*
	Airline					
	Demand	24,239	25,093	25,721	26,364	27,023
	Market Share	*13.9%*	*13.4%*	*13.2%*	*12.5%*	*11.7%*
	Capture	3,376	3,370	3,397	3,307	3,152
	Penetration	*85%*	*84%*	*84%*	*84%*	*84%*
(a)	**Total Room Nights Captured**	**67,525**	**68,942**	**72,817**	**71,113**	**67,756**
(b)	Available Room Nights (365 days * 250 rooms)	91,250	91,250	91,250	91,250	91,250
(c) = (a) / (b)	**Subject Occupancy**	**74%**	**76%**	**80%**	**78%**	**74%**
(d)	Marketwide Available Room Nights	555,220	573,081	583,220	613,565	660,285
(e) = (b) / (d)	**Fair Share**	**16%**	**16%**	**16%**	**15%**	**14%**
(f)	Marketwide Occupied Room Nights	415,018	437,307	455,588	468,296	479,776
(g) = (a) / (f)	**Market Share**	**16%**	**16%**	**16%**	**15%**	**14%**
(h) = (d) / (f)	**Marketwide Occupancy**	**75%**	**76%**	**78%**	**76%**	**73%**
(i) = (c) / (h)	**Total Penetration**	**99%**	**99%**	**102%**	**102%**	**102%**

TABLE 11.10 Projected market mix of the hotel

	Base Year	Year 1	Year 2	Year 3	Year 4
Commercial	55%	60%	61%	61%	61%
MICE	15%	10%	10%	10%	10%
Individual Leisure	20%	19%	19%	19%	19%
Group Leisure	5%	6%	5%	5%	5%
Airline	5%	5%	5%	5%	5%
Total	**100%**	**100%**	**100%**	**100%**	**100%**

of stability. In conclusion, the hotel is expected to reach a stabilised level of penetration (occupancy performance relative to its competitive market) in year 4, with an overall penetration of 102%.

A CLOSER LOOK 11.8: AVERAGE RATE PER OCCUPIED ROOM

One of the most important considerations in estimating the value of a hotel facility is a supportable forecast of its attainable average rate, which is more formally defined as the average rate per occupied room. The average rate can be calculated by dividing the total rooms revenue achieved over a specified period by the number of rooms sold in the same period. The projected average rate and the expected occupancy percentage are used to forecast rooms revenue, which in turn provides the basis for estimating most other income and expense categories.

A hotel's average rate is the weighted average of the various amounts charged to different market segments, such as rack rates,[6] published rates, commercial rates and contract rates. The average rate also takes into account differentials during peak and off-peak periods, including various seasons of the year, holidays and weekends. Different types of room may also command varying rates and thus have an impact on the overall average rate.

In the case of existing hotel, the operating history can be used as a starting point and project average rate based on market conditions and the property's relative degree of competitiveness. This process is outlined as follows:

1. The average rates of competitor properties are considered to determine whether the hotel's rates reflect market conditions, competent management, and buyer's expectations.
2. Factors that may have an impact on future average rate increases are analysed for each market segment, and future growth rates for each segment are estimated.
3. The hotel's average rate is projected for each segment based on the growth estimates. The subject hotel's overall average rate is calculated for each projection year based on the segment average rates. The average rate forecast for the hotel takes into account potential market mix changes.

In forecasting average rate growth, a base underlying inflation rate of 2% has been used. Various market-specific and hotel-specific growth factors have been applied to the average rate of the respective demand segments.

A CLOSER LOOK 11.9: ROOM RATE GROWTH ESTIMATE

Hotel room rate inflation is not necessarily the same as the general economic rate of inflation experienced in the local community. It is impacted more by market conditions, such as the relationship between supply and demand. When hotel room rate inflation is projected into the future, the movement in average rate up to the point where the hotel achieves its stabilised occupancy is generally attributed to property-specific and market-specific factors. After a hotel achieves occupancy stabilisation, most forecasts assume that room rates will continue to increase at the expected general economic rate of inflation for the local market area.

Table 11.11 illustrates the estimated increases in average rate for each market segment.

Although having applied growth rates of 2.5% in year 1 to each segment's rate, the overall change in year 1 was 3.3%; this is because of the slight change in the hotel's market mix towards the higher-paying Commercial segment. Table 11.12 shows how the projected changes in average rate by segment, in conjunction with forecasts of demand by segment, affect the overall average rate.

The forecast of average rate reported in Table 11.13, beginning from year 1, will be used to project the hotel's rooms revenue corresponding to the first projection year for the hotel's forecast of income and expenses.

Projection of Income and Expenses

Using the previously reported projection of occupancy and average rate and based on comparable hotels' financial operating profiles, a 10-year forecast of income and expenses has been developed starting from year 1. An annual inflation rate of 2% has been estimated.

TABLE 11.11 Projected average rate growth by market segment

Market Segment	Base Year Average Rate	Projected Growth Rate Year 1	Year 2	Year 3	Year 4
Commercial	£ 97	2.5%	2.5%	2.5%	2.5%
MICE	£ 86	2.5%	2.5%	2.5%	2.5%
Individual Leisure	£ 63	2.5%	2.5%	2.5%	2.5%
Group Leisure	£ 52	2.5%	2.5%	2.5%	2.5%
Airline	£ 63	2.5%	2.5%	2.5%	2.5%
Total	£ 85	3.3%	2.7%	2.4%	2.5%

TABLE 11.12 Average rate forecast of the hotel by market segment

	Base Year	Year 1	Year 2	Year 3	Year 4
Commercial					
Average Rate Growth	–	2.5%	2.5%	2.5%	2.5%
Captured Room Nights	37,139	41,472	44,276	43,140	41,138
Rooms Revenue	£ 3,617,976	£ 4,141,159	£ 4,531,628	£ 4,525,751	£ 4,423,653
Average Rate	£ 97.42	£ 99.85	£ 102.35	£ 104.91	£ 107.53
MICE					
Average Rate Growth	–	2.5%	2.5%	2.5%	2.5%
Captured Room Nights	10,129	7,159	7,297	7,077	6,718
Rooms Revenue	£ 870,636	£ 630,774	£ 658,975	£ 655,123	£ 637,395
Average Rate	£ 85.96	£ 88.11	£ 90.31	£ 92.57	£ 94.88
Individual Leisure					
Average Rate Growth	–	2.5%	2.5%	2.5%	2.5%
Captured Room Nights	13,505	13,123	13,875	13,719	13,057
Rooms Revenue	£ 851,288	£ 847,862	£ 918,878	£ 931,260	£ 908,497
Average Rate	£ 63.04	£ 64.61	£ 66.23	£ 67.88	£ 69.58
Group Leisure					
Average Rate Growth	–	2.5%	2.5%	2.5%	2.5%
Captured Room Nights	3,376	3,818	3,973	3,870	3,690
Rooms Revenue	£ 174,127	£ 201,854	£ 215,254	£ 214,939	£ 210,081
Average Rate	£ 51.57	£ 52.86	£ 54.19	£ 55.54	£ 56.93
Airline					
Average Rate Growth	–	2.5%	2.5%	2.5%	2.5%
Captured Room Nights	3,376	3,370	3,397	3,307	3,152
Rooms Revenue	£ 212,822	£ 217,710	£ 224,961	£ 224,479	£ 219,318
Average Rate	£ 63.04	£ 64.61	£ 66.23	£ 67.88	£ 69.58
Total					
Average Rate Growth	–	3.3%	2.7%	2.4%	2.5%
Captured Room Nights	67,525	68,942	72,817	71,113	67,756
Rooms Revenue	£ 5,726,850	£ 6,039,359	£ 6,549,695	£ 6,551,552	£ 6,398,944
Average Rate (Before Discount)	£ 84.81	£ 87.60	£ 89.95	£ 92.13	£ 94.44
Average Rate Penetration	112.2%	113.1%	113.3%	113.2%	113.2%
Marketwide Average Rate Growth	–	2.5%	2.5%	2.5%	2.5%
Marketwide Average Rate	£ 75.57	£ 77.45	£ 79.39	£ 81.38	£ 83.41

TABLE 11.13   Forecast occupancy and average rate of the hotel

Year	Occupancy	Average Rate	RevPAR	Average Rate in Base Year Prices
Year 1	76%	£ 88	£ 67	£ 85
Year 2	80%	£ 90	£ 72	£ 86
Year 3	78%	£ 92	£ 72	£ 86
Year 4	74%	£ 94	£ 70	£ 86

The forecast of income and expenses is expressed in inflated pounds sterling as of the date of each projection year. The stabilised year is intended to reflect the expected operating results of the hotel over its remaining economic life, given any or all applicable stages of build-up, plateau and decline in the life cycle of the hotel. Thus, income and expense estimates from the stabilised year forward exclude from consideration any abnormal relationship between supply and demand, as well as any non-recurring conditions that may result in unusual revenues or expenses. For the purposes of determining the hotel's Market Value, it is assumed that the hotel is sold as at the date of value; the projection of income and expenses therefore reflects the achievements of a typical new owner.

Because the hotel is an existing one with an established operating performance, its historical income and expenses experience can serve as a basis for projections.

A CLOSER LOOK 11.10: FORECAST OF INCOME AND EXPENSES

The forecast of income and expenses is intended to reflect the valuer's subjective estimate of how a typical buyer would project the subject property's future operating results. Depending on the dynamics of the local market, a typical buyer's projection may be adjusted up or down.

The model used to project a hotel's revenue and expenses is based on the premise that hotel revenues and expenses have one component that is fixed and another that varies directly with occupancy or facility use. A projection can be made by taking a known level of revenue or expense and calculating the fixed and variable components. The fixed component is adjusted only for inflation, whereas the variable component is also adjusted for the percentage change between the projected occupancy and facility use that produced the known level of revenue or expenses.

Based on the knowledge of the market for hotel accommodation in the city area, and the hotel's expected future market position, a forecast of income and expenses has been developed. The forecast starts on year 1 and represents the opinion of how a competent management company would operate the hotel (Table 11.14 and Table 11.15).

Rooms revenue is determined by two variables – occupancy and average rate – as previously discussed. Analytical details on the nature of the revenue and expense line items presented in the statement of income and expense can be found in the 11th edition of the Uniform System of Accounts for the Lodging Industry (USALI).[7]

TABLE 11.14 Detailed forecast of income and expenses of the hotel

	Base Year (Historical Operating Results)				Year 1				Year 2				Year 3				Stabilised			
Number of Rooms	250				250				250				250				250			
Days Open	365				365				365				365				365			
Occupied Rooms	67,525				69,350				73,000				71,175				67,525			
Occupancy	74%				76%				80%				78%				74%			
Average Rate (£)	84.86				87.60				89.95				92.13				94.44			
RevPAR (£)	62.80				66.58				71.96				71.86				69.89			
Revenues	(£ 000)	% Gross	PAR (²) (£)	POR (³) (£)	(£ 000)	% Gross	PAR (£)	POR (£)	(£ 000)	% Gross	PAR (£)	POR (£)	(£ 000)	% Gross	PAR (£)	POR (£)	(£ 000)	% Gross	PAR (£)	POR (£)
Rooms	5,730	52.8%	22,922	84.86	6,075	53.6%	24,300	87.60	6,566	54.2%	26,264	89.95	6,557	54.1%	26,228	92.13	6,377	53.8%	25,508	94.44
Food and Beverage	4,470	41.2%	17,879	66.19	4,652	41.1%	18,607	67.08	4,933	40.7%	19,734	67.58	4,936	40.7%	19,744	69.35	4,839	40.9%	19,354	71.66
Other Income	659	6.1%	2,636	9.76	597	5.3%	2,387	8.61	619	5.1%	2,474	8.47	626	5.2%	2,504	8.79	628	5.3%	2,513	9.30
Total Revenues	10,859	100%	43,437	160.82	11,324	100%	45,295	163.28	12,118	100%	48,472	166.00	12,119	100%	48,476	170.27	11,844	100%	47,375	175.40
Departmental expenses (¹)																				
Rooms	1,410	24.6%	5,639	20.88	1,436	23.6%	5,745	20.71	1,496	22.8%	5,985	20.50	1,510	23.0%	6,041	21.22	1,508	23.6%	6,031	22.33
Food and Beverage	3,110	69.6%	12,442	46.06	3,175	68.2%	12,699	45.78	3,297	66.8%	13,187	45.16	3,333	67.5%	13,331	46.83	3,339	69.0%	13,354	49.44
Other Expenses	358	54.3%	1,430	5.30	297	49.7%	1,187	4.28	304	49.2%	1,217	4.17	309	49.4%	1,238	4.35	314	50.0%	1,257	4.65
Total	4,878	44.9%	19,511	72.24	4,908	43.3%	19,631	70.77	5,097	42.1%	20,389	69.82	5,153	42.5%	20,610	72.39	5,161	43.6%	20,642	76.42
Departmental income	5,981	55.1%	23,926	88.58	6,416	56.7%	25,664	92.52	7,021	57.9%	28,083	96.18	6,966	57.5%	27,865	97.88	6,683	56.4%	26,733	98.97
Undistributed operating expenses																				
Administrative & General	891	8.2%	3,562	13.19	883	7.8%	3,533	12.74	912	7.5%	3,649	12.50	926	7.6%	3,703	13.01	934	7.9%	3,736	13.83
Marketing	304	2.8%	1,215	4.50	471	4.2%	1,884	6.79	487	4.0%	1,946	6.66	494	4.1%	1,975	6.94	498	4.2%	1,992	7.38
Prop. Operations & Maint.	413	3.8%	1,650	6.11	442	3.9%	1,767	6.37	456	3.8%	1,825	6.25	463	3.8%	1,851	6.50	467	3.9%	1,868	6.92
Utilities	272	2.5%	1,086	4.02	294	2.6%	1,178	4.25	304	2.5%	1,216	4.17	309	2.5%	1,234	4.34	311	2.6%	1,245	4.61
Total	1,878	17.3%	7,514	27.82	2,090	18.5%	8,362	30.14	2,159	17.8%	8,636	29.58	2,191	18.1%	8,763	30.78	2,210	18.7%	8,841	32.73
Management Fees	326	3.0%	1,303	4.82	340	3.0%	1,359	4.90	364	3.0%	1,454	4.98	364	3.0%	1,454	5.11	355	3.0%	1,421	5.26
GOP after management fees	3,777	34.78%	15,109	55.94	3,986	35.2	15,943	57.47	4,498	37.1	17,993	61.62	4,412	36.5	17,648	61.99	4,118	34.8	16,471	60.98

(continued)

TABLE 11.14 (Continued)

	Base Year (Historical Operating Results)				Year 1				Year 2				Year 3				Stabilised			
Number of Rooms	250				250				250				250				250			
Days Open	365				365				365				365				365			
Occupied Rooms	67,525				69,350				73,000				71,175				67,525			
Occupancy	74%				76%				80%				78%				74%			
Average Rate (£)	84.86				87.60				89.95				92.13				94.44			
RevPAR (£)	62.80				66.58				71.96				71.86				69.89			
Revenues	(£ 000)	% Gross	PAR (2) (£)	POR (3) (£)	(£ 000)	% Gross	PAR (£)	POR (£)	(£ 000)	% Gross	PAR (£)	POR (£)	(£ 000)	% Gross	PAR (£)	POR (£)	(£ 000)	% Gross	PAR (£)	POR (£)
Gross Operating Profit (GOP)	4,103	37.784	16,412	60.76	4,326	38.2	17,302	62.37	4,862	40.1	19,447	66.60	4,776	39.5	19,102	67.10	4,473	37.8	17,892	66.24
Fixed expenses																				
Property Taxes	228	2.1%	912	3.38	231	2.0%	924	3.33	236	1.9%	942	3.23	240	2.0%	961	3.38	245	2.1%	980	3.63
Insurance	32	0.3%	128	0.48	33	0.3%	132	0.48	34	0.3%	135	0.46	34	0.3%	137	0.48	35	0.3%	140	0.52
Incentive Management Fee	378	3.5%	1,511	5.59	399	3.5%	1,594	5.75	450	3.7%	1,799	6.16	441	3.6%	1,765	6.20	412	3.5%	1,647	6.10
Reserve for Replacement	326	3.0%	1,303	4.82	340	3.0%	1,359	4.90	364	3.0%	1,454	4.98	364	3.0%	1,454	5.11	355	3.0%	1,421	5.26
Total	964	8.9%	3,855	14.27	1,002	8.9%	4,009	14.45	1,083	8.9%	4,330	14.83	1,079	8.9%	4,317	15.16	1,047	8.8%	4,189	15.51
Net Operating Income (NOI)	2,814	25.9%	11,254	41.67	2,984	26.3%	11,935	43.02	3,416	28.2%	13,663	46.79	3,333	27.5%	13,330	46.82	3,071	25.9%	12,282	45.47

*(1) Departmental expenses are expressed as a percentage of departmental revenues.

*(2) Per Available Room.

*(3) Per Occupied Rooms.

TABLE 11.15 10-year forecast of income and expense of the hotel (years 1 to 10)

	Year 1		Year 2		Year 3		Year 4		Year 5		Year 6		Year 7		Year 8		Year 9		Year 10	
Number of Rooms	250		250		250		250		250		250		250		250		250		250	
Occupied Rooms	69,350		73,000		71,175		67,525		67,525		67,525		67,525		67,525		67,525		67,525	
Occupancy	76%		80%		78%		74%		74%		74%		74%		74%		74%		74%	
Average Rate (£)	87.60		89.95		92.13		94.44		96.33		98.26		100.22		102.23		104.27		106.36	
RevPAR (£)	66.58		71.96		71.86		69.89		71.28		72.71		74.16		75.65		77.16		78.70	
Revenue	(£ 000)	% Gross	(£ 000)	% Gross	(£ 000)	% Gross	(£ 000)	% Gross	(£ 000)	% Gross	(£ 000)	% Gross	(£ 000)	% Gross	(£ 000)	% Gross	(£ 000)	% Gross	(£ 000)	% Gross
Rooms	6,075	53.6%	6,566	54.2%	6,557	54.1%	6,377	53.8%	6,505	53.8%	6,635	53.8%	6,767	53.8%	6,903	53.8%	7,041	53.8%	7,182	53.8%
Food and Beverage	4,652	41.1%	4,933	40.7%	4,936	40.7%	4,839	40.9%	4,935	40.9%	5,034	40.9%	5,135	40.9%	5,237	40.9%	5,342	40.9%	5,449	40.9%
Other Income	597	5.3%	619	5.1%	626	5.2%	628	5.3%	641	5.3%	654	5.3%	667	5.3%	680	5.3%	694	5.3%	708	5.3%
Total	11,324	100%	12,118	100%	12,119	100%	11,844	100%	12,081	100%	12,323	100%	12,568	100%	12,820	100%	13,077	100%	13,338	100%
Departmental expenses (*)																				
Rooms	1,436	23.6%	1,496	22.8%	1,510	23.0%	1,508	23.6%	1,538	23.6%	1,569	23.6%	1,600	23.6%	1,632	23.6%	1,665	23.6%	1,698	23.6%
Food and Beverage	3,175	68.2%	3,297	66.8%	3,333	67.5%	3,339	69.0%	3,405	69.0%	3,473	69.0%	3,543	69.0%	3,614	69.0%	3,686	69.0%	3,760	69.0%
Other Expenses	297	49.7%	304	49.2%	309	49.4%	314	50.0%	320	50.0%	327	50.0%	333	50.0%	340	50.0%	347	50.0%	354	50.0%
Total	4,908	43.3%	5,097	42.1%	5,153	42.5%	5,161	43.6%	5,264	43.6%	5,369	43.6%	5,476	43.6%	5,586	43.6%	5,698	43.6%	5,812	43.6%
Departmental income	6,416	56.7%	7,021	57.9%	6,966	57.5%	6,683	56.4%	6,817	56.4%	6,954	56.4%	7,092	56.4%	7,234	56.4%	7,379	56.4%	7,527	56.4%
Undistributed operating expenses																				
Administrative & General	883	7.8%	912	7.5%	926	7.6%	934	7.9%	953	7.9%	972	7.9%	991	7.9%	1,011	7.9%	1,031	7.9%	1,052	7.9%
Marketing	471	4.2%	487	4.0%	494	4.1%	498	4.2%	508	4.2%	518	4.2%	529	4.2%	539	4.2%	550	4.2%	561	4.2%
Prop. Operations & Maint.	442	3.9%	456	3.8%	463	3.8%	467	3.9%	476	3.9%	486	3.9%	496	3.9%	505	3.9%	516	3.9%	526	3.9%
Utilities	294	2.6%	304	2.5%	309	2.5%	311	2.6%	318	2.6%	324	2.6%	330	2.6%	337	2.6%	344	2.6%	351	2.6%
Total	2,090	18.5%	2,159	17.8%	2,191	18.1%	2,210	18.7%	2,254	18.7%	2,300	18.7%	2,345	18.7%	2,392	18.7%	2,440	18.7%	2,489	18.7%
Gross Operating Profit (GOP)	4,326	37.784	4,862	37.784	4,776	37.784	4,473	37.784	4,563	37.784	4,654	37.784	4,746	37.784	4,842	37.784	4,939	37.784	5,038	37.784
Management Fee	340	3.0%	364	3.0%	364	3.0%	355	3.0%	362	3.0%	370	3.0%	377	3.0%	385	3.0%	392	3.0%	400	3.0%
GOP after management fees	3,986	34.784	4,498	34.784	4,412	34.784	4,118	34.784	4,200	34.784	4,284	34.784	4,369	34.784	4,457	34.784	4,547	34.784	4,638	34.784

(continued)

TABLE 11.15 *(Continued)*

	Year 1		Year 2		Year 3		Year 4		Year 5		Year 6		Year 7		Year 8		Year 9		Year 10	
Number of Rooms	250		250		250		250		250		250		250		250		250		250	
Occupied Rooms	69,350		73,000		71,175		67,525		67,525		67,525		67,525		67,525		67,525		67,525	
Occupancy	76%		80%		78%		74%		74%		74%		74%		74%		74%		74%	
Average Rate (£)	87.60		89.95		92.13		94.44		96.33		98.26		100.22		102.23		104.27		106.36	
RevPAR (£)	66.58		71.96		71.86		69.89		71.28		72.71		74.16		75.65		77.16		78.70	
Revenue	(£ 000)	% Gross	(£ 000)	% Gross	(£ 000)	% Gross	(£ 000)	% Gross	(£ 000)	% Gross	(£ 000)	% Gross	(£ 000)	% Gross	(£ 000)	% Gross	(£ 000)	% Gross	(£ 000)	% Gross
Fixed expenses																				
Property Taxes	231	2.0%	236	1.9%	240	2.0%	245	2.1%	250	2.1%	255	2.1%	260	2.1%	265	2.1%	271	2.1%	276	2.1%
Insurance	33	0.3%	34	0.3%	34	0.3%	35	0.3%	36	0.3%	36	0.3%	37	0.3%	38	0.3%	39	0.3%	39	0.3%
Incentive Management Fee	399	3.5%	450	3.7%	441	3.6%	412	3.5%	420	3.5%	428	3.5%	437	3.5%	446	3.5%	455	3.5%	464	3.5%
Reserve for Replacement	340	3.0%	364	3.0%	364	3.0%	355	3.0%	362	3.0%	370	3.0%	377	3.0%	385	3.0%	392	3.0%	400	3.0%
Total	1,002	8.9%	1,083	8.9%	1,079	8.9%	1,047	8.8%	1,068	8.8%	1,090	8.8%	1,111	8.8%	1,134	8.8%	1,156	8.8%	1,179	8.8%
Net Operating Income (NOI)	2,984	26.3%	3,416	28.2%	3,333	27.5%	3,071	25.9%	3,132	25.9%	3,195	25.9%	3,258	25.9%	3,324	25.9%	3,390	25.9%	3,458	25.9%

Departmental expenses are expressed as a percentage of departmental revenues.

Special attention should be given to the FF&E which are essential to the operation of a hotel, and their quality often influences the standard or grading of a property. Included in this category are all non–real-estate items that are typically capitalised rather than expensed. The FF&E of a hotel are often exposed to heavy use and must be replaced at regular intervals. Periodic replacement of FF&E is essential to maintain the quality, image and income potential of a hotel. Because capitalised expenditures are not included in the operating statement, but nevertheless affect an owner's cash flow, a valuation should reflect these expenses by deducting an appropriate reserve for replacement. Based on industry experience a reserve for replacement of 3% to 4% of total revenue is generally sufficient to provide for the timely replacement of FF&E.

The projection of income and expenses reported in Table 11.14 and in Table 11.15 are intended to reflect how a typical buyer would project the hotel's operating results.

VALUATION

In order to estimate the value of the hotel,[8] a DCFA analysis has been used, estimating the cost of debt and the cost of equity first, rather than a straight Weighted Average Cost of Capital (WACC), based on the premise that Investors typically purchase real estate properties with a mix of equity and debt financing.

Data for the debt component are developed from an analysis of the prevailing interest rates offered in the marketplace coupled with interviews with hotel investors, banks, and other investment institutions. To reflect the appropriate rates and investment yields required by banks, the 10-year swap rate for pound sterling has been reviewed. A risk premium is then added to the yield for the risks associated with a project of this nature. Short-term interest rates at the valuation date in the UK are assumed at 7%. From this information and the perceived risk of the hotel's location, it is considered that a bank will lend up to 60% of the hotel's value as determined by this valuation (LTV).

In order to estimate the value of the hotel's equity component, the loan to value ratio has been considered, together with the operational risk inherent in achieving the projected income stream, the age, condition and expected market position of the hotel, the freehold nature of the site, and the opportunities for competition to enter the market. Given the market conditions at the date of valuation, an equity investor is likely to require an equity yield rate of 20% for a hotel investment such as the subject property.[9]

Inherent in this valuation process is the assumption of a sale at the end of an assumed 10-year holding period:[10] the Terminal Value, also called estimated reversionary sale price, has been calculated by capitalising the projected 11th year's Net Operating Income by an overall terminal cap rate.[11] From this sale price, a percentage has been deducted for the seller's transaction costs and legal fees. On the basis of current yields for Comparable properties,[12] a terminal cap rate of 7% has been estimated, while the seller's brokerage and legal fees have been assumed to be 1.5% of the sale price.

Table 11.16 summarises the key valuation parameters used in the derivation of the value of the hotel by the DCFA.

Using a total property yield (WACC Discount Rate) of 10.7%, Table 11.17 shows the DCFA model. The DCFA value has been adjusted to allow for deductions for stamp duty (4% of value) and legal fees (0.5% of value), which have been treated as purchaser's costs in arriving at the price which would be paid for the hotel.[13]

Overall, therefore, the Market Value of the hotel can be quantified at £ 35,600,000, which equates £ 142,400 per room for the 250-room hotel.

TABLE 11.16   Summary of the valuation parameters

Stabilised Year	Year 4
Inflation	2.0%
Loan to Value	60.0%
Term (years)	10
Cost of Debt	4.5%
Terminal Capitalization Rate	7.0%
Transaction Costs	1.5%
Cost of Equity	20.0%
Discount rate	10.7%

TABLE 11.17   DCFA model

Year	Net Operating Income (£)	Discount Factor @ 10.7%	Discounted Cash Flow (£)
Year 1	2,984,000	0.9033	2,695,574
Year 2	3,416,000	0.8160	2,787,550
Year 3	3,333,000	0.7372	2,456,928
Year 4	3,071,000	0.6659	2,044,981
Year 5	3,132,000	0.6015	1,884,012
Year 6	3,195,000	0.5434	1,736,142
Year 7	3,258,000	0.4909	1,599,255
Year 8	3,324,000	0.4434	1,473,941
Year 9	3,390,000	0.4006	1,357,910
Year 10	53,088,000(*)	0.3618	19,209,681
		Estimated Market Value	37,245,974
		Less: Stamp duty @ 4.0%	*1,489,839*
		Less: Legal fees @ 0.5%	*186,230*
		Estimated Market Value (rounded)	**35,600,000**
Reversion Analysis			
11th Year's Net Operating Income			3,527,000
Capitalisation Rate			7.0%
Total Sales Proceeds			50,385,714
Less: Transaction Costs @ 1.5%			*755,786*
Net Sales Proceeds			**49,629,929**

*10th year net operating income of £ 3,458,000 plus sales proceeds of £ 49,630,000 (rounded)

NOTES

1. Even if based on a real valuation, fictitious names have been used for streets and hotel brands.
2. The hotel can be classified as Upscale, according to the international classification which, based on the actual average room rates, divides the hotel chain scale segments in Luxury, Upper Upscale, Upscale, Upper Midscale, Midscale, Economy and Independent.
3. For in-depth information about hotel valuations, please see also the *Hotel Investments Handbook* by Steve Rushmore: www.hvs.com/article/3237-The-Rushmore-Letter-Hotel-Investments-Handbook.
4. Furniture, Fixtures, and Equipment: generally referred to movable furniture, fixtures, or other equipment that have no permanent connection to the building. An FF&E list includes:
   - Guest room furnishings, including all movable and non-movable furniture, decorative lighting and decorative elements (for example, curtains)
   - All design-elements within the guest areas (lifts, restrooms, hallways)
   - Restaurants, bars and conference facilities complete furnishing
   - Administrative and staff areas furnishing
   - Equipping of all storage facilities, large kitchen appliances
   - Small equipment (silver, glass, porcelain) as well as technical devices for guest entertainment and conference facilities
   - Computer equipment (excluding network) and telecoms user-equipment.
5. RevPAR is calculated by multiplying a hotel's occupancy by its average rate.
6. The official or advertised price of a hotel room, on which a discount is usually negotiable.
7. See www.hftp.org/hospitality_resources/usali_guide
8. Please refer also to www.hvs.com/article/591-Simultaneous-Valuation-A-New-Capitalization-Technique-for-Hotel-and-Other-Income-Properties.
9. Even if the valuer in the case has not explicitly mentioned and described the model, the estimation is implicitly based on a Build-up Approach model.
10. In contrast to what stated in Chapter 9, Subsection 'Choosing the Time Horizon', where the suggested time horizon should be the minimum beyond which the cash flow is stabilised (in this case year 4), the valuer has opted for a 10-year period. The choice of using 10-year or 15-year time horizons is quite common among valuers and it cannot be considered wrong if the estimated going-out cap rate is consistent with the time horizon.
11. Previously mentioned also as the 'going-out cap rate' or 'reversionary yield'.
12. This analysis is not reported in the case study.
13. The choice of adjusting the estimated Market Value for the stamp duty and legal fees, in those countries where those costs vary according to the different Investors, is difficult and therefore not used in market valuation. When it is possible to apply these adjustments, it is indeed even better: the final Market Value obtained is the purchase price that would allow the Investor to reach the equity return used in order to estimate the discount rate in the valuation.

CHAPTER 12

Development Project Appraisal

T he following case study is related to the valuation of a plot of land located in Manhattan, New York City, where the Highest and Best Use (HBU) has been identified in the Development of a luxury residential condominium with retail space at its base. As a complex Development Project which will take a few years to be completed, a Multiple Periods Residual Value Approach is deemed to be the most appropriate valuation method.

DESCRIPTION OF THE PROPERTY

The subject property consists of a development area located in the Financial District neighbourhood of Manhattan in New York City, within major employment centres, transportation nodes, the World Trade Center redevelopment and outdoor recreation areas. This desirable destination creates demand for high-end residential condos that hit the top 10% of the market by price.

The value of a development area is a function of the Building that will be constructed on it, designed to its best permitted use, as described in the Chapter 6, Section 'Residual Value Methods'. The valuation process will therefore rely on the identification of the 'best' use of the area, i.e. the HBU that allows the highest profit.

According to a feasibility study undertaken,[1] the HBU has been identified in a tower of 250 luxury condo units with unrivalled views rising above the retail space located at street level, second floor and basement level. According to the same study, a Building whose concept is developed by a premier architect has unavoidably higher costs associated with building design, top quality materials and luxury interior finishes. However, this should be recovered in the form of higher sales prices considering that, based on market analysis, the contribution of a renowned architect to the sell-out of a top-tier building provides for a 10% to 15% premium.

The base of the residential tower will feature 1,125 m^2 of retail space in a highly visible corner with strong and growing pedestrian traffic. This strategic location will benefit from affluent workers in surrounding office towers, as well as from residents in the area and tourist

---

This case study has been written by **Arianna Mazzanti**.

Arianna Mazzanti is a financial project manager at Milanosesto Development – Prelios Group, which foresees the mixed-use development of over 1 million m^2 of new and renovated spaces and 650,000 m^2 of green spaces on the former Ex-Falck industrial area in Sesto San Giovanni (Milan).

Previously she worked for Bizzi & Partners Development, a global real estate firm active in established and emerging markets across Europe and The Americas. Before moving to Milan, she was based for over three years in New York focusing on real estate projects in the United States, mainly the development of luxury residential buildings with retail space and the conversion of an office building to a condominium.

TABLE 12.1   Area chart

Intended Use	# of units	Rentable / Sellable Area (m²)
Retail	1	1,125
Residential	250	25,728
Total	**251**	**26,853**

TABLE 12.2   Residential units mix

Unit Type	%	# of units	Average size (m²)	Sellable Area (m²)
studio	21.2%	53	50	2,656
1-bedroom	45.2%	113	85	9,573
2-bedroom	22.4%	56	140	7,821
3-bedroom	11.2%	28	203	5,678
Total	**100.0%**	**250**	**103**	**25,728**

TABLE 12.3   Retail areas by floor

Floor	Rentable Area (m²)
Basement	300
Groud	305
Second	520
Total	**1,125**

traffic to Lower Manhattan attractions. Moreover, the proximity to important transportation hubs, covering trains and most of the subway lines, will ensure traffic from commuters and visitors, estimated to total 500,000 people per day.

Close by, the retail portion of the World Trade Center site features approximately 30,000 m² of retail space and includes a selection of prime tenants. Other retail complexes have been developed in the surrounding areas in order to expand the offerings to include luxury fashion, a European-style marketplace, and quick-casual and formal dining.

A breakdown by function is detailed in Table 12.1 to outline the building components and the respective dimensions.

The residential unit mix and average unit size are summarised in Table 12.2.

The retail space is distributed over three floors, as outlined in Table 12.3.

At the date of valuation, the foundation works have been completed[2] and there is no entitlement risk as building permits have been obtained.

CHOICE OF VALUATION METHOD

The choice of a Residual Value Method prevails over the Direct Comparison Approach because the comparable sales do not truly capture the specific features of a Development. Comparable

Land sales would require indeed substantial adjustments, namely: location, views, time of the purchase to account for changes in market conditions, layout of the units, and building configuration.

Among the different approaches of the Residual Value Method, the Multiple Periods Residual Value Approach is deemed to be the most appropriate considering the time horizon to complete the construction and sale of the mixed-use tower. In particular, it takes into account the time value of money when computing the return on invested capital by considering the period in which the capital is invested. The estimated cash flows over time are discounted at an expected rate of return, providing for a more precise measure of the Investor's margin.

The value allocated to the subject property is residual after net proceeds from sales have covered all costs related to the development, including the remuneration for the Development risk and the developer's activity.

A CLOSER LOOK 12.1: MARKET VALUATION AND REAL ESTATE DEVELOPMENT PROJECTS

The subject property represents a typical Development Project. In the real world the current Owner of the area might not have either the amount of capital necessary to pursue the development nor the skills to run it, and therefore the actual project might not coincide with his foreseen HBU development. In Market Value estimation this is not relevant, since the precondition is that some market participants have the available capital to develop the project and, thus, to benefit of the highest Net Present Value of the HBU scenario.

MARKET ANALYSIS

At the date of valuation, overall development activity in the subject district has significantly increased since the recovery from subprime mortgage crisis. Moreover, the public infrastructure projects have been improving Lower Manhattan's accessibility and attractiveness. The current trend of the neighbourhood appears to be positive with rising demand for retail, residential and office spaces. Economic expansion is expected to continue over the next several years as the tech industry drives employment and financial services continue to recover.

The New York City residential market is the largest housing market in the United States. The majority of the market consists of rental units,[3] many of which are governed by rent stabilisation and rent control regulations. However, the rising cost of development sites in Manhattan makes it harder for developers to break-even by pursuing a rental building investment strategy. Consequently, most new developments in Manhattan are condominium projects, unless they are constructed with subsidies, or conversions to condominium.

The luxury segment hits the top 10% of the condominium market by price which on average, at the valuation date, is estimated to stand at over $ 30,000 per square metre in Downtown Manhattan. In the upper tier of the market, units' absorption goes in parallel with construction works. This is usually the result of targeted marketing strategies which start advertising a selected set of units several months prior to project completion to foster demand from the market and to gradually increase the pricing. The placing of inventories during the construction

TABLE 12.4   Comparable condominium developments

Comparable developments	# of units	% of units sold	Average unit size (m^2)	Average sale price ($/m^2)
1	157	63.1%	182	$ 33,874
2	220	5.0%	155	$ 25,629
3	157	46.5%	178	$ 22,647
4	223	3.6%	81	$ 23,056
5	257	5.1%	122	$ 21,905
6	192	7.3%	191	$ 23,853
7	187	35.8%	134	$ 22,109
8	146	79.5%	205	$ 32,109
Average	**192**	**30.7%**	**156**	**$ 25,648**
High	**257**	**79.5%**	**205**	**$ 33,874**
Low	**146**	**3.6%**	**81**	**$ 21,905**

period lowers substantially the market risk and allows for improvements in the financing terms which usually tie to the sales absorption rate, with a positive impact on the project timeline and profit.

The comparable developments exhibit predominantly units sold in the range between 146 and 257 m^2 or 192 m^2 on average. The condominium average sales price ranges from a low of 21,905 $/m^2 to a high of 33,874 $/m^2, or 25,648 $/m^2 on average, which should be adjusted to consider all differences in the design, finishing, location and views to correctly estimate the revenues of the subject property. The main comparable condominium unit sales are reported in Table 12.4.

VALUATION OF THE DEVELOPMENT PROJECT

The Discounted Cash Flow Approach (DCFA) has been determined to be the best approach for evaluating the subject development area. Forecasted sources of revenues and expenses are modelled to reflect expectations of typical investors in the property being appraised.

Choosing the Time Horizon

Considering that, as reported in the Section 'Description of the Property' above, building permits have been obtained at the time of the valuation, the uncertainty related to the overall project timeline is lowered substantially. The choice of the time horizon is based on the typical development schedule for a new residential building, estimated to fall within the range of 18 to 24 months once all approvals are granted and foundations are completed. In this specific case, the valuation allows a period of 30 months for above-grade construction. The contingency on the development schedule takes into account the size and complexity of the project, mainly due to the tight development site footprint which requires considerable coordination efforts during the construction phase.

A CLOSER LOOK 12.2: ABSORPTION RATE AND MARKETING STRATEGY FOR LUXURY RESIDENTIAL DEVELOPMENTS

A key factor in residential developments is the absorption rate: iconic buildings associated with the name of star architects are proved to sell faster than other products in the same location and with a competitive set of finishing. Additionally, distinctive buildings from a quality standpoint and with a higher standing for the amenity space are more attractive in the market if price points and common charges remain at a competitive level. In this scenario, new developments experience the highest absorption rate in the initial phase of sell-out, which overlaps with construction activities.

The usual marketing strategy for developers is to let buyers choose on a limited inventory list compared to the entire set of units being developed, which is then integrated on a rolling basis. Scarcity stimulates demand as people feel that they may not be able to get those units in the future. Furthermore, the selection of units comes from a deep study: pricing the property implies testing the market and to start low enough to create momentum and raise progressively the sales price, but not too low to avoid the product to be perceived of scarce quality. Obviously, the first units to be sold at discount cannot be the most valuable ones. A fair balance is the key to make the project successful: marketing is essential for luxury condominiums.

The sales velocity in the market has been studied considering the main Comparable Properties in the surrounding area. The resulting absorption of units is summarised in Table 12.5.

From the market evidence it has been inferred that on average units will be sold at a pace of 6 units per month for the subject property. Consequently, the absorption period considered in

TABLE 12.5   Sales velocity for Comparable Properties

Comparable developments	# of units	Average # of sales/month
1	157	11
2	220	3
3	157	5
4	223	3
5	257	4
6	192	2
7	187	15
8	146	9
Average	192	6
High	257	15
Low	146	2

the valuation is 18 months after construction completion. Assuming that sales will reasonably begin after a semester the building starts going vertical, with a timeline of 30 months for above-grade construction and 6 units per month absorption rate, at completion the units sold will be 144 out of 250. In other words, 58% of the residential units are assumed to be sold prior to completion. The remaining 106 units will take 18 months to be sold, always considering an average of 6 units per month.

Estimating the Cash Flows

Revenues Estimate Based on the comparable analysis presented in the Section 'Market Analysis', an average price of 30,000 $/m^2 has been considered appropriate, and the average price per residential units results to be approximately $ 3 million.

In addition to the subject's residential units, the property will contain 1,125 square metres of retail space. In order to determine the rent for the retail component, a market analysis has been carried out on comparable spaces in the surrounding area. The resulting average rent for the ground floor is 3,285 $/m^2. However, the subject valuation has to account for the Lower Manhattan revitalisation, highlighted at the beginning of this chapter, and for the fact that the district of the subject property is experiencing a tremendous growth as a retail destination.

The valuation estimates a net retail rent of 1,650 $/m^2, which is a weighted average of a rent of 700 $/m^2 for the cellar space,[4] 3,500 $/m^2 for the ground floor retail space and 1,115 $/m^2 for the second floor retail space. Rent for cellar space commands a substantial discount compared to the ground floor rent, given the loss of visibility and no access to natural light. Likewise, rent for the second floor has a discount compared to the ground floor rent but it is better priced than the basement areas having some visibility and access to light and air.

Typically, in New York City retail tenants sign long-term leases, ranging from 10 to 15 years. The exit timing for the retail component in the subject's valuation is assumed at construction completion, upon the issuance of the Temporary Certificate of Occupancy. Considering market data, the valuation is based on an overall cap rate of 4.75 percent, bringing to a total expected revenue from the retail unit equal to $ 39.1 million as presented in Table 12.6.

Development Costs Estimate It is market practice to refer to Gross Buildable Areas in estimating development costs on a unitary basis. Non-sellable areas typically include lobby and reception, amenity space, mechanical rooms and circulations. The small footprint of the building goes against efficiency, which can be reasonably assumed to be 70% for the residential portion of the building. Retail areas are usually sold for 100% of their built area at minimum, with nil loss factor. The total buildable area and the breakdown for intended use is reported in Table 12.7 and it will represent the base for the calculation of cost estimates.

TABLE 12.6 Retail component valuation with the Direct Capitalisation Approach

Floor	Rentable Area (m^2)	Rent ($/m^2/year)	Net Operating Income
Cellar	300	$ 700	$ 210,000
Groud	305	$ 3,500	$ 1,067,500
Second	520	$ 1,115	$ 579,800
Total	**1,125**	**$ 1,651**	**$ 1,857,300**
		@ 4.75% Cap. Rate	**$ 39,101,053**

TABLE 12.7   Gross Buildable Areas calculation

Intended Use	Buildable Area (m²)	Building Efficiency	Rentable / Sellable Area (m²)
Retail	1,125	100%	1,125
Residential	36,754	70%	25,728
Total	**37,879**	**71%**	**26,853**

Comparable developments incurred in hard costs within a range from 4,960 \$/m² to 11,500 \$/m², or 7,070 \$/m² on average. Taking into account the characteristics of the foreseen development and the estimates made by a third-party engineering company, projected construction costs have been estimated at 8,000 \$/m².

Hard costs typically range between 70% and 80% of total development costs. The subject property hard costs have been estimated at the top end of the range, accounting for 84% of total development costs, which is reasonable for the construction of a tower on a small site footprint. As for the timing, usually forecasts of construction costs tend to have a peak in middle periods and moderated spending in both earlier periods and in the end tail. Consistently, the subject valuation will not apply a linear distribution for hard costs, but more similar to a bell-curve.

An overview of comparable data for soft costs indicates a range from 1,110 \$/m² to 2,153 \$/m², with an average of 1,615 \$/m². For the subject property they have been estimated, including architects, engineering and all other consultants, equal to approximately 1,550 \$/m² and they have been distributed in the DCFA model with the same timing of the hard costs (in similar projects indeed they usually represent 20% of the hard costs).

A CLOSER LOOK 12.3: DEVELOPER'S PROFIT

In addition to the above identified cost items, some valuers also include within the development costs the developer's profit incentive (estimated as a percentage of the total hard and soft costs). While a development management fee to cover for operating and coordination costs is reasonable, the valuer should be careful not to include a development management fee to motivate and compensate the developer for the expertise and the risk associated with the development if that reward component is already included in the discount factor as a risk premium.

Lastly, sales fees are due on gross sales proceeds. It has been considered an average of 4.75% on residential sales (calculated as a weighted average assuming a mix of owners' placed units with no commissions, exclusive broker sales with below-average commissions and sales made by co-brokers with above-average commissions), and a standard 2% on the exit value for the retail unit.

Determining the Discount Rate

In a transparent market such as the New York real estate market, the appropriate discount rate can be selected between the ones inferred from the market instead of building up the discount

TABLE 12.8 Discounted Cash Flow Approach model

	semester	Above-Grade Construction					Post-construction			Total
		1	2	3	4	5	6	7	8	
Positive Cash Flows										
Residential sales revenues	$771,840,000	$0	$0	$0	$0	$0	$555,724,800	$111,144,960	$104,970,240	$771,840,000
% of units closed		*0.0%*	*0.0%*	*0.0%*	*0.0%*	*0.0%*	*72.0%*	*14.4%*	*13.6%*	
Retail sales revenues	$39,101,053	$0	$0	$0	$0	$0	$39,101,053	$0	$0	$39,101,053
% of units closed		*0.0%*	*0.0%*	*0.0%*	*0.0%*	*0.0%*	*100.0%*	*0.0%*	*0.0%*	
Total Positive Cash Flows		**$0**	**$0**	**$0**	**$0**	**$0**	**$594,825,853**	**$111,144,960**	**$104,970,240**	**$810,941,053**
Negative Cash Flows										
Hard costs (8,000 $/m²)		$36,363,840	$72,727,680	$84,848,960	$72,727,680	$36,363,840				$303,032,000
Hard costs distribution in %		*12.0%*	*24.0%*	*28.0%*	*24.0%*	*12.0%*				
Soft costs (1,550 $/m²)	19.38%	$7,045,494	$14,090,988	$16,439,486	$14,090,988	$7,045,494				$58,712,450
Developer's Profit (15% Hard & Soft costs)	15.00%	$6,511,400	$13,022,800	$15,193,267	$13,022,800	$6,511,400				$54,261,668
Sales commissions		$0	$0	$0	$0	$0	$27,178,949	$5,279,386	$4,986,086	$37,444,421
Residential (4.75% of residential sales revenues)	*4.75%*	*$0*	*$0*	*$0*	*$0*	*$0*	*$26,396,928*	*$5,279,386*	*$4,986,086*	*$36,662,400*
Retail (2.00% of retail sales revenues)	*2.00%*	*$0*	*$0*	*$0*	*$0*	*$0*	*$782,021*	*$0*	*$0*	*$782,021*
Total Negative Cash Flows		**$49,920,734**	**$99,841,468**	**$116,481,713**	**$99,841,468**	**$49,920,734**	**$27,178,949**	**$5,279,386**	**$4,986,086**	**$453,450,539**
Net Cash Flows		**–$49,920,734**	**–$99,841,468**	**–$116,481,713**	**–$99,841,468**	**–$49,920,734**	**$567,647,904**	**$105,865,574**	**$99,984,154**	**$357,490,514**
Discount rate	8.00%									
Time factor		*0.25*	*0.75*	*1.25*	*1.75*	*2.25*	*2.75*	*3.25*	*3.75*	
Discount factor		*0.981*	*0.944*	*0.908*	*0.874*	*0.841*	*0.809*	*0.779*	*0.749*	
Discounted Cash Flows		**–$48,969,427**	**–$94,241,707**	**–$105,798,145**	**–$87,260,839**	**–$41,983,391**	**$459,370,334**	**$82,438,020**	**$74,919,021**	**$238,473,866**
Land Market Value	$238,473,866									
Land Market Value (rounded)	**$238,500,000**									

rate by estimating a premium to be added to a risk-free rate selected from investment securities. Therefore, it is common practice to use widely recognised indications from investor surveys as an authoritative source for cap and discount rates, such as the PwC Real Estate Investor Survey[5] and the Real Estate Research Corporation Investor Survey.[6] These surveys are based on the net cash flows to Investors already including the developer's profit, as explained in A Closer Look 12.3.

At the date of valuation, it has been estimated an 8% discount rate,[7] above the average of those surveys, since a higher market risk for a luxury condominium development with prices in the upper tier has been taken into account.

Calculating the Market Value of the Development Project

The DCFA model of the valuation, which summarises the assumptions made in the previous sections, is shown in Table 12.8.

Based upon the analysis performed in this appraisal, the Market Value of the Land is approximately $ 238.5 million.

NOTES

1. Omitted in this case study.
2. Foundation works of the subject property are deemed suitable for several Development Projects, including the identified HBU tower building.
3. These properties, even if Residential, being owned by a single Investor and professionally managed, according to the classification presented in Chapter 2 for analysis purposes may be classified as Commercial Properties.
4. Also known as 'basement floor'.
5. 'A source for capitalization and discount rates, cash flow assumptions, and actual criteria of active investors, as well as property market information', www.pwc.com/us/en/industries/asset-wealth-management/real-estate/library/investor-survey.html
6. www.situs.com/services-2/situs-rerc
7. Please note that when the developer's profit is included in the cash flows as in this case study, the discount rate is lower and does not fully reflect the expected rate of return. As an alternative methodology, the valuer may have not considered the developer's profit in the cash flows and he may have used a higher discount rate reflecting the whole return. Both methodologies are correct, and the choice depends on the local market practice and data availability.

Glossary

The Glossary section reports some of the most frequently real estate terms used in practice and some terms used in the text with the intended meanings given to them by the Authors. The use of capital letters is not intended to confer importance to the individual terms, the definitions of which may not be strictly "rigorous" from a legal or economic point of view, but only to make the text easier to read and indicate unequivocally certain concepts which are often referred to in the text with the same meaning. The authors certainly have no intention of proposing new definitions! Note, furthermore, that the following list does not include terms with meanings that are widely accepted in the relevant literature and in practice (including yield, cap rate, Net Operating Income, etc.) and the definitions or explanations for which can easily be found within the same text.

Break option An early withdrawal clause which allows the tenant to terminate the lease agreement at certain specific time without incurring into penalties.

Brownfield Property that is currently unusable and which in order to generate some utility (Space for which there is a real demand) requires a Residual Value Method (i.e. replacement or refurbishment of the Building by improving its quality or changing its current use).

Buildable Area See "Buildable Land".

Buildable Land Land which fulfils all the legal and/or economic requirements for buildings to be erected for a purpose that complies with existing legislation authorising their construction and the cost of which can be covered.

Building The structure built on the Land and representing the component of the property that loses its utility over time.

Build-Up Approach A method to estimate Property Return Rates which consists in the identification of the main elements according to which the risk of an investment can be defined, in the research of a tool in order to quantify them and, at the end, in a synthesis of those quantities, applying the necessary weighting factors, in order to obtain a single number representative of the intensity of the risk considered.

CapEx Capital investment expenditures, i.e. investments made to improve and increase usability, and therefore value, of the property, by maximising its capacity to generate income. Unlike extraordinary maintenance, which is intended exclusively to maintain the Building in appropriate physical conditions, CapEx are aimed at increasing its quality.

Commercial Business premises in which Space is a means of production to make other goods and services, where strategic control is often of less value.

Commercial Property See "Commercial".

Commercial Space Space which constitutes a means of production for businesses in a broad sense, both private and public, i.e. which is used in a production process by Users.

Comparable Property see "Comparables".

Comparables Properties that are comparable to the property being valued and that compose the comparative set from which comparative data can be derived. If the Sales Comparison Methods are used, the comparative data, at the property level, are the sale prices of transactions involving properties. If the Income Capitalisation Methods are used, the comparative data, at the property level, are the yield rates of assets recently sold (Investment Market) and the rents (Space Market).

Cost Approach Methods Property Valuation methods based on the cost involved in building a property.

Depreciated Cost Approach Methods See "Cost Approach Methods".

Depreciated Cost Methods See "Cost Approach Methods".

Development Project This is the property production activity which involves acquisition of the area (purchase of raw materials) and construction (production process) in a real industrial Residual Value Method in which the raw materials (Land and Building) are used to obtain a final product (the property, i.e. the space available for use) which will be sold to the end client (direct User or Investor).

Direct Capitalisation Approach Valuation model (within the Income Capitalisation Approach Methods) which allows the expected income for a single period to be converted into an indication of value by means of direct capitalisation.

Direct Comparison Approach Valuation model (within the Sales Comparison Approach Methods), which is based on the values of Comparable Properties recently sold.

Discounted Cash Flow Approach (DCFA) Valuation model (within the Income Capitalisation Approach Methods) which allows all future Cash Flows to be converted into a Present Value, discounting every expected future benefit at an appropriate discount rate.

Effort rate The ratio of the rent (or rent and expenses) on the tenant's turnover. In Trade-Related Properties it is an important measure of the sustainability of the rent paid by the tenant.

Expected Rental Value (ERV) See "Market Rent".

Flexible Commercial Property Property used by businesses for whom the use of a specific property is not key to their decisions regarding Space Use, but in which the opportunity to use a certain amount of space with specific characteristics is important.

Greenfield Land on which no Building has ever been built before.

Gross Buildable Area Total floor area including surface areas that cannot be leased or sold (such as lobby and reception, amenity space, mechanical rooms, etc.).

Gross Surface Area The sum of all the surface areas (covered and uncovered) of a property, divided by purpose and floor, as well as by primary and secondary purpose (lift shafts, corridors, utilities areas, etc.).

Headline rent In lease agreements which foresee free-rent periods or step-up rent formulas, it is the rent amount that will be paid by the tenant "at operating speed".

Highest and Best Use (HBU) Any use of the property that is physically possible (i.e. technically achievable), financially sustainable, legally permitted (or allowed by town planning regulations), economically convenient (which offers the best profitability) and which therefore allows the value itself to be maximised.

Income Capitalisation Approach Methods See "Income Capitalisation Comparison Approach Methods".

Income Capitalisation Methods See "Income Capitalisation Comparison Approach Methods".

Income Capitalisation Comparison Approach Methods Property Valuation methods which allow the value of a property to be expressed based on the future Cash Flows and return required.

Income-producing Property Property already built which typically generates rental income/cash flow. This may be a property needing to be upgraded or a property completed but not yet leased.

Investment Market The market in which the ownership of the properties is traded between Owners/Investors.

Investment Property Property whose Owner derives utility not from the end-use of the same, but from the income derived from the offer of the Space Use, i.e. the rental income.

Investment Value (or Worth) *"The value of an asset to the owner or a prospective owner for individual investment or operational objectives"* (RICS, 2017).

Investor The Owner of a property who does not use it directly but who, for investment purposes, benefits from income derived from granting Space Use.

Key money The amount of money paid from a new tenant in order to "buy" the lease agreement from the current tenant of a retail unit (it is common practice especially for High Street Retail units). In this way the new tenant will substitute the old one in all its contractual obligations.

Land The area on which the Building stands, including the building rights and the rights associated with its location.

Market Rent *"The estimated amount for which an interest in real property should be leased on the valuation date between a willing lessor and willing lessee on appropriate lease terms in an arm's length transaction, after proper marketing and where the parties had each acted knowledgeably, prudently and without compulsion"* (RICS, 2017).

Market Value The estimated amount of money, or equivalent means, for which a property should be sold or purchased, as of the valuation date, by a seller and a buyer with no particular ties and both interested in the sale, on a competitive basis, following an appropriate marketing activity in which both have acted in an informed, conscious and unrestricted way. This amount, with certain limits, must reflect the Highest and Best Use of the asset, i.e. a use which is physically possible, financially sustainable, legally permitted and economically convenient for the ordinary market players.

Multiple Periods Residual Value Approach The Residual Value Method applied using a Discounted Cash Flow Approach and therefore taking into account all future Cash Flows converting them into a Present Value, discounting every expected future benefit.

Net Leasable Area See "Net Lettable Area".

Net Lettable Area The surface area of a property that can be leased to one or more tenants; generally, this excludes the surface area of the entrance hall, atrium, utilities area, lift shaft, etc.

Net Sellable Area The equivalent of the Net Lettable Area, but for Residential Properties developed for sales.

No Buildable Area See "No Buildable Land".

No Buildable Land Land which does not fulfil the legal and/or economic requirements for Building (see "Buildable Land").

Non-Flexible Commercial Property Property used and usable only by a specific User which, either for intrinsic characteristics of the Building, or in view of the absence of demand in a particular real estate market, is unlikely to be used by an alternative User.

Off-plan sale Sale of a property (usually residential units) that needs to be built yet, before the Development has started, in order to reduce the market risk of the developer and generate some positive cash flow.

Over rent A situation when the passing rent is above the ERV, thus increasing the chances that the tenant might leave the property or renegotiate its lease agreement at break options or lease agreement expiry.

Owner The person who owns a property and who receives some utility from it, either through direct use or through the income derived from offering the Space Use (i.e. the rental income). In the latter case he can be defined also as the "landlord".

Passing rent The actual rental amount paid by a tenant for a specific property under the lease agreement.

Property Return Rates Rates which express the amount of return expected by Investors and which are needed for the purpose of applying the Income Capitalisation Methods. In the Direct Capitalisation Approach, where the reference amount is the income, the formula requires the use of a cap rate, a measure of income return. It ideally projects the current income into the future, determining the value of the asset. In the Discounted Cash Flow Approach, where the reference amount is the cash flow, the formula requires the use of a discount rate, a total return. It ideally relates future income flows to the present.

Property Valuation The process of estimating the value of a property. In the broadest sense, the term "valuation" involves a judgement on the equivalence of a property (the one being valued) and an amount of money (unit of measurement), given certain conditions and within a certain period of time. Valuing a property, therefore, means expressing its value in an amount of money.

Rent roll This might refer either to a list of properties belonging to an individual or company, stating the rents owed by and received from each tenant, or to the gross income generated by a rented property. In this book it is considered as the synoptic table which summarises the main details of the existing lease agreements for a particular property.

Residential Property (typically apartments, condominium and single-family homes, etc.) in which the Space is residential and is a consumer good.

Residential Property See "Residential".

Residential Space Space which constitutes a final consumer good for its User, without being used directly to produce other goods or services.

Residual Value Method The process of applying the Income Capitalisation Approach Methods based on the estimated value of the property and the respective costs.

Sales Comparison Approach Methods Property Valuation methods according to which the value of an asset is obtained based on the identified prices of transactions that can be defined as comparable.

Sales Comparison Methods See "Sales Comparison Approach Methods".

Single Period Residual Value Approach The Residual Value Method applied on a single period process. The sale value of the property that can be built and its construction costs are gathered in a single period, without directly considering the time required for the actual construction and sale of the property.

Space See "Space Use".

Space Market The market in which the "Space Use" property is traded when there is a separation between Users and Owners/Investors.

Space Use In the sense of the physical use of a property, it is the utility produced by it, which depends on many factors associated with the Building (e.g. size, shape, quality, efficiency) and the location (e.g. centrality, connection, accessibility), in other words, the Land.

Trade-Related Commercial Property Property in which the company's production activity is directly connected to the Space and consistent with the product/service offered, as in the case of hotels and retail premises.

Trade-Related Property See "Trade-Related Commercial Property".

Trading Operation Operations in which a property is sold in a short period of time, either as a result of a strategic decision or because market conditions have changed and led to an unexpected Capital Gain.

Under rent A situation when the passing rent is below the ERV.

User The person who benefits from the "Space Use" in exchange for an amount of money (rent). This may be the Owner of the property, in which case the opportunity cost rather than the rent has to be considered, i.e. the cost of renouncing the opportunity to receive an amount of money from a third party.

Weighted Lettable Area The surface area resulting from the application of weighting factors, estimated by the valuer, to the various areas of the Net Lettable Area (such as archives, technical rooms or parking spaces), in order to obtain a single uniform piece of data for each use of the property.

Yield Capitalisation See "Discounted Cash Flow Approach".

Bibliography

Accetta G. (1998), 'Supporting Capitalisation Rates', *Appraisal Journal*, Vol. **66**, n. 4, pp. 371–374.

Akerlof G.A., Shiller R.J. (2009), *Animal Spirits: How Human Psychology Drives the Economy, and Why It Matters for Global Capitalism*, Princeton University Press, Princeton, NJ (USA).

Akerson C.B. (1984), *Capitalisation Theory and Techniques. Study Guide*, Appraisal Institute, Chicago, IL (USA).

Appraisal Institute (2001), *The Appraisal of Real Estate*, 12th edition, Appraisal Institute, Chicago, IL (USA).

Appraisal Institute (2002), *The Dictionary of Real Estate Appraisal*, 4th edition, Appraisal Institute, Chicago, IL (USA).

Barber A. M. (1992), 'Understanding Direct Capitalisation', *The Canadian Appraiser*.

Baum A., Machmin D., Nunnington N. (2017), *The Income Approach to Property Valuation*, Routledge, London (UK).

Beracha E., Skiba H. (2014), Real Estate Investment Decision Making in Behavioral Finance, in H. Kent Baker, V. Ricciardi (eds.) *Investor Behavior: The Psychology of Financial Planning and Investing*, Wiley, New York (USA).

Black F., Scholes M. (1973), 'The Pricing of Options and Corporate Liabilities', *Journal of Political Economy*, Vol. **81**, n. 3, pp. 637–659.

Bond S., Wang K.K. (2005), 'The impact of cell phone towers on house prices in residential neighborhoods', *Appraisal Journal*, Vol. **73**, n. 3, pp. 256–277.

Borghi A. (2008), *La finanza immobiliare. Il mercato, la valutazione, gli strumenti e le tecniche di finanziamento*, Egea, Milano (Italy).

Bourassa S.C., Hoesli M., Sun J. (2004), 'What's in a view?', *Environment and Planning A*, Vol. **36**, n. 8, pp. 1427–1450.

Bourassa S.C., Hoesli M., Sun J. (2005), 'The price of aesthetic externalities', *Journal of Real Estate Literature*, Vol. **13**, n. 2, pp. 165–188.

Boydell S. (1998), *An analysis of the investment appraisal of enclosed regional shopping centres – an Australian perspective*, Liverpool John Moore University, Liverpool (UK).

Boyle M.A., Kiel K.A. (2001), 'A survey of house price hedonic studies of the impact of environmental externalities', *Journal of Real Estate Literature*, Vol. **9**, n. 2, pp. 117–144.

Bravi M., Rossi M. (2013), 'Real Estate Development, Highest and Best Use and Real Options', *Firenze University Press*, XLI Incontro di Studio del Ce.S.E.T., pp. 479–498.

Brealey R.A., Myers S.C., Allen F. (2016), *Principles of Corporate Finance*, 12th edition, Mc Graw Hill, New York (USA).

Breidenbach M., Mueller G.R., Schulte K.W. (2006), 'Determining Real Estate Betas for Markets and Property Types to Set Better Investment Hurdle Rates', *Journal of Real Estate Portfolio Management*, Vol. **12**, n. 1, pp. 73–80.

Brown G.R., Matysiak G.A. (2000), *Real Estate Investment – A Capital Market Approach*, Financial Times Prentice Hall, Upper Saddle River, NJ (USA).

Brueggeman W.B., Fisher J.D. (2010), *Real estate finance & investments*, McGraw Hill Education, New York (USA).

Capozza D.R., Li Y. (2002), 'Optimal Land Development Decisions', *Journal of Urban Economics*, Vol. **51**, pp. 123–142.

Clayton J., Ling D.C., Naranjo A. (2009), 'Commercial Real Estate Valuation: Fundamentals Versus Investor Sentiment', *The Journal of Real Estate Finance and Economics*, Vol. **38**, n. 1, pp. 5–37.

Coleman C., Crosby N., Mcallister P., Wyatt, P. (2013), 'Development appraisal in practice: some evidence from the planning system', *Journal of Property Research*, Vol. **30**, n. 2, pp. 144–165.

Copeland T., Tufano, P. (2004), 'A Real-World Way to Manage Real Options', *Harvard Business Review*, March.

Crosby N., Mcallister P. (2004), 'Deconstructing the transaction process: an analysis of fund transaction data', in *Liquidity in Commercial Property Markets: Research Findings*, pp. 22–39, Investment Property Forum, London.

Damodaran A. (2012), *Investment Valuation: Tools and Techniques for Determining the Value of Any Asset, University Edition*, 3rd edition, Wiley Finance Series, John Wiley & Sons Inc., New York (USA).

Des Rosiers F. (2002), 'Power lines, visual encumbrance and house values: a microspatial approach to impact measurement', *Journal of Real Estate Research*, Vol. **23**, n. 3, pp. 275–301.

Di Pasquale D., Wheaton C.W. (1992), 'The markets for real estate asset and space: a conceptual framework', *Real Estate Economics*, Vol. **20**, n. 2, pp. 181–198.

Ellwood L.W. (1959), *Ellwood tables for real estate appraising and financing*, Ballinger Publishing Company, Pensacola, FL (USA).

Fedrizzi S.R., Morri G., Pavesi A.S., Soffietti F., Verani E. (2014), 'A value creation tool in the sustainable building field: the LEED certification' (Italian original title: 'Uno strumento per la creazione di valore nella realizzazione di edifici sostenibili: la certificazione LEED'), *Territorio Italia*, Vol. **1**, pp. 35–44.

Fernandez P. (2015), 'CAPM: An Absurd Model', IESE Business School, University of Navarra, November 19.

Fernandez P. (2017), 'CAPM: The Model and 307 Comments About It', IESE Business School, University of Navarra, October 17.

Ferrero C. (1996), *La valutazione immobiliare*, Egea, Milano (Italy).

Fisher J., Martin R. (1994), *Income Property Valuation*, Dearbon Real Estate Education, La Crosse, WI (USA).

Geltner D.M., Miller N.G., Clayton J., Eichholtz P. (2013), *Commercial Real Estate: Analysis and Investments*, 3rd edition, OnCourse Learning, Mason, OH (USA).

Goddard G.J., Marcum B. (2012), *Real Estate Investment: A Value Based Approach*, Springer, New York (USA).

Gordon M.J., Shapiro E. (1956), 'Capital Equipment Analysis: The Required Rate of Profit', *Management Science*, Vol. **3**, n. 1, pp. 102–110.

Gunnelin A., Hendershott P. H., Hoesli M., Soederberg B. (2003), 'Determinants of Cross-Sectional Variation in Discount Rates, Growth Rates, and Exit Cap Rates', *Research Paper n. 90*, FAME – International Center for Financial Asset Management and Engineering.

Guthrie G. (2009), 'Evaluating Real Estate Development Using Real Options Analysis', *Social Science Research Network, pp.* 1–21.

Hoesli M., Morri G. (2010), *Investimento immobiliare*, Hoepli, Milano (Italy).

House G.C. (2004), 'Demand for Real Estate: Capital Flows, Motivations, and the Impact of Rising Rates', *Institute for Fiduciary Education*.

Hui E.C., Fung H. H. (2009), 'Real estate development as real options', *Construction Management and Economics*, Vol. **27**, n. 3, pp. 221–227.

IFEI – Institut Français de l'Expertise Immobiliere (1993), *Charte de l'Expertise en Valuation Immobilière*.

Janssen J., Kruijt B., Needham B. (1994), 'The Honeycomb Cycle in Real Estate', *Journal of Real Estate Research*, American Real Estate Society, Vol. **9**, n. 2, pp. 237–252.

Kauko T., D'Amato M. (2008), *Mass Appraisal. An International Perspective for Property Valuers*, Wiley-Blackwell, New York (USA).

Kelly W., Epley D.R., Mitchell P. (1995), 'A Requiem for Ellwood', *The Appraisal Journal*, Vol. **63**, n. 3, pp. 284–290.

Keynes J.M. (1921), 'A Treatise on Probability', *Journal of the Institute of Actuaries*, Vol. **53**, n. 1, pp. 78–83.

Knight F.H. (1921), *Risk, Uncertainty, and Profit*, Schaffner & Marx, Houghton Mifflin Co., Boston, MA (USA).

Lancaster K.J. (1966), 'A new approach to consumer theory', *Journal of Political Economy*, Vol. **74**, n. 2, pp. 132–157.

Lind H., Nordlund B. (2014), 'A transparent Two-Step Categorization of Valuation Methods', *The Appraisal Journal*, Vol. **82**, n. 3, pp. 244–251.

Ling D.C., Naranjo A. (1997), 'Economic risk factors and commercial real estate returns', *Journal of Real Estate Finance and Economics*, Vol. **14**, n. 3, pp. 283–307.

Lucius D.I. (2001), 'Real Options in Real Estate Development', *Journal of Property Investment & Finance*, Vol. **19**, n. 1, pp. 73–78.

Mcdonald J.F. (2015), 'Capitalisation rates for commercial real estate investment decisions', *Journal of Property Investment and Finance*, Vol. **33** n. 3, pp. 242–255.

Morri G., Artegiani A. (2015), 'The effects of the global financial crisis on the capital structure of EPRA/NAREIT Europe index companies', *Journal of European Real Estate Research*, Vol. **8**, n. 1, pp. 3–23.

Morri G., Benedetto P. (2017), *Valutazione Immobiliare – Metodologie e casi*, EGEA, Milan (Italy).

Morri G., Cristanziani F. (2009), 'What determines the capital structure of real estate companies? An analysis of the EPRA/NAREIT Europe Index', *Journal of Property Investment & Finance*, Vol. **27**, n. 4, pp. 318–372.

Morri G., Mazza A. (2015), *Property Finance: an international approach*, Wiley, New York (USA).

Morri G., Soffietti F. (2013), 'Greenbuilding sustainability and market premiums in Italy', *Journal of European Real Estate Research*, Vol. **6**, n. 3, pp. 303–332.

Myers S. C. (1977), 'The Determinants of Corporate Borrowing', *Journal of Financial Economics*, Vol. **5**, n. 2, pp. 147–175.

Pagourtzi E., Assimakopoulos V., Hatzichristos T., French N. (2003), 'Real estate appraisal: a review of valuation methods', *Journal of Property Investment & Finance*, Vol. **21**, n. 4, pp. 383–401.

Pomykacz M., Olmsted C. (2013), 'Options in Real Estate Valuation', *Appraisal Journal*, Vol. **81**, n. 3, pp. 227–238.

Reenstierna E.T. (2008), 'An Argument for Establishing a Standard Method of Capitalisation Derivation', *The Appraisal Journal*, Vol. **76**, n. 4, pp. 371–376.

Renigier-Biłozor M., D'Amato M. (2017), 'The Valuation of Hope Value for Real Estate Development', *Real Estate Management and Valuation*, Vol. **25**, n. 2, pp. 91–101.

RICS Guidance Note (2010), *Discounted Cash Flow for commercial property investments*.

RICS (2017), *RICS Valuation – Global Standards 2017 (Red Book)*.

Rosen S. (1974), 'Hedonic prices and implicit markets: product differentiation in pure competition', *The Journal of Political Economy*, Vol. **82**, n. 1, pp. 34–55.

Schulz R., Wersing M., Werwatz A. (2014), 'Automated valuation modelling: a specification exercise', *Journal of Property Research*, Vol. **31**, n. 2, pp. 131–153.

Sirota D., Barrel D. (2003), *Essentials of Real Estate Investment*, 6th edition, Dearbon Real Estate Education, La Crosse, WI (USA).

Strickland T. (1999), 'Extracting Overall Capitalisation Rates from the Market – A review of Basic Considerations', *Assessment Journal*, September/October, pp. 17–21.

TEGoVA – The European Group of Valuers' Association (2016), *European Valuation Standards*, 8th edition.

Thebee, M. A. J. (2004), 'Planes, Trains, and Automobiles: The Impact of Traffic Noise on House Prices', *The Journal of Real Estate Finance and Economics*, Vol. **28**, n. 2–3, pp. 209–234.

Wang K., Grissom T. V., Chan S. H. (1990), 'The Functional Relationship and Use of Going-in and Going-out Capitalization Rates', *The Journal of Real Estate Research*, Vol. **2**, n. 5, pp. 231–245.

Williams J.T. (1991), 'Real Estate Development as an Option', *Journal of Real Estate Finance and Economics*, Vol. **4**, n. 2, pp. 191–208.

Wincott D. (1991), 'Terminal capitalisation rates and reasonableness', *Appraisal Journal*, Vol. **59**, n. 2, p. 253–260.

Wincott D.R., Hoover K.A., Grissom T.V. (1996), 'Capitalisation Rates, Discount Rates and Reasonableness', *Real Estate Issues*, Vol. **21**, n. 2, pp. 11 ss.

Wurtzbach C.H., Miles M.E. (1987), *Modern Real Estate*, 3rd edition, Wiley, New York (USA).

Wyman D., Seldin M., Worzala E.M. (2011), 'A new paradigm for real estate valuation?', *Journal of Property Investment & Finance*, Vol. **29**, n. 4, pp. 341–358.

Index

Printed and bound by CPI Group (UK) Ltd, Croydon, CR0 4YY

16/04/2025

14658507-0001